Desk 88

Desk 88

EIGHT

PROGRESSIVE

SENATORS

WHO CHANGED

AMERICA

Sherrod Brown

FARRAR, STRAUS AND GIROUX | NEW YORK

Farrar, Straus and Giroux
120 Broadway, New York 10271

Grateful acknowledgement is made for permission to reprint the "Seven Advices" of Rumi, from
Love's Ripening: Rumi on the Heart's Journey, translated by Kabir Helminski and Ahmad Rezwani,
© 2008 by Kabir Helminski and Ahmad Rezwani. Reprinted by arrangement with The Permissions
Company, LLC, on behalf of Shambhala Publications Inc., www.shambhala.com.

Library of Congress Cataloging-in-Publication Data
Names: Brown, Sherrod, 1952– author.
Title: Desk 88 : eight progressive senators who changed America / Sherrod Brown.
Other titles: Desk eighty-eight, eight progressive senators who changed America
Description: First edition. | New York : Farrar, Straus and Giroux, 2019 | Includes
    bibliographical references and index.
Identifiers: LCCN 2019021224 | ISBN 9780374138219 (hardcover)
Subjects: LCSH: Brown, Sherrod, 1952-—Political and social views. | United States.
    Congress. Senate—Biography. | Legislators—United States—Biography. | United
    States—Politics and government. | Progressivism (United States politics)—History.
Classification: LCC E176 .B887 2019 | DDC 328.73/0922 [B]—dc23
LC record available at https://lccn.loc.gov/2019021224

Designed by Richard Oriolo

www.fsgbooks.com
www.twitter.com/fsgbooks • www.facebook.com/fsgbooks

1 3 5 7 9 10 8 6 4 2

FRONTISPIECE: Photograph of the drawer of Desk 88 (courtesy of the U.S. Senate Collection)

To my late mother, Emily Campbell Brown,
a small-town Southern girl who taught my brothers
and me about service and justice.

To Connie, who makes the fight every day.

And to our future warriors for justice:
Clayton, Leo, Jackie, Carolyn, Milo, Ela, and Russell.

CONTENTS

Desk 88

Prologue

THE ORIGINS OF DESK 88

We must come to see that human progress never
rolls in on wheels of inevitability.

—Martin Luther King, Jr.

F INALLY, IT WAS THE FRESHMEN'S TURN. Ten of us—nine
Democrats and one Republican—wandered around the big hall,
surveying where we might sit. We talked about location: which
row to sit in, whom to sit next to, which desk was closest to the front—it
was all perhaps a bit too reminiscent of high school.

It suddenly occurred to me: there were no bad places to sit. No pillars
to sit behind. No obstructed views. We were on the floor of the United
States Senate.

At the freshman orientation a couple of months earlier, senior senators had shared with us some stories and traditions of the Senate. One of those traditions—reminiscent of middle school—is that most senators at some point in their careers carve their names in the drawers of their desks in the Senate chamber.

So, a bit sheepishly, with these carvings and this history in mind, I pulled out drawer after drawer in desk after desk, pushing aside the clutter of stationery, legislation printouts, and committee reports to read the names that were carved on the inside bottom of each drawer.

At the fourth desk I approached, something felt different. I knew almost every name carved in the drawer. I read through the names of Desk 88—Black of Alabama, Gore of Tennessee, Lehman of New York, McGovern of South Dakota, and—I broke off, curious. Between McGovern and Ribicoff of Connecticut, the desk drawer had only one word: Kennedy. No state, no first name. I called out to Senator Edward Kennedy and asked him to look at the desk. "Ted, which brother's desk was this?"

He looked down at Desk 88. "It must be Bobby's," he said. "I have Jack's." I had found my Senate home. My chief of staff, Jay Heimbach, informed the clerk of the Senate that Desk 88 was the one I wanted.

WHAT DREW ME to the names at Desk 88 was the idea that connected them: progressivism. It's a political ethic that had driven not only my votes in Congress (I joined the House of Representatives in 1993 and reached the Senate in 2007) but also my decision to run for office in the first place. Over the past century, progressives have stood for labor rights, civil rights, stronger antitrust laws, women's rights, a higher minimum wage, health and safety regulations, a steeply graduated income tax, child labor protections, and workers' compensation. More recently, progressives have fought for abortion rights, universal health care, strong environmental laws to combat climate change, equal rights for gay and transgender Americans, gun safety laws, consumer protections, and a ban on political contributions from corporations.

Progressives of all generations, and certainly those who sat at Desk

88, share a revulsion at injustice and wage inequality and wealth disparity; most progressives are bound together by a deep respect for the dignity of work and, in Tolstoy's words, "the fundamental religious feeling
that recognizes the equality and brotherhood of man." Progressives typically share a common suspicion of concentrated power, especially private
power.

Some of those who sat at Desk 88 played crucial roles when the country was in the midst of progressive times. Others, at great risk to their
political careers, espoused progressive principles in more difficult eras,
when the country was in a particularly conservative, sometimes dark and
angry mood.

Often the great achievements of the occupants of Desk 88 took place
somewhere else—in the ornate hearing rooms of the Russell Senate Office Building, in union halls or church basements, at veterans' lodges or
in school auditoriums. But sometimes—and there are examples in this
book—the desk itself bore witness to a turning point in progressive history. The greatness of these senators was most evident when they spoke
out and fought against the special interests that have always had too
much influence in our government.

Like most legislators throughout U.S. history, the senators of Desk
88 have been disproportionately white and male. The Senate historian believes that no woman has yet called Desk 88 hers. Even as this book cel-
ebrates the men who articulated and achieved progressive goals, its final
chapter will acknowledge the work still to be done and highlight a new
generation of progressives working for equality and opportunity.

Progressive movements arouse the public as they fight the abuse of
power by oil companies, Wall Street, the tobacco industry, and huge
pharmaceutical firms. They challenge the dominance of the big banks and
Big Oil and the gun manufacturers, and they attack entrenched racism
and sexism. They want to reform a broken system under which powerful
interest groups almost always have their way in the halls of Congress and
in state legislatures across the country. They speak out against what William Jennings Bryan labeled "predatory wealth."

Fundamentally, progressives want an America where the voiceless are heard in the government, where those without wealth or power have a government that represents *them*. And as progressives fight for civil rights and women's rights, for LGBTQ rights and labor rights—in short, the fight for equality is what defines a progressive—we know that progress has never come easy, even in the United States of America.

Almost two decades ago, I addressed a Workers Memorial Day rally in Lorain, Ohio. I stood in front of a fifty-foot-high pile of black iron-ore pellets where the Black River empties into Lake Erie. After the event, the steelworker Dominic Cataldo handed me a lapel pin depicting a canary in a birdcage. "This pin," he told me proudly, "symbolizes our decades-long fight for worker safety." Ever since, I've worn my canary pin to honor the millions of Americans who have fought for traditional American values, and to celebrate the dignity of work. In the early days of the twentieth century, more than two thousand American workers were killed in coal mines every year. Miners took a canary into the mines to warn them of toxic gases; if the canary died, they knew they had to escape quickly. It was a warning system built out of desperation. With no trade unions strong enough to help and no government that seemed to care, the miners were on their own.

Americans—in their churches and temples, in their union halls and neighborhood organizations, in the streets and at the ballot box—fought to change all that. Our progressive forebears convinced our government to pass clean air and safe drinking water laws, to approve auto safety rules and protections for the disabled, to enact Medicare and civil rights and consumer protections, to create Social Security and workers' compensation, to sponsor medical research and build airports and highways and public transit and municipal water and sewer systems. Every accomplishment, every step forward, came in the face of entrenched and powerful opposition—from Big Oil and Wall Street, from tobacco companies and pharmaceutical firms, from industries that poisoned our air and fouled our rivers. Tens of millions of Americans now live longer and healthier lives because activists all over our nation fought for our American values of fairness and economic justice.

History shows that progressives—and progressivism—are at their best when they appeal to a sense of community. To progressives, it was always about *public* health and *public* safety and *public* education and *public* works. But too often, in modern America, we see, as John Kenneth Galbraith noted, "private opulence and public squalor." We see a government that provides tax cuts for those who least need them, and starves public services—medical research, city parks, health care, child care, water and sewer systems, public transit, neighborhood schools, rural broadband—for everyone else.

Progressivism is not just about government playing a positive role in people's lives—though it is that, from civil rights to workers' rights, from clean air to support for children and the disabled, from minimum wage to Medicare. It is about more than the government standing with those with less privilege. It is also about a civic culture defined by fairness and reason, and tolerance for opposing viewpoints. About voting rights and fair play. About campaigns where the candidate with the most money does not necessarily win. About a political system that encourages participation. About a government and an economic system that work to generate safety and opportunity for the many, not concentrate wealth in the hands of the few. And about the dignity of work.

The lessons we learn from Desk 88 are still instructive for our country. Consider the question of war and peace. On March 7, 1968, Robert F. Kennedy stood at his desk on the floor of the United States Senate to deliver his strongest and most poignant speech in opposition to the Vietnam War. "Are we like the God of the Old Testament," he thundered, "that we can decide in Washington, D.C., what cities, what towns, what hamlets in Vietnam are going to be destroyed?" He rejected President Lyndon Johnson's justification for fighting that war, that if we don't engage with and defeat the Communists in Vietnam, they will overrun all of Southeast Asia, then invade Hawaii, then attack San Francisco. That same reasoning, New York's junior senator asserted, was used by the Soviets and the Nazis in 1939 and 1940 when they invaded, conquered, and then divided up Poland and the Baltic states.

More than three decades later, Johnson's arguments were employed, this time by a Republican president, in justifying an attack on Iraq, the expansion of government wiretapping and library searches, fast-track trade-negotiating authority, and tax cuts for the wealthiest Americans—

of course, any excuse will do. We must fight them over there, President George W. Bush and Vice President Richard Cheney warned us, so we don't have to fight them here. Neither Presidents Kennedy and Johnson in Vietnam nor President Bush in Iraq had heeded the words of the nineteenth-century Prussian general Carl von Clausewitz, who wrote that, in war, a nation should "never take the first step without considering what may be the last."

The misuse of fear can shape domestic politics as well. In his last address at the National Prayer Breakfast, in February 2016, President Obama instructed us: "Fear does funny things. Fear can lead us to lash out against those who are different or lead us to try to get some sinister 'other' under control. Alternatively, fear can lead us to succumb to despair, or paralysis, or cynicism."

Most of the time, the fear of change has the upper hand in politics. Ralph Waldo Emerson told us that history is a contest between the Conservators and the Innovators. Conservators—those with privilege and wealth, who want to hold on to what they have—are vastly outnumbered. But they long ago figured out how to consolidate power: exploit the fear of people who would benefit from change by convincing them that change is too risky. Conservators routinely warn the public that big government—those people in Washington—will take away what they earned with their hard work: a small house, a moderate income, a barely middle-class lifestyle. "Fear always springs from ignorance," Emerson noted. So often, those who have little often line up with the Conservators.

With great skill, conservative leaders have learned to distract the public with fear and prejudice because they know they lack public support on the fundamental issues. They attack government regulation as they feed Wall Street. They talk about crime as they underfund public schools. They rail against government spending on the least privileged as they lavish tax cuts on the most privileged. They ridicule welfare recipients and food stamp beneficiaries as they pad corporate welfare accounts and subsidize large corporate farms. At their best, the senators at Desk 88 fought back against this fear-mongering. "Self-anointed patriots," as Tennessee Senator Albert Gore, Sr., called them, raise the specter of Communism, terrorism, or immigration to make people forget that the conservative elite are, in fact, taking advantage of *them*.

Fear has played a central strategic role in the Republican Party since at least World War II. It was Communism in the 1940s, 1950s, 1960s, and 1970s. It was crime in the 1960s, 1970s, and 1980s. It was the fear of terrorism in the George W. Bush years. It was integration and immigration—people we do not know, religion we do not understand, and cultures we find alien—through much of our history.

PERHAPS IT SHOULD not have shocked the GOP establishment when, after decades of Republican dog whistles about race via "states' rights" and being "tough on crime," Donald Trump's bark captured the Republican base in 2016. Trump's ideas, after all, were not so different from those of others in his party—just less polished. During the desperate flight of hundreds of thousands of refugees from the Middle East in 2015, presidential candidate Jeb Bush—the national media's Designated Thinking Man—proclaimed we should accept in our country only "Christian Syrians." A few days later, Trump said that our government should bar all Muslims from entering the United States. Fido's yap yielded to the Doberman's full-throated roar. Of course, Trump was more explicit than established Republicans wanted him to be in his racist, xenophobic, and misogynist comments. But the overwhelming majority of Republican officeholders, many of whom disavowed his individual comments, endorsed him nonetheless. Some even endorsed him, unendorsed him, then endorsed him again. And almost unanimously they have continued to enable and support him well into his presidency.

THE STATE OF THE UNION

I came to the United States Senate at the close of an era. Voters in 2006 spoke a resounding "no" to the conservative Bush-Cheney policies of deregulation, tax cuts for the most privileged, runaway budget deficits, giveaways to favored corporations, and expansionist foreign policy. The conservative era, ushered in by the Reagan landslide of 1980, had run its course, and had imposed a substantial cost on our country.

The far right had shown contempt for a government of the people, for the people. Beginning with Republican House Majority Leader Tom DeLay—with his K Street Project*—conservatives used government to enrich their political allies. Huge tax cuts were bestowed on the super-wealthy and on favored Washington special interests. Medicare was partially privatized, reaping tens of billions of dollars for well-connected pharmaceutical and insurance companies. An energy bill written by the Koch brothers and their billionaire allies was signed into law, further enriching much of the Republican money base. Friends of the president and the vice president made billions of dollars providing services in Iraq, most notably Vice President Cheney's former employer Halliburton, which received tens of billions of dollars in unbid contracts. And military spending—but not veterans' benefits—knew few limits.

The last quarter century was a period of exploding budget deficits and, perversely, a starving of many government services, at least those programs that didn't serve K Street. It was a time of burgeoning trade deficits and a shrinking manufacturing workforce. The damage is especially evident in our cities, rural areas, and inner-ring suburbs—where crumbling bridges, potholed streets, badly maintained water and sewer systems, and decaying public transit systems endanger both safety and prosperity.

In the 1950s, 1960s, and 1970s our country built some of the best public works in world history. Yet despite the fact we are a wealthier country today, we have failed to modernize or even maintain them. We as a nation spend 2.4 percent of our gross domestic product on infrastructure, while the European Union spends more than 5 percent, and China expends 9 percent on domestic and foreign projects.

The fervor behind tax cuts for the richest Americans—and cuts in spending—robbed our nation of much more than reliable highways and bridges. The neglect of public health, the compromising of worker safety

---

*Many of Washington's most influential and profitable lobbying firms are located near or on K Street in the District of Columbia.

and environmental regulations, and the shredding of protections for consumers and the investing public have all imposed dire costs on our country. Today, millions of poor, working class, and middle-class students are unable to acquire an education without taking on oppressive debt. My wife, Connie Schultz, whose utility-worker father had little money to send four children to college, graduated from Kent State University with less than $1,200 in debt in 1979. In those days, tuition costs were lower because state governments provided more funds for state universities, Pell Grants were more plentiful, Stafford Loans more accessible, the GI Bill more generous. The cost of attending Kent State for in-state students today? Twenty-two thousand dollars per year.

The budget deficit exploded during the Reagan-Bush years, reaching one billion dollars a day. The Clinton years—with tax increases, spending cuts, and economic growth—saw the huge budget deficits turn to surplus. But then, beginning in 2001, the new self-professed conservative in the White House, George W. Bush, again ran up billion-dollar-a-day deficits with tax cuts for the most privileged, the unpaid-for war in Iraq, and a giveaway to the pharmaceutical and insurance industries in the form of a Medicare drug benefit.

What did these deficits achieve? To get some perspective: during the eight years of the Clinton presidency, the nation enjoyed a net increase of twenty million private-sector jobs; during the eight years of the second Bush presidency, the nation saw a net increase of fewer than one million private-sector jobs.

And something else happened: an expanding chasm between the very rich and the middle class. The link between worker productivity and worker pay began to weaken in the 1970s, with the second Clinton administration an exception to the pattern. During the mild economic growth of the Bush II years, that link was severed. Profits went up, but wages didn't; productivity rose dramatically, yet workers' security was compromised. Average income for American workers, adjusted for inflation, dropped $2,000 in the first seven years of the Bush presidency, and that was before the economic meltdown. And while the median wage was flat, the median wage for African American workers sharply declined. Though the Obama presidency and Congress saved America from economic catastrophe, and began a turnaround that has lasted a decade, the forces that widen inequality remain unchecked. Simply put, workers—and this includes as many as three-fourths of employed Americans—are not sharing in the wealth they create for their employers.

Conservatism has had no answer to the question of the growing gulf between the most privileged and everyone else; or more precisely, it has had the same answer it always did: more deregulation, more tax cuts for the wealthy, more privatization of government services. All were tried in the Bush years. All made the problem worse.

Conservatism has had its chance, winning far more political battles since 1980 than it lost—some at the ballot box, some in state legislatures, some in the halls of Congress, and others in an increasingly conservative, activist Supreme Court. Republicans have been a majority on the United States Supreme Court for more than four decades. But conservatism today is more about interest group politics than a coherent value system. Voters felt a betrayal as interest group conservatism—especially in the corporate wing of the Republican Party—overreached. In the Bush years, the Medicare drug law was written by and for the pharmaceutical companies. The energy bill was drafted by and for oil and gas interests. Health insurance rules were essentially promulgated by and for the insurance industry. And trade agreements were negotiated by and for Wall Street and the multinational corporations that were reaping record profits by outsourcing jobs.

Of course, conservatives' trickle-down economics did benefit some people: executives with strong political ties. More lobbying contracts, more lax regulation, and more goodies and perks for the favored few all but guaranteed campaign contributions that kept the conservative, increasingly southern Republicans in power. All good for monied Washington interest groups, but not so much for a beleaguered American public.

Three years into the Trump administration, Republicans—with a minority of voters behind them, but assisted by redistricting, voter suppression, the arcane electoral college, and bold power plays by the Republican leader in the Senate—still hold on to power. Far more Americans voted for a Democrat for president in 2016, far more Americans voted for

Democrats for the Senate in 2016 and 2018, yet Republicans control the Senate, the White House, and the Supreme Court. But their power will not last.

THE PROGRESSIVE ERAS

The occupants of Desk 88 have seen three great progressive eras since 1900, with—arguably—a fourth one snuffed out by the GOP's retaking of Congress in 2010. Each lasted only a few years and was fueled by an immense burst of energy from a demanding public. Each brought an electoral backlash that forced progressives to play defense as entrenched interest groups rallied to roll back progressive gains. Each progressive era helped to generate extraordinary amounts of wealth for the American people, creating a huge middle class that no other country in world history had seen. In short, these three progressive eras put government on the side of the vast majority of the American people. If progressives are going to govern successfully once again, they will need to heed the lessons of how past victories were won.

THE FIRST PROGRESSIVE ERA

The first era saw a restless stirring among the voters in both major political parties. Precipitated in part by the populist side of Theodore Roosevelt's presidency, it also resulted in a significant change to the United States Senate. In 1912, Congress passed and sent to the states a constitutional amendment to provide for the direct election of United States senators. Until then, senators were chosen by state legislatures, many of whom were in thrall to their state's agricultural or industrial interests and corrupt political machines. Idaho Senator William Borah hailed the direct election of senators as "the most effective means of taking from organized wealth the control of the Senate, and indeed our national politics."

The election year 1912 was a watershed for the progressive movement with the four-way race among the incumbent Republican President William Howard Taft, the Bull Moose Party nominee Theodore Roosevelt, New Jersey Democratic Governor Woodrow Wilson, and the Socialist

Party nominee Eugene V. Debs. A sitting president, a former president, a future president, a national labor leader—all running on platforms defined by various degrees of progressivism.

Within a few years of Woodrow Wilson's victory, Congress passed the Clayton Act, which established the Federal Trade Commission to reduce the power of the "money trust," abolished child labor in manufacturing, helped small farmers get access to credit, set up a federal workers' compensation program, and confirmed the progressive Louis Brandeis as the first Jew on the United States Supreme Court. Congress and the states passed and ratified constitutional amendments to give women the right to vote and to permit a progressive income tax.

THE SECOND PROGRESSIVE ERA

President Franklin Delano Roosevelt's First Hundred Days was the most exciting time in congressional history, and launched the second progressive era of the twentieth century. The problems were immense: unemployment levels were as high as 25 percent; banks were failing; millions lived in squalor in the cities and in rural America. And FDR followed a presidency that seemed indifferent to these problems. It was clear that Herbert Hoover's tighten-your-belts-and-balance-the-budget conservative brand of governing was not working. In 1931, President Herbert Hoover announced, "We cannot legislate ourselves out of a world economic depression." Maybe not, but he and the Republican majority in the United States Senate were not even going to try.

FDR's First Hundred Days began on March 9, 1933. Congress gave Roosevelt almost everything he asked for. "We ground out laws so fast," Arizona Democratic Senator Henry Fountain Ashurst noted in his diary, "that we had no time to offer even a respectful gesture toward grammar, syntax, and philology." And most of the time, Republicans—badly outnumbered and psychologically cowed—went along . . . meekly. The Republican leader Charles McNary of Oregon shrugged in early 1934, "The majority of the Republican members of the Congress will continue warmly to support those measures fashioned materially to improve the economic conditions of the country."

And then the Democrats gained ten more Senate seats in the 1934 midterm elections. They now had sixty-nine seats in the ninety-six-member chamber. Almost two dozen belonged to southerners who were skeptical or hostile to FDR's growing belief in an activist federal government. Still, there were two southern senators—Alabama's Hugo Black, who sat at Desk 88, and Majority Leader Joseph Robinson, who had been Al Smith's running mate in the 1928 presidential election—who played major roles in moving FDR's progressive agenda forward. The Arkansan Robinson was FDR's most loyal Senate supporter as he shepherded the president's programs through the Senate, and Black, as chairman of the Education and Labor Committee beginning in 1935, helped to lead the charge on labor issues.

The second progressive era—from 1933 to 1938—gave the country Social Security and a minimum wage, public power and the Tennessee Valley Authority, protections for consumers and small investors against Wall Street predators, and an eight-hour workday and collective bargaining for workers. Tens of millions of Americans benefited almost immediately. Hundreds of millions still do. Sitting at Desk 88, several senators—Hugo Black, but also Theodore Green of Rhode Island, Herbert Lehman of New York, and Glen Taylor of Idaho—would play their part in creating a social contract Americans still depend upon today.

THE THIRD PROGRESSIVE ERA

The century's third progressive era came in the 1960s and brought, in the words of one-term Michigan Congressman Paul Todd, "the happy Congress," the 89th Congress, when Minority Leader Gerald Ford and the Republicans "were not at all vitriolic."

Sitting on the back porch of their farmhouse just outside Kalamazoo with his wife, the former Kalamazoo mayor Caroline Ham, Todd told me a year before he died that he and his colleagues were not thinking about making history. "We just knew what needed to be done," he said. But in just two years, 1965 and 1966, they may have accomplished more than any other Congress of the last century: passage of Medicare and Medicaid, which have provided health insurance for more than 250 million Americans; the Higher Education Act, which gave millions of young people the opportunity to go to college; the Voting Rights Act, which enfranchised millions of southern black citizens; the Elementary and Secondary Education Act, which helps tens of millions of less advantaged schoolchildren learn to read; and the Immigration and Nationality Act, which opened up immigration from the developing world. In 1964, leading into the presidential election, Congress passed the Civil Rights Act and the Wilderness Act, which protected 9.1 million acres, and created the Office of Economic Opportunity, which led to the Job Corps and Head Start.

Several progressive legislators—all Democrats—who sat at Desk 88 during their Senate careers made significant contributions to the progressive victories of the 89th Congress. As a member of the Finance Committee, Connecticut's Abraham Ribicoff played a leading role in the creation of Medicare; before his election to the Senate in 1962, he had served as President Kennedy's Secretary of Health, Education, and Welfare. Vance Hartke, a labor Democrat from Indiana elected to the Senate in the landslide of 1958, worked to pass the Civil Rights Act in the 88th Congress and the Voting Rights Act in 1965. Alabama's Lister Hill, who was elected to the Senate in 1938, the year after Senator Hugo Black vacated the seat to ascend to the Supreme Court, wrote the Hill-Burton Act, which assisted local communities with hospital construction in exchange for those hospitals serving the indigent. He also helped to create the National Institutes of Health, the finest research facilities in the world.

Each of these three progressive eras in the twentieth century saw a burst of legislative activity lasting only a few years. But the impact for the country—civil rights and Social Security, minimum wage and antitrust enforcement, Medicare and education—was, and still is, profound. As the political philosopher Hannah Arendt observed, "The good things in history are usually of very short duration, but afterwards have a decisive influence over what happens over long periods of time." Undoubtedly, there will be another progressive era for our country. What form it takes and when it happens is up to us: How do we honor the dignity of work by ensuring that it is rewarded with a living wage and secure retirement? How do we make up for our failures in earlier progressive eras to address racial inequality? How do we respond to climate change? How do we reform a court system that puts far too many men of color in prison? How do we overcome decades of discrimination in housing, employment, and access to credit? What do we do about wealth inequality?

In *Desk 88*, we learn from one hundred years of progressive successes and progressive failures. We should never romanticize our history or hearken back to the good ol' days in the United States Senate; after all, in the 1950s—in the days of Herbert Lehman and Glen Taylor and the early years of Albert Gore, Sr., and William Proxmire—ninety-five white men and one white woman could not or would not pass legislation extending voting rights to millions of black Americans.

When I first opened the drawer of Desk 88, I saw immediately the bold block letters carved by Hugo Black. Alongside his name were those of perhaps two dozen other United States senators, all Democrats, many forgotten, some known for one or two accomplishments. For this book, I chose eight senators whose achievements and ideals are worth highlighting, and who inform my work in the Senate today. Each of them fought for the dignity of work and against disparity in wealth, and all of them believed that if you work hard, you should have a decent standard of living. They not only subscribed to progressive ideals, but also worked hard to build the future that the labor leader Sidney Hillman described: "We want a better America, an America that will give its citizens, first of all, a higher standard of living so that no child will cry for food in the midst of plenty."

They are:

- Hugo Black of Alabama, whose ambition took him from membership in the Ku Klux Klan to the United States Senate, where he helped to lift millions of black and white American workers out of poverty;

- Theodore Francis Green of Rhode Island, who to his New England aristocratic friends was a traitor to his class when he brought democracy—and security and prosperity—to hundreds of thousands of Rhode Island workers;

- Glen Taylor of Idaho, an entertainer who sang his way to the Senate and ended up in Bull Connor's Birmingham jail because he addressed integrated audiences and spoke out on civil rights;

- Herbert Lehman of New York, who brought his state the Little New Deal and showed its previous governor how to uplift millions;

- Albert Gore, Sr., of Tennessee, whose ambition led him to vote against civil rights but who was defeated a decade later because he stood courageously for civil rights and against the Vietnam War;

- William Proxmire of Wisconsin, who didn't much care what his colleagues thought of him, but who never gave up on anything—from his own political future to the United Nations Genocide Convention—until his mission was accomplished;

- Robert F. Kennedy of New York, whose eyes were opened by an undernourished Mississippi child, and who then spent the rest of his short life afflicting the comfortable;

- George McGovern of South Dakota, who, in the face of personal and political setbacks, fed the poor in the United States and all over the world, and was personally recognized by Pope John XXIII for his compassion.

These eight senators helped to create a Democratic Party that looks out for ordinary Americans, whether they punch a time clock, work construction, sit behind a desk, treat patients in a hospital, or raise children at home. The occupants of Desk 88 played a role in every progressive era, and all those years in between when progressives fought to hold on to their gains. Some had moments of greatness; some simply did their jobs. Each of the senators at Desk 88 contributed to a better nation, a kinder society, and a more progressive America.

Theirs are the stories of Desk 88.

1.

Hugo Black

FINDING LIGHT IN THE SHADOWS

SERVED IN THE UNITED STATES SENATE 1927–1937

Every minute of my time that is possible to use, I am devoting to
a study of questions, with a view to alleviating human suffering
and to an adjustment of the machinery in such way that our
government can continue to be a real people's government.

—Senator Hugo Black of Alabama

A YOUNG, AMBITIOUS HUGO BLACK thought he had to choose between the Ku Klux Klan and the Big Mules. He chose the Klan.

The Big Mules were the steel and coal interests, the utility executives and the corporate lawyers, the bankers and the wealthy planters and the railroad men. Most Alabamans, black or white, resented the Big Mules. Steelworkers, miners, railroad workers, and the unemployed all watched the Big Mules feed at the trough, while they could imagine no way out of their hardscrabble lives. They knew that they were creating great wealth for their bosses, and they were equally sure they were sharing in almost none of it.

The future governor Bibb Graves described the social and economic structure of 1920s Alabama this way: Little mules were straining and sweating to pull the heavy, loaded hay wagon up the road. Tied to the back of the wagon were two Big Mules, strolling along happily, contentedly munching the hay. Graves pledged to hitch the Big Mules to the wagon, force the Big Mules to shoulder a heavier portion of the tax burden, and give the little mules some relief.

The Klan was a group of hooded terrorists. Murderously anti-black. Violently anti-immigrant. Viciously anti-Catholic and anti-Semitic. At the peak of its powers in the Alabama of the mid-1920s, when Black was elected to the United States Senate, the white-robed Klansmen spread terror throughout the state. Some estimated that half of Birmingham's registered voters belonged to the Klan. Klansmen saw themselves as protectors of all things American. Many shop windows advertised their owners' Klan membership with "TWK" (Trade With a Klansman) signs in their windows. James Esdale, Grand Dragon of the Realm of Alabama, boasted, "We had the best people in the state." The Jefferson County (Birmingham) sheriff belonged. So did hundreds of preachers. As did prominent businessmen. And scores of politicians. And the future senator and Supreme Court justice Hugo Black.

Black told a friend years later, "I would have joined any group if it helped me get votes."

Hugo Black's 1920s Ku Klux Klan membership dogged him—as it should have—for the rest of his life. Although he resigned his membership soon after he took the Senate oath of office from Vice President Charles G. Dawes, his affiliation with the terrorist group was not—at least in his first term—far from the minds of many of his colleagues. Maybe they believed, as Black probably told them repeatedly, that he would not have been elected without support from the Klan. And they surely knew that he had put his political ambitions above any real principles of social justice—a fairly common affliction in that august ninety-six-member body. A number of northern liberals referred to him privately as "that Kluxer."

Black would later argue that his Klan membership was passive: no violence, no exhorting others to terrorism, little demagoguery about race or religion. Besides, he insisted, he could never have sided with the Big Mules. Because he chose a political career, it had to be one or the other.

Hugo Black joined the Ku Klux Klan at the age of thirty-seven. One of fifteen hundred inductees at a 1923 ceremony with five thousand Alabama Klansmen and seventy-five hundred Klansmen from other southern states, he became more active than he would ever acknowledge— marching in parades in small towns in all corners of Alabama, donning the Klan's eye-slitted mask and pointed hood, speaking at inductions and local Klaverns. But there was, as far as anyone knows, no violence or calls to violence in Black's activities. And there was some evidence that he joined the Klan in part because a Jewish friend encouraged him to "keep down the few extremists."

Still, his record, at least during his first six-year term in the United States Senate, was hardly a paean to racial harmony or social justice. He voted with thirteen other southerners to cut off aid to Washington, D.C.'s Howard University, then a fledgling African American institution of higher learning. He helped to filibuster an anti-lynching bill. He proposed a couple of times to suspend all immigration. On the floor of the United States Senate, he pronounced, "I think the United States has the right to select the race and nationality in the type of immigrants who come into this country." And Black refused to endorse the Democratic candidate Al Smith for president in 1928, the first Roman Catholic nominee of a major party in American history. Black would say only, "Vote the Democratic ticket."

So how does a former Klansman make his way into a book about senators' contributions to a progressive America? Perhaps because Hugo Black later strived to make up for his Klan membership. He transformed from a member of the KKK into a Supreme Court justice who firmly opposed it. He was recognized during his last couple of years in the Senate as one of the great progressives in a progressive Senate in that progressive era, a giant among giants. Joseph Alsop and Turner Catledge, prominent national columnists, described Black as "an absolute anomaly, an intellectual leftist liberal from below the Mason and Dixon line . . . probably the most radical man in the Senate."

Grover Cleveland Hall, editor of *The Montgomery Advertiser* and a 1928 Pulitzer Prize winner for his exposure of KKK activities in "editorials against gangsterism, floggings, and racial and religious intolerance," wrote that Black "is a radical of the Norris, La Follette, Holmes, Brandeis school—perhaps the first genuine philosophical radical that the deep South has sent to the Senate."

He was the first of FDR's eight appointees and, in his thirty-four years on the court, he outlasted all of them save William O. Douglas; he was the most senior justice on the court by the late 1940s. Though he wrote the infamous 1944 decision permitting the internment of Japanese Americans, he most often strongly championed civil rights and civil liberties, and consistently supported the First Amendment, even when joining only Douglas in a two-man dissent. He was the author of *Gideon v. Wainwright*, ordering the lower courts to provide counsel to indigent defendants. And in 1971 he authored, in his last time writing for the majority, the Pentagon Papers decision in spite of President Richard Nixon's ominous warning that permitting the publication of the government's confidential analysis of the Vietnam War would threaten national security. "No Justice in our history," fellow progressive Supreme Court Justice William J. Brennan, Jr., intoned, "had a greater impact on our law or on our constitutional jurisprudence."

Not least, the former Klansman was a driving force in the unanimous 1954 *Brown v. Board of Education* ruling that struck down racial segregation in the nation's public schools. When that decision was announced, Justice Black was burned in effigy in his home state. A candidate for governor said, "Justice Black is not fit to try a chicken thief." He, a sitting Supreme Court justice, was disinvited to his 1956 law school reunion at the University of Alabama.

Hugo Black, Jr., in his book *My Father*, described the reaction of much of the Alabama establishment—newspapers, politicians, citizens: "[They] looked on Daddy as 'a traitor to the South.'" Hugo Jr. was planning a run for Congress but decided against it in light of the 1954 ruling. A few years later, the young Black moved his family and his law practice to Florida.

Hugo Black is a complicated but necessary inclusion in a book about great progressives who sat at Desk 88. He was an avid reader of history. He surely knew of America's nativist past—from the Know-Nothing party of the 1850s, to the Chinese Exclusion Act of 1882, to the Immigration Act of 1924. He had rejected the KKK, yet he and his colleagues on the Supreme Court could not escape that nativist past when handing down the decision to force more than one hundred thousand Japanese Americans into internment camps during World War II.

Black's early life is a cautionary tale for ambitious young public officials. A populist and a progressive from his earliest days, he had the courage to fight for the least privileged—as a lawyer and as a judge. But as a young man, he let his ambition flip his progressive populism onto its ugly, racist underbelly. Ambition kept him from understanding that real populism is never racist, never anti-Semitic, never pushes some people down to lift others up.

BLACK WAS BORN on a winter day in 1886 in rural Clay County, Alabama, thirty miles from the Georgia state line, the last of eight children. His father was a Confederate soldier who later operated a general store; his mother, a postmistress. Lafayette Hugo Black (Lafayette was his father's middle name; Hugo was his big sister's idea after she read a Victor Hugo novel) was a voracious reader as a little boy. He was called Hugo by his family, and although his name was inscribed as LaFayette Hugo Black in the family Bible, he took as his name throughout his life Hugo Lafayette Black. As a small boy, as early as six, he was a regular observer at the county courthouse.

At fifteen, he temporarily dropped out of high school to show solidarity with his sister, who had been mistreated by school authorities—it was the future jurist's "first dissent," in the words of the Black biographer Roger Newman. Hardly missing a beat, young Hugo hurried through college and law school, set up a practice in the small town of Ashland, Alabama, then moved on to Birmingham and specialized in labor law and personal injury work. Birmingham was one of the fastest-growing cities in America: its population had increased from 38,000 in 1900 to 133,000 in 1910 to 179,000 in 1920.

Black was later appointed a police court judge, was elected Jefferson County (Birmingham) prosecutor in 1914, resigned three years later, and then served as a captain during World War I. After the war, he returned to his law practice, representing injured coal miners and the widows of steelworkers killed on the job. Birmingham, the industrial center of the South, had far too many of both. Black, then only in his thirties, was becoming known as the best trial lawyer in Alabama. Always better prepared in court than anyone else, he was beating the Big Mules consistently, and he won their begrudging respect. He preferred jury trials, where ordinary, almost always white, people rendered their verdicts; he knew that decisions rendered by judges drawn from a legal system closely aligned with banks and coal conglomerates and utility companies were less likely to go his working-class clients' way.

On May 25, 1925, two-term Senator Oscar Underwood indicated he would probably not run for reelection in 1926. A fixture in Alabama politics since his election to the United States House of Representatives in the mid-1890s and two-time presidential candidate, the sixty-three-year-old Underwood had attacked the Ku Klux Klan at the 1924 Democratic National Convention: "It is either the Ku Klux Klan or the United States of America. Both cannot survive. Between the two, I choose my country." Hugo Black was off and running, but so were others: a former governor, the son of a former United States senator, a former state supreme court justice, a wealthy coal operator by the name of Lycurgus Breckenridge Musgrove. All the others were personally wealthy or had ties to the monied establishment, the Big Mules. All, of course, were white and campaigning before an almost entirely white electorate—in a state about one-third African American.

Hugo Black's candidacy threatened the Alabama power structure. Typically, candidates came from the ruling class and belonged to the right clubs in Birmingham and Montgomery and Mobile. And once in office, they represented those who put them there—the banks and the utility companies, the coal companies and the steel industry. Still today, throughout the South, Republican politicians, most of them born into privilege, see it as their life's work to help their social class, to help those with privilege get more of it. But Black was not like the other candidates. They stood for office. He ran. He scurried around the state, visiting every corner of Alabama. He met farmers and factory workers, clerks and laborers, teachers and secretaries. He denounced the power trusts and railroads and the banks—"organized money," he called it.

And he did it with a sense of humor. He told the story of meeting a boy at a crossroads in southern Alabama. Black asked him directions to get to Andalusia. The boy shrugged his shoulders. "Andalusia or Montgomery—which way is which?" The kid shook his head. "You don't know much, do you?" the future senator retorted.

"No," the boy said. "But I ain't lost."

Many years later, author Clifton Fadiman told a story about Justice Black's sense of humor during his days on the court. Once he was attending the obligatory funeral for an acquaintance whom he intensely disliked. A colleague, arriving late, slid into the pew next to the jurist and asked how far along the service was. Black whispered, "They've just opened for the defense."

Black could make a crowd roar with laughter, but campaigning was serious business. As he challenged the Big Mules and all they represented, the Alabama press was increasingly antagonistic. Black spoke of his dream of "the sunlight of justice to all and special favor to none." Most of the state's newspapers labeled him a demagogue and accused him of fomenting and inciting the public.

Like many progressives, Black liked reporters but had little use for editors and publishers, calling them "merchandisers of the First Amendment" and labeling their newspapers "propaganda for the privileged." He saw a world engaged in a Manichean battle between the comfortable and the dispossessed where wealthy interest groups like the Big Mules— cheered on by editorial pages—too often had their way with politicians. Newspaper editors and publishers accused him of class warfare, as newspaper management so often does when politicians challenge the security and contentment of their social class. So much for the journalistic ethic of comforting the afflicted and afflicting the comfortable.

In the end, Black won the Democratic primary fairly handily, besting second-place finisher John H. Bankhead II—who later joined Black as Alabama's junior senator—by more than thirty thousand votes. In the general election, he exceeded 80 percent of the vote in the one-party state of Alabama. Black was off to Washington.

His first term was nothing unusual, nothing special. The first couple of years in office, especially in those days, usually found a new senator quietly working, making few waves, and rarely taking to the floor to speak. In the early days, senators waited for years to address their colleagues. In 1878 Kansas Senator Preston Plumb, according to Senate Historian Richard Baker, thought he should be the exception. Following a long-winded speech noted more for its length than for its substance and delivery, Plumb was scolded the next day by *The Washington Post*: "The awful example of Senator Plumb should not be lost upon the new Senator of the Future. An important part of the decorum of the Senate is a rule that no Senator shall open his mouth except to vote, or take a drink, until he has been in there three years."

Hugo Black's friend Montana Democrat Burton Wheeler later said of Black's early years, "He hardly took part in anything. He just sat at his desk, quietly greeting everyone and looking around." He got along well with his colleagues, made no waves, and did not try to attract too much attention to himself. He was elected by his Democratic Party peers to be secretary of the Democratic Caucus, an achievement that perhaps reflected the potential that his colleagues saw in him. And while not yet a leader or even an activist, he was assiduously learning the Senate and its ways.

The Senate did not start its work, in those days, until late in the new calendar year. Between the November 1926 election and the beginning of the congressional session in December 1927, Black spent much of his time reading history, law, politics, government—anything that he thought would make him a better senator. The Black biographer Gerald Dunne recalled that Black "made the Library of Congress his postgraduate school."

His most important teacher may have been Senator George Norris of Nebraska. Born near Clyde, Ohio (a town immortalized by Sherwood Anderson's *Winesburg, Ohio*), Norris was a nationally revered progressive leader when Black came to the Senate. The young Alabama senator watched Norris, a nominal Republican, as he convinced others—in the cloakroom and in the Senate chamber—by force of logic. Norris was persuasive and effective, Black noticed, because he knew more than anyone else about the subject at hand, and he looked at his work with an unusually long-term view of its impact. Norris was consistently true to his beliefs, and his Senate colleagues knew it. Their mentor-protégé relationship evolved into a friendship that lasted until Norris's death in 1944.

Near the end of Black's first term, he was beginning to find his courage. He knew the 1920s had been a decade of profligacy, avarice, and corporate acquisitiveness—and with the Crash of 1929 came a huge amount of human suffering, brought on largely by Wall Street greed.

As the country began reckoning with the Crash and President Hoover's response, Black cited the injustice of salaries as high as $100,000 for railroad executives, as high as $250,000 for bankers, and, in at least one case, a $1 million bonus. He called particular attention to the workings of the Reconstruction Finance Corporation, which Hoover had formed in January 1932 to support economic recovery. Black noted that board members of public corporations seeking loans from the Reconstruction Financing Corporation were receiving as much as $50,000 a year for attending one meeting a month. His amendment to the Reconstruction Financing Corporation appropriations bill was simple: no one who worked for a corporation that was a beneficiary of RFC largesse could receive, as salary and bonuses, more than the vice president of the United States, who earned $15,000 a year at the time.

To Black, it was about the dignity of work; workers should have a decent standard of living. Rising to speak in the Senate chamber on January 25, 1932, he thundered, "I think that wages are entirely too low in this country and that that is largely responsible for the huge concentration of wealth which has taken its toll from every precinct and nook and cranny of this Nation and unjustly and unduly enriched a certain exclusively privileged few." Why, he asked, should we "take the money out of the pockets of the taxpayers—their dimes, their quarters, their dollars, which they have made by hard toil—put it into a pool, and supply it to business enterprises that pay salaries ranging as high as $250,000 per year"? A business "has no right to protest if the Government, which supplies the money for its business, insists that it shall run its business in an economical manner."

As for those businesses that did not take federal money, Black wanted them left alone. "Conduct your own affairs. Operate your own business. Pay your own salaries; but we leave it to you to stand or to fall upon your own energy, upon your own perseverance, upon your own business cunning, and your own business acumen."

As 1932 wore on and the economy worsened, unemployed World War I veterans came to Washington to request early payment of the bonus promised to them by the federal government. Leaders of the Bonus Expeditionary Force, or Bonus Army, asked for a meeting with President Hoover. He refused, pointing out that the 1924 legislation creating the bonus specified that the money was payable in 1945 or upon the veteran's death, whichever happened first. At Hoover's urging, the Congress decisively defeated a measure to pay the bonuses earlier. Then Hoover dispatched General Douglas MacArthur and his troops to remove the veterans and their families from the makeshift shacks in which they'd been camped for almost two months, many near the White House. Their shacks were set afire, the Bonus Army and their families were teargassed, and most fled without their belongings. Two babies were killed. Two veterans and two police officers also died. Black was the only United States senator who publicly criticized Hoover for sending in troops: "As one citizen I want to make my public protest against this militaristic way of handling a condition which has been brought about by widespread unemployment and hunger."

All in all, Black was not satisfied with his first term in the United States Senate. Still a young man—he was forty-six at the end of it in 1932—he had been too quiet, too detached. He had been in the minority, and served with two presidents he did not much respect. He confided to his wife, Josephine, that he was much too preoccupied with home-state politics and too little concerned with fighting for his own beliefs.

His second term—with a new progressive president, a new Democratic majority, and a likely committee chairmanship—would indeed be different. Black figured out—more than most of his colleagues—that serving as a United States senator was about much more than drafting amendments, sponsoring bills, speaking on the Senate floor. He saw corruption all around him—from the Big Mules in Alabama to the interest groups in Washington—and he knew that he would have to build a case, a public case, to fight it.

He began what he called "the probe"—a series of hearings aimed at powerful, influential, and mostly untouchable interest groups. Black achieved a great deal when he legislated at Desk 88, but his reputation was established in the ornate committee rooms of the Capitol and the Senate Office Building.

In Alabama, Black had watched the unfolding of the 1924 investigation by Montana Senator Thomas Walsh, which brought down top officials in the Harding administration in the Teapot Dome scandal, and a 1931 investigation by a New York judge that resulted in several convictions and the removal from office of New York Mayor Jimmy Walker.

"The power of the probe," Black wrote, "is one of the most powerful weapons in the hands of people to refrain the activities of powerful groups who can defy every other power. That is because special privilege thrives in secrecy and darkness and is destroyed by the rays of pitiless publicity."

Perhaps more than anyone before him, Senator Black learned how to use "the probe": discovering corruption, shining a powerful spotlight on it, focusing the public's attention on it through public hearings, writing legislation to clean it up. The probe was often ostentatious, sometimes overdone, but always newsworthy. "Great reputations have been made in investigations," he wrote in 1936. He did it first with the Air Mail Scandal, as chairman of a Special Committee to Investigate Air and Ocean Mail Contracts. The hearings opened in January 1934. Quickly, he found evidence of a cover-up, almost always worse than the crime itself. The Air Mail reform was signed into law.

And the Air Mail probe—with its unearthing of the destruction of documents, unsavory behavior by executives and lobbyists, and corruption by contractors—led to much more. He pursued lobbying reforms (he called Washington lobbyists "the pressure boys"), and then the biggest fish of all, the utilities' holding companies. By the beginning of Black's second term, the eight largest utility holding companies controlled more than 70 percent of the investor-owned utility industry. Although the lobbying reform passed the Senate, it died in the House. But the Public

Utilities Holding Company Act (PUHCA, as it was known for decades) was signed into law on August 26, 1935, by a very appreciative Franklin Roosevelt, who called it "his greatest legislative triumph." The new law forced divestiture upon the giant holding companies, and set up effective state regulation of the now smaller power companies. It would remain on the books until the 1990s, when it was repealed by a pro–utility company Republican Congress.

The investigations conducted by Black confirmed what so many Americans thought: much of the economic and social pain that Americans were suffering was a result of the greed and profligacy of the owners of capital and their stooges who populated the halls of Congress and the corridors of the statehouses. And the only way to fix that was the regulatory zeal of the New Deal.

Black directed his anger at the situation, at injustice and inequality—and rarely at the people who wittingly or unwittingly perpetrated the status quo. And government needed prodding—aggressive, outspoken prodding—by progressives like him. The Big Mules did not need his help, but the miner, the injured railroad worker, and the retired steelworker did. "Power tends to shrink into the hands of fewer and fewer people," he told his son Hugo Jr. He warned of "the combined power of organized wealth and its organized propaganda."

And, as Black believed, if the House and especially the Senate spoke too often with an upper-class accent, the courts were the aristocracy. Federal judges were usually drawn from the ranks of business lawyers who represented banks, utilities, and industrialists. "In almost all instances, judges in the federal courts have been men, who whether by instinct or by environment, have not been sympathetic enough with the plain people, and been too sympathetic with wealth and privilege."

Early in his career—as a judge sentencing an unemployed miner to prison for theft and as a lawyer representing an injured steelworker—Black saw the connection between crime and poverty. By late 1932, according to the president-elect, Franklin Roosevelt himself, Birmingham was the hardest-hit town in Depression America. "Forty percent of the population was on relief of some kind, some kind of relief job, on support from government," Black said. He called on the federal government to provide unemployment insurance. We can no longer rely just on "individual initiative and rugged individuality" and "leave it to you to stand or fall upon your own business cunning and acumen."

Seeing the devastation that the Depression was wreaking on his constituents in Alabama, and knowing personally so many workers and farmers who had lost their jobs and their homesteads, he thought to himself: if only we could find a way to get people back to work.

Sitting at Desk 88 in the Senate chamber in December 1932, he went to work. Black—a skilled legal draftsman—wrote legislation to establish a six-hour workday, a thirty-hour workweek. There were simply not enough jobs, he believed, unless everyone worked less. Black predicted that millions of new jobs would be created. Two prominent economists labeled the bill "revolutionary in its economic and social implications." The Black biographer Roger Newman wrote that Hugo Black "was a New Dealer before the New Deal."

After FDR took office in March 1933, Black—joined by House Labor Committee Chairman William Connery, Jr., a Massachusetts Democrat—reintroduced the bill. The committee report accompanying its committee passage was strong: "Our economic structure cannot be rehabilitated until our people can work at fair wages and thus buy the things they need." Black understood something that so many in our country still do not: that low prices, brought on by deflation in the days of the Great Depression or by the globalization of the twenty-first century, cannot substitute for an economy that puts its emphasis on job creation and good wages. He knew how dignity of work meant that a hard day's labor should provide a decent standard of living.

In April, the Senate quickly passed the bill, 53–30. Black predicted that it would supply six million men with work, on the theory, according to *Time* magazine, "that the employer who wants to keep his production at current levels must hire 25% more workers to obey the law." American Federation of Labor president William Green, a former state senator from Coshocton, Ohio, rejoiced over the news: "It's the first constructive measure yet passed dealing with unemployment. It strikes at the root of the problem—technological unemployment."

In the end, a much diluted version of his jobs bill, but with a minimum wage included, was subsumed into a very complicated National Industrial Recovery Act, which passed and was signed by President Roosevelt in June 1933. To the surprise of only a few, the conservative, business-dominated Supreme Court struck it down as unconstitutional two years later.

The monied interests pushed hard against Black and Roosevelt and the New Deal. Former President Hoover, in his 1934 book *The Challenge to Liberty*, called Roosevelt's program a "step off the solid highways of true American Liberty into the dangerous quicksands of governmental dictation." The New Deal embodies a "philosophy which leads to the surrender of freedom," Hoover continued. "The whole philosophy of individual liberty is under attack," perhaps leading our nation to fascism.

But to those politicians and newspaper publishers and editors—and there were hundreds and hundreds—who attacked Roosevelt, the writer John Steinbeck had this to say: "Those men who attack him now, and attack his memory, do not hurt his name at all, but simply define themselves as the mean, the greedy, the selfish, and the stupid. Roosevelt's name is far beyond the reach of small minds and dirty hands."

In the spring of 1937, as the chairman of the Senate Education and Labor Committee, Black, along with Connery (who died only a few months later, after the bill's introduction), proposed a stronger, more comprehensive labor reform. Many of Black's fellow southern Democrats—members of Roosevelt's party, of course, but much more conservative than their western and northern Democratic colleagues—were opposed. There were almost no southern Republicans in the House or Senate in those days. "Cotton Ed" Smith of South Carolina led the opposition to Black's labor legislation, claiming that the South did not need higher wages and better worker conditions, because the cost of living was so much less in their states; and besides, it would hurt southern businesses. Black, holding up pay vouchers showing mill worker wages of less than ten cents an hour, indignantly retorted, "I subscribe to the gospel that a man who is born in Alabama, and who can do as much work as a man born in any state in New England, is entitled to the same pay if he does the same work."

But something else was happening in Washington. The elderly, ultra-conservative justices of the Supreme Court had spent the past several years striking down New Deal legislation, and FDR was eager to put his own stamp on its deliberations. In March, he proposed a controversial plan to pack the court with new justices who would presumably uphold his economic agenda. The plan received a frosty response from congressional representatives of both parties, but soon the impasse began to break. Supreme Court Justice Willis Van Devanter, a conservative judge who had consistently voted to strike down New Deal measures, announced his retirement in May. Senate Majority Leader Joseph Robinson, whom everyone expected FDR to appoint to the court, collapsed and died in his Washington apartment in July. And Roosevelt wanted a reliable ally on the court.

The successful probes, the unrelenting questioning of witnesses at these hearings, and Black's legislative record of support for FDR initiatives surely enhanced his reputation with the president of the United States. Perhaps most important, FDR and Black shared the same enemies, the strongest bond two politicians can have.

And close they were. In the early 1960s, when Justice Black was seated next to Marcelle and Patrick Leahy at a Georgetown Law School lunch, Black told the future Vermont senator a story about Roosevelt and the 1936 election. Then-Senator Black was watching the returns with the Roosevelt strategist James Farley and the president himself. "I called him Franklin," he told the Leahys.

Early returns showed that FDR was losing Maine, but, as more returns came in, it was apparent that he was losing little else. Black thought about the old political adage "As Maine goes, so goes the nation." Back then, Maine was considered a political barometer, because its governor's race was held in September and the winner's party usually won the presidential race two months later.

It became apparent that the Republican nominee, Kansas Governor Alf Landon, had won only two states, Maine and Vermont. Black joyously quipped, "As Maine goes, so goes Vermont." Farley, according to Black, then "took the quote" and called it his own. History has in fact attributed "as Maine goes, so goes Vermont" to Farley. And Black was still disputing it twenty-five years later at an awards lunch with a young law student and a Veterans Administration nurse.

In July, Roosevelt suffered the greatest defeat of his presidency when a Senate made up of a huge Democratic majority soundly rejected his court-packing plan. FDR's answer? Nominate his friend the senior senator from Alabama, who was one of the few supporters of the court-packing plan.* Black was in lockstep with Roosevelt on virtually all economic issues, and he would be easily confirmed. It had, after all, been fifty-five years since a senator or former senator had been nominated by the president. Former Mississippi Senator Lucius Quintus Cincinnatus Lamar, who had been a colonel in the Confederate Army, was nominated by President Grover Cleveland. Only six other sitting United States senators—Oliver Ellsworth, John McKinley, Levi Woodbury, Edward White, James Byrnes, and Harold Burton—have moved directly to the United States Supreme Court. Burton, a Republican who held my seat, was Harry Truman's first appointment to the nation's highest court. The last former senator to go to the Supreme Court was Indiana Democrat Sherman Minton, named to the court by Truman in 1949.

Roosevelt—knowing that Black and his strong views evinced passionate feelings among detractors and supporters—wrote his nomination in longhand, kept it from most of his staff, and sent it to the Senate.

The opposition to Black—inside and outside the Senate—was furious. Former President Herbert Hoover, perhaps still smarting over his landslide loss of half a decade earlier, said that the court was "now one-ninth packed." *The Washington Post*, true to its anti-labor sentiments past and present, lambasted Black for "extreme partisanship." One senator remarked, "If the president had searched the country for the worst man to appoint, he couldn't possibly have found anyone to fill the bill so well."

But FDR told James Farley, the chairman of the Democratic National Committee, "They'll have to take him." And the presidential advisor Harold Ickes, understanding both Roosevelt's reason to appoint him and the enmity of Black's enemies, quipped, "The economic royalists fume and squirm."

---

*Republican New Hampshire Senator George Moses wrote, "Senator Walsh of Massachusetts told me . . . that there are only three members of the Senate who are really in favor of the President's plan—they being La Follette of Wisconsin, Black of Alabama, and Minton of Indiana. The first two of these are extreme radicals, and the third is very much of a nitwit."

Opposition Republicans forced the nomination to committee, but couldn't stop him. Only a few days later, he was confirmed 63–13. His political opponents outside the Senate reminded the country again of his past affiliation with perhaps America's most opprobrious organization, but were unable to prove that he was actually a member of the Klan, a distinction that may have saved his nomination. After the confirmation, a rather sardonic joke made the rounds in Washington: "Hugo won't have to buy a robe. He can dye his white one black."

Justice Hugo Black served on the United States Supreme Court longer than all but four jurists—Douglas, Stephen Johnson Field, John Marshall, and John Paul Stevens—in our nation's history, and was widely regarded as one of the twentieth century's most influential justices. His decisions and persuasiveness on civil rights were especially notable. American history will remember the older Justice Black, during the Cold War, as perhaps our nation's preeminent civil libertarian. But the younger Justice Black—writes Norman Thomas in 1961 in *Great Dissents*—"when war was hot, wrote the opinion sustaining the evacuation of Japanese and Japanese Americans on the West Coast without trial or hearing, the single worst judicial blow to civil liberties in my [Thomas's] generation." Neither excusing nor condemning Black, Thomas concluded, "The method of war always corrupts the freedom for which it has sometimes been fought." He left the court eight days before his death in 1971, the longest serving senior justice in Supreme Court history.

AFTER BLACK LEFT the Senate in August 1937 and joined the court, the labor legislation that he had written and that came out of his Education and Labor Committee continued to wend its way through the legislative process. Although the bill passed the Senate by a comfortable margin, it stalled in the House. According to Robert Byrd's *The Senate*, it was the election of the populist and progressive Joseph Lister Hill, who had campaigned for Black's Senate seat on a platform of higher wages, that moved enough southern congressmen to support the legislation. Hill, who sat at Desk 88, served in the Senate from Alabama for more than thirty years, until his retirement in 1969.

Although somewhat watered down, the Fair Labor Standards Act was signed by President Roosevelt the next year. The FLSA set a national minimum wage, established a forty-hour workweek and overtime pay when an employee exceeds those hours, and prohibited child labor. The FLSA, coupled with the Wagner Act creating the National Labor Relations Board, helped put buying power in the hands of millions of workers. Probably no legislation in twentieth-century America did more to create a strong middle class than the Wagner Act and the Fair Labor Standards Act: Higher wages, collective bargaining, and a strengthened union movement came together to raise the standard of living for tens of millions of Americans.

In the spring of 2016, I sat in the office of Jason Bristol, a Cleveland labor lawyer and human rights activist. Under the glass on his desk was a pamphlet printed in 1938, sent by Labor Secretary Frances Perkins to millions of employers and employees. The cover read:

A Ceiling For Hours
A Floor For Wages
And A Break For Children

A minimum wage of 25 cents an hour was to go into effect on October 24, 1938; 30 cents an hour beginning in October 1939; 40 cents an hour beginning in October 1945. Beginning in October 1938 the standard workweek would be forty-four hours; in October 1939 it would be forty-two hours; and after October 1940 the standard workweek was to be no more than forty hours. Beyond those hours, employers were required to pay one and a half times the regular rate. And "oppressive child labor," defined in the statute, was banned immediately.

The impact of Black's Fair Labor Standards Act continues to this day. The FLSA has been amended significantly more than a dozen times in the past seven decades, usually but not always to expand workers' rights. The minimum wage has been increased dozens of times, but not often enough to keep pace with the cost of living.

Equal pay for women was added in 1963. Farm workers were included in the Act in 1966, domestic workers in 1974, and migrant workers in 1983. That these workers, predominantly people of color, had been excluded for decades speaks to the influence of southern Democrats whose price to support the New Deal was the preservation of southern white privilege. FLSA amendments prohibited age discrimination in 1967. And as a new member of the House of Representatives in 1993, I cast my first vote on a major piece of legislation when we expanded the FLSA to allow for caregivers to take uncompensated time off through the Family and Medical Leave Act.

Occasionally, the FLSA has been weakened by a Congress especially beholden to conservative business interests. In 2004 the Bush administration promulgated a rule that rolled back some of the gains that workers and their advocates had earned over several decades by reclassifying low-level supervisors and making them ineligible for overtime pay. But the central tenets of the Act remained inviolate.

On January 25, 2007, I delivered my maiden speech on the Senate floor. Standing at the desk of the majority leader—where Joseph Robinson, Lyndon Johnson, Mike Mansfield, Harry Reid, and now Chuck Schumer have led their party—I asked to be recognized. First-term Illinois Senator Barack Obama was presiding. Edward Kennedy, chairman of the committee that Hugo Black had chaired seven decades earlier, sat nearby. Robert Byrd, a few months away from becoming the longest-serving senator in American history, sat directly behind me. Looking at Senator Obama, I began, "Mr. President." (He may have liked the way that sounded.) I then spoke in support of amendments to the Fair Labor Standards Act, to increase the minimum wage from $5.15 an hour to $7.25 an hour.

Six months later, a minimum wage increase, the first in ten years, was signed into law by President Bush. Twenty-one months later, the acting presiding officer was elected president of the United States.

THOUGHTS FROM DESK 88

L IKE HUGO BLACK, my mother was a child of the segregated South. Born almost one hundred years ago in a small town of maybe four hundred people, she at a young age found segregation and its white privilege first confusing, then confounding, then repugnant.

After college and a year of teaching English in rural Florida, she moved to Washington, D.C., to be part of our nation's war effort. She went to work as a secretary at the Office of Strategic Services (OSS), which after the war transmogrified into the Central Intelligence Agency. Near the war's end, she met my father at an officers' club dance at Washington's Mayflower Hotel. Their unbeknownst connection went back further than that: their ancestors, less than one hundred years earlier, had fought against one another in the Civil War. My mother's great uncle fought in the Confederate Army at Missionary Ridge near Chattanooga; my father's grandfather was part of the Union Army that charged up the mountain in that epic Civil War campaign known to history as the Battle Above the Clouds.

My father, a physician, had recently returned from overseas duty and was stationed at Fort Belvoir, Virginia. A Republican from Mansfield, Ohio, he had voted against Franklin Roosevelt five times (somehow, as a twenty-one-year-old senior at Ohio's Denison University, he voted twice; not that many people voted for Hoover even once). My mother, nine years younger, a Democrat from Mansfield, Georgia, had voted for FDR the only time that she was old enough, in 1944.

Like millions of young couples who survived the painful upheaval of World War II and looked to the future with anxious anticipation, they fell in love. And, sensing the world closing in—he was thirty-five; she, not quite twenty-six—they planned a life together.

In 1946 the Republican doctor from Mansfield, Ohio, married the Democratic teacher from Mansfield, Georgia, and they settled in the small north-central Ohio city of forty thousand people where he had grown up. Now an Ohio transplant, the small-town Georgia woman who had always been a Democrat never even considered voting in 1948 for the *southern* Democrat—Strom Thurmond, the standard bearer for the States Rights Democratic Party. She voted for Truman, the *national* Democrat. My father continued supporting Republicans over the next two decades, proud of his 1964 vote for Barry Goldwater and his conscience of a conservative.

Millions of southern white voters switched from the national Democrats to the segregationist Dixiecrat Thurmond in 1948 and rarely looked back—many voting for Eisenhower in 1952 and 1956 and Nixon in 1960, overwhelmingly supporting Goldwater in 1964, and Wallace in 1968 and Nixon in 1972. Like Black, my mother went in the other direction. She pulled away from her family's ideological roots and became a national Democrat as she and her more conservative husband were raising my older brothers and me in the 1950s and 1960s.

More important to her than politics was her social activism. She joined and later became the local president and then the state president of the Young Women's Christian Association, asserting that the YWCA did more to empower women and advance civil rights than any long-standing organization in America, with the exception of the Urban League and the NAACP. She was drawn to the style and the politics of Congressman Ron Dellums, the young fiery Berkeley Democrat whom she heard speak to the YWCA convention in New York. And after she picked up Congresswoman Shirley Chisholm at the Cleveland airport to drive her to a YWCA speech in Mansfield, my mother couldn't stop talking about the charismatic Brooklyn Democrat, the first African American woman ever elected to Congress and the first black female to win presidential nominating delegates.

No issue informed my mother as much as race. While the busing controversy raged in the 1960s in the national media, my mother talked of a different kind of forced busing, the forced busing of her childhood in the segregated South. Black children were bused past a new, all-white school to attend a distant, underfunded black school. Separate but equal, they said. Black children were given books that were tattered and dated after being discarded by the white schools . . . if the black children were provided with any books at all.

My mother, now middle-aged, organized interracial dialogues at area junior high and high schools to encourage students who went to school together to actually talk to each other and share their stories. And she told us about her childhood, about race and class and privilege, and how she and her sisters, even though they were middle-class at best, enjoyed far more privilege and opportunity than any black child in her native Newton County, Georgia.

She taught my brothers and me always to address older black men and women with their honorific titles: Mrs. Rogers, Mr. Fields, Mrs. Christian. She had seen far too many white children in rural Georgia call older black men Jimmy and Johnny and older black women Betty and Hattie Lou. To this day—as a tribute to my mother and because of her teachings—I ask older African Americans, regardless of their professions, their last names, and then address them as Mr. or Ms.

My mother knew next to nothing about unions—after all, her parents were farmers and her husband was a physician. But she intuitively understood that people banding together could enhance their collective power, raise their standard of living, and demand justice. And she saw trade unionists, people like the United Auto Workers' Walter Reuther and the Brotherhood of Sleeping Car Porters' A. Philip Randolph, standing alongside and marching with civil rights heroes, and that was the cause she cared most about. She knew that Dr. King was martyred in Memphis advocating for exploited sanitation workers.

Her unrelenting activism continued. In 2004, dissatisfied with the grassroots efforts of the John Kerry presidential campaign, she recruited a friend, loaded a card table and two folding chairs into her trunk, and drove to the poorest parts of Mansfield, Ohio, where she sat—day after day—in front of grocery stores, registering voters. Within a month, the two of them registered more than nine hundred voters. She kept the names and phone numbers of the new voters and called them on Election Day to make sure they voted.

At the age of eighty-seven, this shy white girl from the segregated South was the first in my family to go to work as a volunteer to elect America's first African American president, months before the Ohio Democratic primary. January 20, 2009, was the last day she got out of bed and sat up to watch television, sitting with my oldest brother, Bob, seeing history made. She died two weeks after the inauguration. Watching Barack Obama take the oath of office was the last good day of her life.

My father's politics by the end of the 1960s had begun to change. His conservatism was gently challenged by my mother, confronted by my Navy anti-war brother Bob and my father's namesake, Charlie, and made indefensible by his own dislike of President Nixon and Vice President Agnew. My dad was surely one of the few Ohio voters who cast ballots for the landslide losers Barry Goldwater in 1964 and George McGovern in 1972.

My father, no more talkative at home than most men of his generation, never bragged about his overseas World War II service. His patients swore by him, often telling me how much time he spent with them, listening to their stories and empathizing with their pain. They told me that they would often leave his office not with an expensive prescription that they had to fill at Mansfield's Drive-In Pharmacy, but with a handful of drug samples to help cure them. He had the reputation—I think because he was a good listener—of being the best diagnostician in town. He looked askance at doctors who thought of themselves as business-men first and physicians second. He believed that practicing medicine was above all a great privilege. He taught me that service is always a great privilege.

He had no interest in joining the country club or attending the social events of Mansfield's upper crust. We lived in a middle-class neighbor-hood, and my brothers and I attended Brinkerhoff Elementary, Johnny Appleseed Junior High, and Mansfield Senior High School—all good, solid public schools, and all part of a safe, loving, gentle upbringing.

What my dad loved most—other than his family and his patients—was our family farm. In 1819, under the Northwest Ordinance of 1787, President James Monroe signed a deed to Robert Brown, which is hang-ing in his great-great grandson Bob's living room, for a 160-acre tract of land in Richland County, Ohio. Although for three generations our family lived in town and another family farmed the land, Charlie, Bob, and I worked there every summer—milking Guernseys, baling hay, cleaning out the barn, working the fields. My former chief of staff Mark Powden, a Vermonter, told me, upon hearing that we were some of the few dairy farmers still milking those smallish reddish-brown cows, "The farmers who milk Guernseys are too lazy to milk Holsteins and too proud to milk goats." In the summers in the late 1960s and early 1970s, I was paid $125 every two weeks for sixty-to-seventy-hour workweeks. It's where I learned to work. It's when I first understood the dignity of work.

In the mid-1950s, national public health officials announced that there was a new vaccine that could finally end the fearsome scourge of polio. They asked physicians with young children to vaccinate them, and to be public about it, illustrating that the medical profession saw little risk and great benefit in the polio vaccine. My father was photographed in the *Mansfield News-Journal* giving my oldest brother, Bob, then a first-grader, the Salk vaccine. Although this was to be perhaps the most significant public health victory in mid-century America, the hidebound

American Medical Association refused to endorse it, even though my dad and other physicians had implored them to. My father, to my political delight decades later, immediately resigned from the AMA and never rejoined.

Both my parents—she a teacher, he a doctor; she a liberal, he a conservative; she a Democrat, he a Republican; she a southerner, he a northerner—taught me, by their actions and from their admonitions, that the role of government was to help the little guy; the big guys can take care of themselves.

From all that have come my values and my progressive politics.

My belief in my generation and my idealism in high school—organizing Mansfield's first Earth Day with John Todd and Paul McClain on April 22, 1970; cofounding a black culture club with my classmate Wilbert Turner at Mansfield Senior High School; joining my parents and brothers at an anti-war demonstration—were challenged by a sobering incident when I was in college.

My parents, not rich but solidly upper-middle-class, told their three sons to apply to the best schools that would accept us: Bob went to Princeton and Harvard Law School; Charlie went to Denison and Yale Law School; I went to Yale. On a warm spring evening in May 1972, the dormitories emptied as hundreds of my fellow Yale students took to the streets. They had watched President Nixon announce another attack on North Vietnam—this time mining the harbors of Haiphong—a further escalation of a war that he had promised four years earlier to wind down. The reaction on American college campuses was swift and furious.

The students surged down Elm Street, through the campus, past the New Haven Green. The New Haven police set up barricades to keep the student protestors out of the New Haven business district. These young men and women, most of whom had never been confronted by law enforcement, stopped. On one side of the wooden barricades were several hundred students protesting a war in which they and their brothers would likely never have to serve. On the other side were several dozen working-class men in blue, some of whom may have served in Vietnam, and others whose sons might have been fighting there at that moment. The men in blue were paid to protect the property of the downtown business owners, businessmen who came from the same social class as most of the students' parents.

I had been a participant in a number of peaceful anti-war marches and demonstrations over the previous couple of years. I had also been trying, with a small group of other students, to sign up volunteers to go door-to-door in New Hampshire and New York for the anti-war presidential candidate George McGovern.

But this demonstration didn't feel right. I watched a couple dozen or so students taunt the police. Then they began to jeer and chant, "Off the pigs. Off the pigs. Off the pigs." The working-class cops, stolid and silent, appeared to be accepting of the world as it was. The privileged students, with law school or medical school or high-paying jobs in their immediate future, were shouting out slogans of protest against their world. That lesson in the blindness that can come with privilege and class has stuck with me ever since. More than four decades later, I saw that same obliviousness to privilege in the Brett Kavanaugh hearings. A graduate of Yale College and Yale Law School twenty years after I was on campus, Kavanaugh was nominated for the United States Supreme Court in 2018. I knew a number of students at Yale with his background, his demeanor, his social class, his expectations in life, and his reaction to criticism. Many showed little interest in those outside their social class, and exhibited little empathy for those with less privilege (which is about 99 percent of the public). Kavanaugh's angry reaction to criticism of his behavior was all too familiar.

I remember a kid in my dorm who came from a wealthy, well-known family. One day he asked to borrow my guitar; two days later he returned it—damaged, after he had left it out in the rain. No apology. No contrition. No offer to replace it. The kind of situation that, in his first two decades of life, Daddy had apparently taken care of. Students like Kavanaugh never seem to pay a price for bad behavior.

It was a bit later when I began to think more about the police officers' working-class world. I had not grown up in it, and Yale did not exactly have a blue-collar tinge to it. Abraham Lincoln—in defiance of his staff's exhortation to stay in the White House and preserve the union, win the war, and free the slaves—declared that he needed to get out and "get my public opinion baths." He knew he would be a better president, no matter the immediate task at hand, if he knew the hearts and minds—and the lives they lived—of the people he governed. The lessons of Lincoln would become my second lesson about privilege and class.

During college I worked on three campaigns: for Congressman Allard Lowenstein's reelection in New York; for Henry Parker, the first black Democratic nominee for mayor of New Haven; and for George McGovern for president. They all lost. But during my senior year in college, Richland County Democratic Chairman Don Kindt asked me to run for state representative in my hometown of Mansfield. We had met during the McGovern campaign in Mansfield. He had no one else to challenge the Republican incumbent, and he thought I might run and lose and then be ready to serve on the Mansfield City Council.

I was unopposed in the May Democratic primary—apparently no one else thought they could win. I voted absentee while still in school, graduated, and spent the summer and fall going to picnics and parades, knocking on doors, speaking at union halls. But mostly, I learned how to listen, to hear stories from a retiree forced to choose between heating her home and buying her medicine, from a pastor who couldn't explain to a parishioner why her neighborhood was redlined by a local bank, from a student who could not afford college. Listening and fighting for them helped me become a better candidate, and helped me win. I beat the incumbent, M. Joan Douglass, by 2,100 votes.

Early in my first term in the Ohio House of Representatives—I was twenty-two—the legislature had adjourned on a Thursday night. With no votes and no committee hearings on Friday, I headed home to my district in Richland County, about an hour's drive north. With no scheduled appointments the next day, I drove across town to the United Steelworkers hall; their members had always made me feel welcome. Although they had endorsed my candidacy the year before, and I had many times met with and talked to the union's officers and activists, I didn't really know them; I did not know their personal stories; and even though I had gone to high school with their sons and daughters, I didn't really know much about their lives.

Thus began my political education. At USW Local 169 and at the

United Auto Workers Local 549 halls, I learned about the history of trade unionism, and how in 1958 the most powerful corporations in Ohio had tried to destroy the union movement with a "right to work" initiative (the right to work for less, as good trade unionists always reminded the public)—and how those Ohio corporations failed miserably on the ballot. I learned how union workers made steel and how they built cars. I learned that strikes are always an act of back-against-the-wall desperation, because workers never make up for the wages lost, no matter how good the contract and how briefly they are on the picket line. And I learned that, to a trade unionist, strikebreakers—scabs—are the lowest form of human life.

Mansfield in the 1970s was a blue-collar town of 50,000 in a county of 120,000—home to tens of thousands of mostly union workers at Fisher Body, Westinghouse, Tappan Stove, Ohio Brass, Mansfield Tire, and dozens of machine shops, tool-and-die operations, and small assembly plants. They worked hard; most willingly accepted six-day workweeks and the overtime pay that came with them. Most of these workers, especially those lucky enough to carry a union card, had a shot at the American Dream. They owned a modest home; they could buy a new car every four or five years; they could send their children to Mansfield's campus of Ohio State University or to North Central Technical College.

Few of these workers, white and black, expected to have the opportunity that this doctor's kid did. But they understood—intuitively, I would say—that their high school daughter, their son at John Sherman Junior High could have more than they did. Their challenge, to grasp the American Dream and launch their children upward, was more difficult than it was for my parents. More things could go wrong for them: a layoff, a strike, a workplace injury, an illness in the family—each with more devastating consequences than life deals a more affluent white family. And of course African American workers had greater challenges because of decades of racial discrimination.

I learned about luck—where you were born, how much education and income your parents had, what neighborhood you lived in and what school you attended. I understood how much good luck I had, and how little some of these workers had.

And they told me what they read—books and articles and newspapers, stories about strikes and heroes of the labor movement. Over the years, I came to realize that the best books about workers and their unending struggle for dignity and a decent standard of living were novels: Wallace Stegner's *Joe Hill*, and Emile Zola's *Germinal*, and Pietro di Donato's *Christ in Concrete*, and John Steinbeck's *The Grapes of Wrath*.

IN THOSE DAYS—it was the 1970s—most Americans understood that you built a society and an economy from the middle class out. Trickledown economics had been discredited four decades earlier, in the Hoover administration. If workers were paid good wages, they were good consumers. And companies could sell their products. Executives were paid well, but nothing close to the three-hundred-to-one or four-hundred-to-one CEO-to-worker ratios of more recent times. Workers realized that their union cards were their ticket to the middle class and the map to a better future for their sons and daughters. It was a time, in large part because of the union movement, when Americans believed that all work that provides a decent standard of living has dignity, that their children's lives would be better than their own.

But of course the 1970s turned into the 1980s with very different politics, increasing animus from corporate America toward unions, and a reenergized conservative movement. Emerson reminded us a century earlier that Conservators resist change, want to preserve the status quo, want most of all to hold on to their wealth and privilege and status. History tells us that the Conservators—those with privilege and wealth who have lawyers and accountants and lobbyists in state capitols and in Washington—win more often than they lose. Conservators, in the words of John Kenneth Galbraith, are "engaged in one of man's oldest exercises in moral philosophy, that is the search for a superior moral justification for selfishness."

Progressive eras—those periods when Social Security and the right to collective bargaining are enacted, when Medicare and civil rights laws are passed, when food safety rules are created and child labor is prohibited—are bright, meteoric, and short-lived . . . as brief as three or four or five years. And then the Innovators are forced to play defense to preserve the gains of the progressive era. The conservatives return, shouting Stop. No. Enough. Repeal. And we try to hold on to what we created, to protect the public gains.

As we see, in decade after decade, it's easier for the conservatives. History tells us that the burden is always on those who want change. The Conservators, the privileged, always have more money on their side. Their advocates are many: their lawyers and accountants and public relations teams, much of the economics profession, the CEO class, and most newspaper editors and publishers—all who already have great influence in our communities and in our major institutions. The Conservators have a sympathetic media, not just the message enforcers at *The Wall Street Journal* and the cheerleaders at Fox News. Not just the automatons on talk radio. They also enlist the consistently conservative daily newspapers found in Anytown, USA. After all, newspaper owners and publishers want to protect their place in society too. With a wink and a nod, and I assume a chuckle, *The Wall Street Journal*, perhaps the most influential newspaper in America, and Fox News, the nation's most watched cable network, attribute all of society's ills to the influence of the mainstream liberal media. Wherever, and whatever, and whoever they are.

In Washington the Conservators are the lobbyists, the corporate-funded think tanks, the conservative politicians, and the most pro-corporate Supreme Court in my lifetime—even before the appointments of Gorsuch and Kavanaugh. The Conservators' fund-raising apparatus, especially now with the *Citizens United* Supreme Court decision opening the dark money spigot, is a world without end. Often these elected officials and judges—most born to privilege themselves—have chosen, as their primary mission as public servants, to help the privileged get more privilege.

And how they love to base their views in pseudo-facts about Adam Smith, the Scottish philosopher and writer who wrote *An Inquiry into the Nature and Causes of the Wealth of Nations* in 1776. That classic, from which much conservative thought is derived, is not what its twenty-first-century acolytes like to tell us. Smith, whose last job was tariff collector in Scotland, understood that government had an important role to play in society: to build roads and parks and schools, to provide education for its citizens, to tax tobacco and alcohol to raise revenue. He was just as concerned with the "moral sentiments" that foster sympathy between strangers as with the self-interest of merchants and entrepreneurs. And, oh, the "invisible hand" on which all conservative, marketplace economics rests? It appeared in the nine-hundred-page *Wealth of Nations* just three times.

Innovators reach back in history too, but with a firmer grasp. The Innovators believe in using the tools and power of government for progressive change. Franklin Roosevelt, the greatest Innovator to occupy the White House, brought to the American people Social Security and collective bargaining, minimum wage and overtime laws, rules for the banking system and assistance to the poor. Each of these steps was taken in the face of powerful, well-funded, entrenched special-interest opposition. Government, Republican President Theodore Roosevelt used to say, is the only counterweight to the private power of special interests. The fights are difficult and arduous, the outcome always uncertain. "Nothing," the great Protestant theologian Reinhold Niebuhr said, "that is worth doing can be achieved in our lifetime . . . And nothing we do, however virtuous, can be accomplished alone."

And, as Coretta Scott King reminded us, "Struggle is a never-ending process. Freedom is never really won. You earn it and win it in every generation."

Fundamentally, much that happens in Congress—and has happened in Congress for 230 years—is about that struggle. As I talked with steelworkers at Local 169 on Longview Avenue, or listened to Reverend Archie Johnson at Mt. Calvary Baptist Church in Mansfield, or watched elderly Ohioans anguish over paying their heating bill during cold Shelby winters, I thought a lot about that battle between the Innovators and the Conservators.

More than four decades ago, as a young elected official with what I hoped was a long political career in front of me, I knew that I would throw in with the Innovators.

2.

Theodore Francis Green

A TRAITOR TO HIS CLASS

SERVED IN THE UNITED STATES SENATE 1937–1961

As long as I got beaten, my conservative friends tolerated
my liberal views as an amiable idiosyncrasy,
as though I had taken up Buddhism.

—Senator Theodore Francis Green of Rhode Island

TO YANKEE REPUBLICANS IN NEWPORT, Rhode Island, Theodore Francis Green was a traitor to his class. Just like his hero Franklin Delano Roosevelt. But Green's old friends didn't realize it until he was sixty-five years old.

Green's "political aptitudes," as *U.S. News & World Report* observed in 1957, "were slow in revealing themselves." Before his sixty-fifth birthday, he had won just one election, becoming state representative a full quarter century earlier, in a district of fewer than a couple of thousand voters. Not that he hadn't tried. For as long as there have been democracy and competitive elections, candidates have faced a series of hundreds of little humiliations—answering insulting questions, listening to know-it-alls, pleading for campaign help, and enduring nasty comments, the occasional insufferable ally, bad food, and biased editorial boards. For Green, who lost races for Congress in 1920 and for governor of Rhode Island in 1912, 1928, and 1930, the humiliations surely multiplied.

But in his role as a citizen—and a champion of progressive causes— he tallied victory after victory. John Pastore, Green's junior colleague during Green's later service in the Senate, told a story on the floor of the Senate: T. F. Green—not yet an officeholder, not even a candidate—was speaking to Portuguese immigrants at the Providence Public Library in 1917. There, he laid down these six minimum conditions of good citizenship:

First. Knowledge of English;
Second. Establishment of a home;
Third. Thrift;
Fourth. Interest in education;
Fifth. Respect for religious truth; and
Sixth. Interest in honest and intelligent voting.

Green was born into a wealthy family in 1867 in Providence. A sickly child, he was afflicted with pleurisy, typhoid, and malaria, which may have accounted for his lifelong obsession with physical fitness. A son of privilege—Brown University, Harvard Law School, stints at universities in Bonn and Berlin—he was a bit of a Renaissance man: multilingual, successful in business, infantry commander in the Spanish-American War, attorney and president of the American Bar Association, collector of Chinese art, professor of Roman law.

For more than a decade, Green was president of the J&P Coats Company, a thread manufacturer employing five thousand workers in Pawtucket. He established a plant recreation program, a cafeteria, and an infirmary. And to the chagrin of other captains of industry, he insisted on decent wages and better working conditions for his employees.

It was not until he was sixty-five that the "Brahmin Democrat" T. F.

Green—the grandnephew, great-grandnephew, great-great-grandnephew, and great-grandson of Rhode Island congressmen and senators—won his first major election, for governor of Rhode Island and Providence Plantations.

Then everything changed. "As long as I got beaten," Green said, "my conservative friends tolerated my liberal views as an amiable idiosyncrasy, as though I had taken up Buddhism. But when I won and began to get results and make reforms, they were angry. Many cut me on the street, turned their backs on me in the clubs."

And reforms he made. They did not come right away, because in 1933 he faced a grotesquely gerrymandered Republican legislature. He knew that, if he were to accomplish the kinds of change that FDR was making in Washington, he needed more reliable allies and far more political clout in Providence.

For years, Rhode Island had been a state of Yankee Protestant mill-owners who were virtually all Republicans, and Catholic immigrant millworkers, almost always Democrats. Green's lieutenant governor, and later governor, Robert E. Quinn spoke in a 1972 oral history of his Irish aunts working in the Pawtuxet Valley cotton mills for one dollar a day. Illinois Senator Paul Douglas, in describing the importance of T. F. Green, said, "That state was dominated by a relatively small group of very wealthy men who, while they did not run for office themselves, managed the state, either directly or indirectly."

"Ethnicity was destiny," *The Providence Journal*'s Scott MacKay and Jody McPhillips wrote more than a half century after Green's time as governor. These first- and second-generation immigrants "learned at the dinner table to spit 'millowner.'" Quinn recalled that "my father used to think it was a crime for any Irishman to vote for the Republican ticket."

By the 1930s, Rhode Island was the most urban and most Roman Catholic state in the United States. And the immigrants—Irish, Italian, French-Canadian, and Portuguese—fought hard for a bigger say in the state's governance, speaking out in their parishes, organizing unions, forming political clubs. But the conservative political establishment would not let them in.

The Democrats could win statewide elections. There were, after all, far more millworkers than there were millowners. But the legislature continued in Republican hands, because the monied interests made sure of it. Every community in Rhode Island—from Providence and its 275,000 people to West Greenwich with its 485 residents—had one senator, magnifying the small-town Protestant Republican vote while preserving the power of the millowners. "No state outside the south did so much to restrict the right to vote as Rhode Island," wrote the political scientist Duane Lockard. For more than one hundred years, property ownership was a requirement to register; in fact, Rhode Island was among the last states to keep in place a property requirement for voting.

And the legislature wielded far more power than the governor, probably more than in any state in the country. Since 1901, the Rhode Island Senate had been dispensing virtually all state government jobs, choosing commissioners, judges, and other major and minor administrative positions. The governor, especially if he were a Democrat, was no more than a figurehead. A third of a century later, Robert Quinn recalled, "The rotten borough system meant that the old Republican organizations through towns like West Greenwich, Exeter, Richmond, and New Shoreham and Little Compton, and so forth, controlled the State of Rhode Island."

The Great Depression, the 1934 elections, and the events of January 1, 1935, changed all that. The Depression hit Rhode Island (especially its immigrant populations) even harder than it did most other states, and afflicted most painfully—as economic downturns almost always do—the working poor. They suffered in a state dominated by conservative business interests, with little assistance and few services provided to low-paid wage earners.

Even with gerrymandered senate districts, the popularity of President Roosevelt and the Democrats and the disdain for Republicans that so many workers felt brought the Rhode Island Senate to almost a draw on Election Day 1934. Green was reelected decisively to a second two-year term, Democrats won the House easily, and Democrats won twenty of forty-two state senate districts. And Green, Quinn, and their allies felt certain that two of the Republican senate "victories" had been stolen.

Within days of his November 1934 reelection, Green decided he had

had enough. He and his advisors began to hatch plans to end the decades-long rule of minority Republicans. It was clear that the system was rigged when Democrats won overwhelming majorities and had solid public support, but the system did not allow their voices to be heard. After weeks of discussions, they were ready.

On January 1, 1935, Governor Green, Lieutenant Governor Robert Quinn, United States Attorney J. Howard McGrath (who was to become attorney general of the United States under President Truman), party officials, and Democratic legislators gathered at the governor's residence to execute their plan. Everyone had a role to play; everyone got his assignment. And at 10:00 a.m., when the Rhode Island Senate convened, they acted. The Bloodless Revolution—about to be immortalized in the history lessons of Rhode Island schoolchildren—was launched.

Lieutenant Governor Quinn, the senate's presiding officer, swore in only forty of forty-two senators that day. Two Republicans who were to represent Portsmouth and South Kingstown had been challenged by Democrats. The seated senators found themselves in a 20–20 deadlock, and it fell to Quinn to cast the deciding vote. They ended up forming an oversight committee comprised of two Democratic senators and one friendly Republican to examine the votes from the two contested elections. The fraud was easy to spot, and the outcomes were overturned.

The State of Rhode Island and Providence Plantations was now—after decades of minority rule—governed by the majority of its citizens. The senate reconvened that evening at 7:15, with a 22–20 Democratic majority, ready for action. Senator William Troy brought up five bills for immediate consideration. In only fourteen minutes—amid Republican howls of protest—the senate voted to merge eighty-eight state commissions into ten state departments, to oust the entire Providence safety board, to reorganize the finance commission, and to vacate the office of the Providence sheriff. All five justices of the Rhode Island Supreme Court resigned when promised lucrative pensions. Green replaced the five Republicans with three Democrats and two Republicans.

Apparently, Washington took notice. Two years later, in the wake of the failure of FDR's court packing efforts, the Congress passed legislation granting to Supreme Court Justices over the age of seventy, with ten years of service, full pay upon retirement. Four conservative United States Supreme Court justices left by 1941—Devanter in 1937, Sutherland in 1938, Butler in 1939, and McReynolds in 1941; so did three liberal ones—Cardozo in 1938, Brandeis in 1939, and Hughes in 1941.

By 8:00 p.m. on that fateful January day in 1935, the Rhode Island House of Representatives passed all five bills and sent them to the governor. Green promptly signed them. John Pastore, who had been sworn in that morning to his first term as a state representative, said that day was the most exciting of his long, storied career as a state legislator, governor, and United States senator.

The right-wing publisher of the *Chicago Tribune*, Colonel Robert R. McCormick, had a different take on the Democratic takeover in a state almost a thousand miles away. He was so incensed about the end of Republican rule in Rhode Island that he, in an editorial, labeled Rhode Island "a state of rogues" and then ordered a star cut out from the American flag that flew over the *Tribune* headquarters. He later replaced it with a new flag when he was informed that he was likely to be charged with flag desecration. One of the twentieth century's great novelists, Upton Sinclair, wrote in *A World to Win* in 1946: "As for Willie Hearst and Bertie McCormick, they are two spoiled children who inherited vast fortunes and have used them according to their furious prejudices and resentments."

But it was really never about process for T. F. Green. It was about fighting the malefactors of great wealth and enacting a progressive agenda in tandem with President Roosevelt's New Deal—raising living standards and improving workers' lives. Using New Deal funds as leverage, he modernized the court system, transformed an antiquated, lethargic state bureaucracy into an effective instrument of social and economic change, and launched expansive public works programs.

At Green's urging, the Democratic legislature established a minimum wage, restricted working hours for women and children to forty-eight hours a week, set up a workers' compensation program and state unemployment insurance system, and provided a retirement plan for state employees. And to strengthen the labor movement, injunctions against strikes were made more difficult for employers to secure.

During his fourth year as governor, T. F. Green was beginning to attract a national following. He made a seconding speech for President Roosevelt's nomination for a second term. He took on the Republican nominee, Alf Landon, after Republican National Committee Chairman John D. M. Hamilton visited Providence. On July 26, 1936, he joined the governors of Oregon, Pennsylvania, Nebraska, Iowa, and Illinois on a national radio broadcast. Capturing the ebullient optimism of FDR himself, Green enthused, "With cash in her pocket and new hope in her heart, Rhode Island is on her way."

In October 1936—campaigns were much, much shorter in those days—the sixty-nine-year-old Green announced for the Senate against two-term Republican and anti–New Deal Senator Jesse Metcalf, the seventy-five-year-old former chairman of the Senate Education and Labor Committee, and part owner of *The Providence Journal*. With Governor Green's personal popularity, a newly resurgent Rhode Island Democratic Party, a rather feckless Republican incumbent, and the FDR landslide, it was not much of a race. Green's victory helped produce a United States Senate with seventy-six Democrats, sixteen Republicans, and four independents.

The 1936 election, the most one-sided in American history, saw Franklin Roosevelt defeat Kansas Governor Alf Landon in forty-six of forty-eight states and Democrats win huge victories in statehouses and courthouses all over the United States. Landon was nominated at the Republican National Convention at Cleveland's Public Auditorium, the same auditorium where my 2006 victory celebration was held. Eighty years later, the GOP returned to my hometown of Cleveland for its national convention.

The senior senator in Rhode Island at the time of Green's election, Democrat Peter Gerry, also came from great wealth and had ancestors who were members of Congress. His great-grandfather Elbridge Gerry—congressman, governor of Massachusetts, vice president of the United States—played his role in American political folklore when, as governor, he drew a redistricting map that resembled a salamander. The term gerrymander has been with us ever since.

Peter Gerry, thirteen years Green's junior, had served in the House and Senate for twenty-four years by the time the sixty-nine-year-old Green took his Senate oath of office. Gerry, in the words of chronicler John Gunther, was one of the most reactionary men in official Washington, and Green became one of the most progressive.*

Right from the start, Green was an enthusiastic New Dealer and a gushingly loyal FDR supporter. He found his way onto the Appropriations Committee, a rare accomplishment for a freshman. He was an avid proponent of Senator Hugo Black's wages and hours legislation, having lived by its principles when he was an employer, and the low-cost housing bill during his first year in the Senate. He advocated for work and farm relief, and even backed Roosevelt's doomed court-packing efforts.

He supported civil rights, in a state with few black voters. He later voted for the censure of Senator Joseph McCarthy, in a state with a very large number of Irish-Catholics, something his next door Irish-Catholic neighbor in Massachusetts, Senator John F. Kennedy, could not bring himself to do. And he stood strong on issues of immigration and civil liberties, as the country moved to the right after World War II.

But first and foremost, T. F. Green was an internationalist. He spoke five languages, had studied in Germany as a young man, was a veteran of the Spanish-American War, and traveled perhaps more widely than any of his colleagues before coming to Washington.

In 1939, his third year in the Senate, Green was appointed to the Foreign Relations Committee. He aggressively supported a buildup of military might as dark war clouds began to gather over Europe. He wanted a revision of neutrality laws and passage of a lend-lease act so that the United States could build up Great Britain's military by lending or leasing it war supplies—even though America in the late 1930s was mostly an isolationist nation.

After the war, Green was a reliable advocate of Truman's foreign pol-

---

*In a chart prepared in February 1946 by *The New Republic*, Gunther tells us, Green was one of only four senators "with a perfect one hundred percent progressive voting record." The other three were Abe Murdock of Utah, James Tunnell of Delaware, and Hugh Mitchell of Washington State. Gunther enthused: "What an enormously diversified country is the United States, even in respect to an item so small as this. Green is a traction magnate and millionaire aristocrat; Tunnell a public school teacher who became a vigorously successful bank president; Mitchell is the son of a civil servant; Murdock, a poor boy, was born on a farm."

icy. He called the United Nations "the last great hope for mankind." He supported the Marshall Plan, the North Atlantic Treaty Organization (NATO), and, later, United States involvement in Korea.

Although fastidious in his dress and sometimes annoyingly correct in grammar and speech, Green did not lack for a sense of humor. When asked how many square miles our country's smallest state occupied, he declined to say, observing, "It varies so much from high tide to low tide."

When chairing a meeting, the renowned journalist Allen Drury wrote in *A Senate Journal*, Green looked "like a peasant leftover from the Nineties, with his walrus mustache, his sharp-boned face with its sharp shaft of nose, his scholarly eyes and kindly expression, his dignified schoolteacherly way of speaking, his long coat, and his busy, shuffling walk."

In 1951, John Pastore joined Green in representing Rhode Island in the U.S. Senate. Though Pastore, who had been the first Italian American governor in the United States, stood less than five and a half feet tall, he may have been the best orator in the Senate, and with his voice and his intelligence he was said to have intimidated almost everyone he dealt with, including his elder Green.

The Washington lawyer Paul Quinn, who grew up in Rhode Island and still spends a lot of his time there, was a staff person in the Senate in the 1960s. Quinn, who is not related to former Governor Quinn, told me that few people commanded the attention of his fellow senators like Pastore when he took to the Senate floor to speak. Capitol Hill visitors would flock to the Senate gallery when they heard that Pastore might be addressing his colleagues.

One day, when the Senate was considering the Civil Rights Act of 1964, Louisiana Senator Russell Long, a staunch opponent of civil rights, was the concluding speaker in opposition to the bill. Pastore, a senior member of the Commerce Committee, was scheduled to follow Long and be the last speaker before the vote was taken. (The Commerce Committee managed the legislation because the chairman of the Judiciary Committee, Mississippi Senator James Eastland, was one of the Senate's most virulent segregationists.)

As Quinn recounts it, Long spoke in flowery terms about the Old

South, about respect and values and tradition, and about southern women and patriotism. After ten or fifteen minutes, he took a seat in the first row to await Pastore's concluding address. The presiding officer offered the Rhode Island senator the same amount of time. All eyes on him, Pastore strode to the front of the chamber. Walking up to Long's seat, the five-foot-four Pastore leaned over his desk, looked directly into his eyes, and shouted, "So what!" He then called for the vote, and won.

In 1956 Theodore Francis Green became the oldest person ever to serve in the United States Senate, eclipsing Vermont Republican Justin Morrill, who died in 1898 at the age of eighty-eight. Morrill had, upon his death, served in the Senate longer than anyone in the nation's history.

Green had always worked hard to stay fit—and was proud of it. He did not drive. He owned a car only once, when he was governor, because he thought he had to, but he usually walked the nearly three miles to the Senate Office Building. A lifelong bachelor, he drank a single cocktail every day, never smoked, played tennis into his late eighties, and frequently worked out in the Senate gym or at the YMCA. In his successful race for governor in 1932, to attest to his vitality and fitness for the job and perhaps to address issues of his sexuality, the then-sixty-five-year-old Green bought a full-page ad in *The Providence Sunday Journal* showing the muscular candidate stripped to the waist, chopping down a tree and hauling a heavy boulder.

In May 1957, Green became the oldest person ever to serve in the federal legislature in either chamber, when he surpassed the record held by North Carolina Democratic Congressman Charles Stedman, who died in office in 1930. When Green assumed the Foreign Relations chairmanship, he still had a reputation as a tough questioner. His mind grasped details, and he had a vast knowledge drawn from decades of voracious reading, years of extensive traveling, and hundreds of meetings with foreign leaders. He had strong and well-reasoned beliefs as a staunch progressive: about China, third world aspirations, and the prudent use of United States military force.

Late in T. F. Green's career, conservative Georgia Democrat Walter George, three-term chairman of the Senate Foreign Relations Committee, retired. Under the Senate's inviolate seniority system, it was now Green's turn. In January 1957, Theodore Francis Green—at the age of eighty-nine, the oldest man ever to serve in the Senate—ascended to the chairmanship of the Foreign Relations Committee. Foreign Relations was the Senate's most sought-after committee, exceeding the stature and importance of the Finance Committee and the Appropriations Committee in those days of a smaller, less expansive federal government.

But Green's eyesight was failing, his hearing diminishing, and his attention span declining. And, perhaps most important, he was unable to handle his committee's legislation on the floor of the Senate, a crucial responsibility for any chairman. As much as fellow senators and staff, and perhaps even the press, respected Green and wanted him to succeed, grumbles and complaints began to ripple across Capitol Hill.

In the next Congress, by early 1959, the honeymoon was over. *The Providence Journal*, the largest and most prestigious paper in Green's state, editorialized that Rhode Island's senior senator should relinquish his committee duties: "Reports from Washington increasingly suggest that Senator Green no longer has the physical capacity, the mental vigor, or the depth of insight to discharge his duties as the national interest demands." He should, they opined as respectfully as they could, perform "a final and unique service" by giving up his chairmanship.

Majority Leader Lyndon Johnson stepped in. No committee chairman in Senate history, as far as anyone knows, had stepped down in the middle of a session. But LBJ didn't care much for tradition. Always the operator, the Master of the Senate (the title of Robert Caro's brilliant book about the majority leader and his aggressive leadership style) went to see Green in his office, only hours after the editorial appeared. LBJ wanted Green to relinquish his chairmanship, but the majority leader did not want it to appear that either the Democratic leadership or *The Providence Journal* was trying to force Green to quit.

Johnson flattered Green, expressing his support for the octogenarian chairman, flashing his anger at the newspaper's presumptuousness, and offering any assistance Green wanted. Later in the day, back in Green's office, the chairman notified the majority leader, in the face of Johnson's vociferous but less than sincere protestations, that he would indeed step down, as long as he retained his seniority and his committee assignment. Johnson of course assented.

But just getting his way was never quite enough for Lyndon Johnson. The next morning, perhaps to make sure Green had no time to change his mind, he convened a meeting of the Foreign Relations Committee that Johnson himself decided to chair—more precedent-shattering behavior by the majority leader. Sixteen of seventeen committee members were in attendance. Green read a letter aloud from him to Johnson asking that he be relieved of his duties, then turned over the meeting to the majority leader. With great flourish, Johnson made clear that he wanted Green to stay, but that Green believed he could no longer perform his duties adequately.

Other senators, almost every member of the committee, praised Green and urged him to stay. Proving that insincerity could be bipartisan, Republican Senator George Aiken moved that the committee ask Green to reconsider his decision. Seconded by Senator J. William Fulbright,* the heir apparent, the motion carried by a unanimous show of hands.

The charade—and the famous "Johnson Treatment"—continued:

GREEN: I thank you gentlemen from my heart for your expressions of confidence and friendship, but I certainly cannot take any action reversing my letter.

JOHNSON: The members of the committee said what I said, only more eloquently than I, and they have repeated what I said yesterday afternoon—more touchingly, I think. They voted unanimously to ask you to continue.

GREEN: Who did?

JOHNSON: The committee.

GREEN: I didn't know they had.

---

*After Fulbright assumed the chairmanship, Senate rules and tradition forced him to give up his chairmanship of the Banking Committee; he was succeeded by the ultraconservative segregationist Democrat Willis Robertson, father of the far right evangelist politician Pat Robertson, as chairman of the Senate Banking Committee.

JOHNSON: Just a few minutes ago. They now ask unanimously for
you to reconsider.

GREEN: Is that what you were doing?

JOHNSON: You remember what I told you.

GREEN: I would certainly not be brash enough to turn it down
if it were put to the meeting here. I appreciate it highly, and I
ought to give it serious consideration. It didn't occur to me that
it would be this way.

Johnson, recognizing the turn of events, called for a short recess. In
the back room, Green's aides convinced him to stick with his decision.
A few minutes later, Green announced to the committee: "I am deeply
touched by it all, but I still feel that it is my duty to my country, to the
committee, and to myself, to stick to my decision." Chief of staff of the
Foreign Relations Committee Carl M. Marcy recalled years later, "Everybody present breathed a sigh of relief."*

Green's health continued to decline; he underwent two eye surger-
ies and announced in January 1960 that he would not be a candidate for
his fifth term. He retired at age ninety-three and died five years later in
Providence.

Perhaps even the indomitable LBJ could have heeded the age-old
admonition "Be careful what you wish for." T. F. Green was replaced as
chairman of the Foreign Relations Committee in January 1959 by its next
senior member, fifty-two-year-old J. William Fulbright. Less than a decade later, Fulbright was President Johnson's most prominent Vietnam
War critic, prompting the exasperated president to complain, "Why, I
made that man chairman!"

---

*Carl M. Marcy remarked in a 1983 interview that "Senator Green was a perfect gentleman. He
could always make appropriate remarks at a dinner or when called upon. He was of the old, old
school in many respects. I traveled abroad with him several times. I remember two incidents
in Paris. One morning before breakfast I bought some French newspapers and gave them to
Senator Green. He asked if I had paid for the papers. When I said yes, he said, 'Well don't forget
to charge the Committee.' It was a nickel or a dime, or the equivalent in francs. On another
occasion, he looked out of the window one day and he pointed out the Eiffel Tower and said,
'The first time I was here that hadn't been built.'"

THOUGHTS FROM DESK 88

A MONTH OR SO AFTER Theodore Francis Green was elected to the United States Senate, employers in all forty-eight states in the union sent letters to their employees informing them of a new responsibility and a new opportunity. To the millions of workers across the country, it may not have sounded like much of an opportunity.

A few days after Christmas 1936, Howard L. Boyd of York, Pennsylvania, an employee of Pennsylvania Gas and Electric, opened a letter from his company's vice president. It outlined a new program called Social Security "that Congress had passed on August 14, 1935." The Company, the letter read, "is required to deduct 1% of your wages beginning January 1, 1937; 1½% beginning January 1, 1940; 2% beginning January 1, 1943; 2½% beginning January 1, 1946; and 3% beginning January 1, 1947. These deductions, which are matched by your Company, are designed to provide for Retirement at Age 65."

Most workers had no idea what this new program was. While most of these workers had voted to reelect President Roosevelt only six weeks before, and many of them had listened to FDR's fireside chats, few were following the political machinations that produced the Social Security Act in far-off Washington, D.C.

It is also safe to say that, in many of the families who received these letters from their employers, few of their parents and grandparents had even lived to the age of sixty-five. So what good would this Social Security program be to them? And while they trusted Roosevelt, did they believe that in a decade or two or three when someone else was president their money would be available for their retirement?

Many workers around the country heard from their employers, as Boyd did (as recounted several decades later by his son Richard), "you know, they're killing the free enterprise system by taking your money." Or these boys in Washington don't have any idea what they're doing. Or the government is a bunch of thieves, you know, and you'll never see that money. The United States Chamber of Commerce, always with a keen sense of history and unparalleled prescience, said that Social Security was a plan "to Sovietize America."

A couple of months earlier, some had already seen a pre-election warning in their paychecks: during the 1936 election, the Republican National Committee convinced many employers to put flyers in pay envelopes warning workers that, the following January, the government in Washington would take money from them, and that they should vote for Republican Alf Landon because he would stop it. "We must repeal," the GOP nominee said. "The Republican Party is pledged to do this." But there was ample evidence that the public liked what Roosevelt was doing; as we've seen, he carried forty-six states, losing only Maine and Vermont.

On January 31, 1940, Ida May Fuller went to her mailbox in Rutland, Vermont. She opened her mail and found the first Social Security check ever issued—number 00-000-001—for $22.54. Social Security has never missed a payment since. Ever. For eight decades.

Thirty-five years later, Lyndon Johnson flew to Independence, Missouri, to sign the law creating Medicare, to provide health care for the elderly, and to give the first Medicare card to Harry Truman, who as president had asked the "do-nothing" Congress to enact a similar program in 1948. FDR had tried to enlist Congress, under the Social Security Act, to include health care for pensioners. He had failed. So had Truman. So did Kennedy (Eisenhower didn't try). It wasn't so easy for President Johnson either.

Opposition to government health care came from every conservative corner of the nation. Using their tried-and-true formula to protect their wealth, they tried to scare the public. Insurance companies, less influential in 1965 than they are in today's Congress, sent their lobbyists to Capitol Hill to argue that government health insurance was a violation of our free enterprise system. The John Birch Society, then less than a decade old but already well established on the fringes of the far right, and the ideological grandfather of the modern Tea Party, called the Medicare proposal a Communist plot. Texan H. L. Hunt, perhaps the richest man in the world and a major Republican contributor, said that Medicare "would literally make the President of the United States a medical czar with potential life or death power over every man, woman, and child in the country." And private citizen Ronald Reagan, speaking for the American Medical Association, warned that if Congress passed "eldercare," as some called it, "one of these days you and I are going to spend our sunset years telling our children, and our children's children, what it once was like in America when men were free."

Workers' compensation. Social Security. Unemployment insurance. And now Medicare. Another social insurance program was just too much for Barry Goldwater, Strom Thurmond, and the American conservative movement.

Through most of world history, prosperity and economic security have reached only a limited few. The British seventeenth-century philosopher Thomas Hobbes intoned that life for most was "nasty, brutish, and short." Workers and peasants were exploited. Leisure was nonexistent for most people. Workers' and peasants' and slaves' lives were shortened because of the conditions in the factory or on the plantation. No safety net existed in times of want and hunger and illness. Retirement security was virtually unknown. Taxes and levies were oppressive, but mostly on peasants, workers, and small shopkeepers. Governments—almost always selected by the few and rarely chosen by the many—were made up of the wealthiest families, who gave little and took much from the people whom they governed.

Social insurance—as we know it today—began in the 1880s with Prussian Chancellor Otto von Bismarck. Although an ultraconservative German nationalist, Bismarck understood that economic security would help build a more productive economy and a stronger German state. He may not have cared much about the dignity of work, but he understood that providing security to tens of thousands of German workers could undercut any political gains that the socialist parties might make against him. Upon introduction to the Reichstag of his social insurance program, and calling his social insurance proposals "practical Christianity," Bismarck declared, "The real grievance of the worker is the insecurity of his existence; he is not sure that he will always have work, he is not sure that he will always be healthy, and he foresees that he will one day be old and unfit to work." An interesting side benefit for Prussia as it built security for its workers was a sharp decline in emigration to America; German workers who might have been tempted to try their luck in the United States in the 1880s and 1890s were more inclined, because of the social insurance available for them and their families, to stay in Prussia.

At the same time, Leo XIII, known to history as the Labor Pope, encouraged governments to pass social welfare legislation, to honor the rights of working people, to respect the dignity of work. Leo's 1891 encyclical *Rerum Novarum* ("Of the new things"), or *Rights and Duties of Capital and Labor*, was the pope's response to industrialization and the exploitation of factory and mine workers. *Rerum Novarum* is considered the foundational text of modern Catholic social teaching. "Let the working man and the employer make free agreements . . . and respect the dignity of workers . . ." The encyclical prescribed formation of trade unions and collective bargaining, and condemned child labor and working long hours.

In the ensuing years, other nations, notably Great Britain in 1911, introduced unemployment insurance. In the 1920s and 1930s a number of American states set up workers' compensation programs to assist injured workers, and to keep those workers from bringing suit against employers for workplace injuries. But not until the Great Depression did the United States provide old-age benefits and unemployment insurance. From FDR to LBJ, Democrats built an American version of a social insurance temple with the solid pillars of Social Security and unemployment insurance, and workers' compensation and Medicare. Senators like Black and Green played important roles in erecting it.

Call social insurance a progressive principle. Or call it our Judeo-Christian ethic. Or call it a sense of community, or an American value. Our system of social insurance—Social Security, Medicare, unemployment insurance, workers' compensation—has given opportunity to our workers and security to our families. Nearly every worker pays in. And almost everyone is eligible for help when they need it: illness, workplace injury, death of the breadwinner, disability, medical care for the sick, a pension for the retired, a safety net for the laid-off worker. And that is—still today—what the big fights in Washington are so often about. The 1930s and Social Security. The 1960s and Medicare. And efforts by Trump and Senate majority leader Mitch McConnell of Kentucky in 2017 and 2018 to transfer hundreds of billions of dollars from working families to the wealthiest 1 percent of the population.

Republicans never much liked the social insurance temple or its individual Social Security and unemployment insurance and Medicare pillars. Conservatives say that they can spend their money better than the government can; they argue that the American people's generosity, and America's rich texture of charitable institutions—from churches to major foundations—could take care of the sick and the elderly and the disabled. They have promised to do so many times, but it never seems to work out the way they told us.

Many Republicans opposed the creation of Social Security and unemployment insurance in the 1930s. A majority of House Republicans opposed Medicare in 1965. Since the early 1980s, well-funded conservatives—CEOs, editorial boards, far-right think tanks, talk radio and Fox News—have worked to build opposition to America's Social Security and Medicare and unemployment insurance. And since the newly energized Republicans of the Reagan years and the emboldened party of the Gingrich years, the GOP has aggressively tried to cut, scale back, limit, privatize, cap, block grant, voucherize (take your pick, Dear Reader) all things social insurance.

Since the creation of Medicare in 1965, the Republicans had never had a majority in the House of Representatives—until the 1994 elections. One of Speaker Gingrich's first actions in 1995—for the first time in forty years the House of Representatives had a Republican Speaker—was to attempt to cut Medicare and begin its privatization. "Now, we don't get rid of it in round one because we don't think that that's politically smart, and we don't think that's the right way to go through a transition," he intoned. "But we believe it's going to wither on the vine because we think people are voluntarily going to leave it—voluntarily." And during his 1996 presidential campaign, Republican Kansas Senator Bob Dole bragged about his 1965 opposition to the creation of Medicare when he was a young Kansas congressman. The Clinton White House and minority Democrats in Congress mobilized, and Gingrich soon realized that Medicare had too much public support to privatize it.

Newt Gingrich was a smart strategist and tactician; after all, he figured out against the odds a path to the majority for his Republican Party, the first GOP majority in forty years. But not only did he believe that he was the smartest guy in the room, a typical Washington affliction; he thought he was smarter than the whole room. Nobody is. Nobody. That was his downfall.

The Gingrich Medicare defeat aside, by the turn of the millennium, conservatives thought they were winning the social insurance fight; since Reagan's presidency, there had been an effort by conservative think tanks and far-right monied interests, with their Wall Street allies, to convince future generations that Social Security was "unsustainable" (their favorite word to describe all social insurance, but never the defense budget) and that it would not be there for them when they retired.

The billionaire funders Joseph Coors and David and Charles Koch had, in the mid-1970s, founded the Heritage Foundation and the Cato Institute, respectively, think tanks whose primary mission was to shrink government, in part by undermining social insurance. In 1983, for example, Stuart Butler and Peter Germanis of the Heritage Foundation wrote for the Cato Institute's *Cato Journal* that Social Security opponents should pursue "a Leninist strategy" to "restructure [Social Security] into a predominantly private system." And while Heritage and Cato and their billionaire funders may—or may not; the human mind works in funny but necessary ways—have been driven mostly by an ideological antipathy to social insurance, there were huge benefits for "banks, insurance companies, and other institutions," all of which of course would help them build their "Leninist coalition" to discredit and undermine Social Security. And undermine it they did.

According to a *USA Today* poll in October 2013, only 11 percent of eighteen- to twenty-four-year-olds expected to receive Social Security when they retired in four or five decades. Some conservative politicians claim that young people think there is a better chance that Elvis is alive than that they will get a Social Security check when they retire. George W. Bush, in his first term, rammed a partial Medicare privatization bill through a reluctant Congress—the Republican House passed it in a middle-of-the-night, hold-the-roll-open-for-two-hours two-vote margin—in the name of a Medicare drug benefit.

Then the election of 2004—it was hardly a landslide; Kerry's razor-thin loss in one state, Ohio, made the electoral college difference—gave President Bush the confidence to use his political capital to give the CEO class, Wall Street, and the party's billionaire libertarian funders what they had wanted for decades: to privatize Social Security and accelerate the dismantling of the welfare state and the end of social insurance. Bush proposed private accounts for Social Security. Many of Washington's "serious people" and the "most responsible" talking heads—followed by lots of very important newspaper editors (few of whom really needed Social Security)—added their upper-class harmony to the chorus; there was, after all, a Republican House and a Republican Senate and a Republican president, and we all know that Social Security was "unsustainable."

Brings to mind Timothy Crouse's classic 1972 campaign book *The Boys on the Bus* about reporters covering presidential politics: when one bird flies off the telephone wire, they all do.

The reaction was swift, and unexpected—at least by President Bush and Vice President Cheney and *The Wall Street Journal* editorial board—in its fury. Even Montana Senator Max Baucus, the senior Democrat on Finance, usually a reliable Bush ally on the big things—the Iraq War, Medicare privatization, tax cuts, environmental rollbacks, trade agreements—pushed back hard in defense of Social Security.

A dispirited Democratic Party—after all, we had lost everything in the 2004 election—was suddenly jolted awake. House and Senate Democrats organized like we had never seen. Democrats—conservatives and moderates and liberals—held news conferences and spoke at rallies; we wrote editorials in newspapers; we used social media as never before. And an enraged public, across the ideological spectrum, said an emphatic no. The public intuitively understood that Social Security, as FDR's grandson James Roosevelt, Jr., wrote, "could not be better managed. It returns more than 99 cents to beneficiaries on every dollar collected . . . I dare you to find a private retirement plan that can claim that."

In a matter of only a few weeks, President Bush's privatization scheme was dead. Five years later, when the economy imploded, the nation could only imagine what would have happened if privatization had been enacted and people's private accounts decimated.

President Bush and his conservative advisors had forgotten one big thing: the public has always loved Social Security; they do not want it to change; they like it the way it is. In fact, the only real criticism *from the public* is that the cost of living adjustment (the COLA) is inadequate in keeping up with rising costs. It is important for the Washington pundits to know—although most don't seem to care to—that the average Social Security check (in 2019 dollars) is little more than $1,450 per month, and that more than one-half of America's elderly population derives more than half their income from Social Security. In Ohio, for a third of our senior citizens, Social Security is just about their entire income.

While the defeats of Gingrich's Medicare privatization campaign and Bush's Social Security scheme were irrefutable, Republican animus toward social insurance—especially Medicare and Social Security—won't let them stop. The Republican Speaker's budget, the CEO-funded organization Fix the Debt,* and Senate Finance Committee efforts to undermine Social Security Disability—all continue to try to dismantle America's social insurance safety net.

After all, the most significant difference between the two parties— the Manichean political struggle over most of the last century that Emerson predicted when he warned that Conservators will desperately fight to hold on to their privilege—is about the importance of government and the role of social insurance. Whenever conservatives have the opportunity to undermine or weaken America's social insurance system, they have taken advantage of it. Candidate Donald Trump may have broken with GOP tradition and campaigned as a defender of Social Security and Medicare, but once in office, he aligned with conservative orthodoxy and the Republican establishment to attack Medicaid and undermine the nation's social insurance. They just can't help themselves. All of them.

But progressives don't want to just play defense, to just defend Social Security and Medicare and unemployment insurance. It's why elections matter. We will continue to work to expand social insurance and expand the safety net; after all, it's what we stand for. In March 2017, at Ohio State's John Glenn College of Public Affairs, I unveiled our Working Too Hard for Too Little plan to strengthen the dignity of work. It calls for an increase in the minimum wage, an updating of the overtime rule, stronger penalties for employers who engage in wage theft, and providing sick leave and paid family leave. Until we succeed, progressives will not rest.

---

*A particularly rich development: the longtime CEO of the Eaton Corporation, a Fortune 500 company and a major Cleveland employer, fashioned himself a balanced-budget crusader as he lectured anyone who would listen—and he expected everyone to listen—that Social Security was unsustainable, that we had to cut spending, that we had to achieve a balanced budget. His company "moved" its corporate headquarters to Ireland in a tax-evading "inversion," avoiding $165 million in federal taxes. His annual compensation was $11 million. To my knowledge, only one Clevelander was paid more handsomely at the time: LeBron James of the Cleveland Cavaliers.

3.

Glen Taylor

THE SINGING COWBOY FROM KOOSKIA

SERVED IN THE UNITED STATES SENATE 1945–1951

At one time, I stated on the floor of the Senate
that I was going to vote my convictions, as though I never
expected to come back. All I can say is that I did vote
my convictions, and I did not come back.

—Senator Glen Taylor of Idaho, last words on the Senate floor

N O OTHER DEMOCRATIC SENATOR would do it. But Idaho's
Glen Taylor was like no other senator.

It was January 3, 1947. Ohio Senator Robert Taft and the
new Republican majority were ecstatic. Fifteen years in the minority, and
now they were ready to govern. In only a decade, the Senate had gone
from a 76–16 Democratic majority (with four independents) to a 51–45
Republican majority. But before business could be conducted, there was
the matter of Theodore Bilbo.

An ultra-segregationist Democrat from Mississippi, Bilbo had just been reelected to a third term as senator after serving as governor for eight years. He was unquestionably the United States Senate's most virulent racist: "If I can succeed eventually in resettling the great majority of the Negroes in West Africa . . . I propose to do it." When criticized by Eleanor Roosevelt, he countered, "I might entertain the notion of crowning Eleanor Queen of Great Liberia."

Allen Drury called him "evil and ruthless" and "the most hated man in the District" of Columbia. John Gunther called him "the worst miscreant in American public life." As chairman of the District of Columbia Committee from 1945 to 1947—Senate courtesy and the seniority system allowed such a virulent racist to be the de facto mayor of Washington, D.C., an increasingly African American city—Bilbo aimed to force homeless people to move out of Washington. "I'm getting [the Negro] used to moving, so that after the war he will be ready to move to West Africa."

A few weeks after the Mississippian's 1946 reelection, the Senate Special Committee to Investigate Senatorial Campaign Expenditures brought Bilbo before it to defend his campaign behavior. Seriously ill from cancer, he told the committee that, during his campaign, he had called on "every red-blooded American who believes in the superiority and integrity of the white race to get out and see that no nigger votes." He warned against "Northern niggers teaching [Southern blacks] how to register and how to vote." And he offered assistance to circuit clerks, the state's voter registrars, to "think up questions enough to disqualify undesirables" from voting under Mississippi's literacy test laws. Most of the witnesses were African American and told a very different story, speaking of Bilbo's appeals to racism and how he encouraged violence. At around the same time, the Senate Special Committee to Investigate the National Defense Program launched its own inquiry into Bilbo; it found that he had received a number of illegal gifts, including a Cadillac and a swimming pool for his Mississippi home. Both committee reports were sent to the Senate in early January 1947.

The five-person Campaign Expenditures Committee, made up of Democratic senators from South Carolina, Louisiana, and Oklahoma and Republican senators from New Hampshire and Iowa, recommended on a party line vote that Bilbo be seated. Shame on those three Democrats, many northern liberals—and much of the rest of the country—thought.

Three weeks later, on January 3, 1947, Senator Glen Taylor acted. After Connecticut Republican Raymond Baldwin was sworn in, the clerk of the Senate, following alphabetical order, called the name Theodore G. Bilbo. At Desk 88, Idaho's senior senator rose to object.

Taylor, with fewer than one thousand African Americans in his state, had already established a record of support for civil rights legislation during his first two years in the Senate. He had helped to lead the unsuccessful effort to break the southern senators' filibuster of the Fair Employment Practices Commission in 1946.

"I send to the desk a resolution to which I wish to address myself," Taylor pronounced. Marquis Childs, a columnist for *The St. Louis Post-Dispatch*, and later the first winner of the Pulitzer Prize for Commentary (the same Pulitzer category that my wife, Connie Schultz, won in 2005), captured the scene. "If Hollywood had written the script, the drama on the first day the Senate met could not have been sharper . . . From the back row on the Democratic side, the young hero sprang up. It was perfect typecasting. Glen Taylor, Senator from Idaho, could be played by James Stewart or Gary Cooper."

Holding the floor for an hour—amid catcalls and interruptions from southern Democrats and some of their conservative Republican allies—the third-year senator laid out his case: "We are not only on trial collectively, we are on trial individually . . . What a hypocritical and blasphemous gesture we would witness today, if Mr. Bilbo were to stand in our midst and place his hand on The Holy Bible and swear fealty to democratic institutions, to free elections, to the rights of citizens." Taylor spoke of Bilbo's membership in the Ku Klux Klan, mentioning a radio speech when the Mississippian proudly pronounced, "once a Klansman, always a Klansman."

Marquis Childs: "As though any further drama was needed. At the peroration of Taylor's speech, Bilbo came over and sat down a few feet from the speaker. He sat there glowering up with an arrogance rarely equaled in Senate history."

Many Republicans, led by Taft and first-termers Kenneth Wherry of Nebraska and Homer Ferguson of Michigan, saw an opportunity to curry favor with the increasing numbers of black voters in northern cities. They introduced their own resolution to deny Bilbo his seat. According to Kate Scott, the assistant historian of the United States Senate, Minority Leader Alben Barkley resolved the stalemate by asking that Bilbo's credentials be tabled without action while he underwent surgery.

Bilbo was never sworn in for a third term in the United States Senate. He died in a New Orleans hospital eight months later at the age of sixty-nine.

THERE WAS LITTLE doubt about Glen Taylor's political courage. In addition to his outspoken support for civil rights, he battled for labor rights, knowing there was never a strong organized trade union presence in his state. And in 1948—when virtually all of his political advisors and every pundit in Idaho and in Washington, D.C., told him that it would destroy his chances of reelection—he accepted the Progressive Party vice presidential nomination with Henry Wallace.

AND HE HAD nothing to fall back on to support his family. After each of his defeats—in 1938 for Congress; in 1940, 1942, 1954, and 1956 in losing Senate bids; and in 1950 when he lost reelection to the United States Senate—Taylor struggled financially: as a country musician in a Western band, as a construction worker, as an actor, as a sheet metal worker in a munitions plant, as a toupee maker, as a carpenter.

One of thirteen children and the son of a mostly itinerant Disciples of Christ minister, he learned the Golden Rule: "Think how you would feel on the other end," his father told him. Although Taylor was a spiritual man who was baptized more than a dozen times as a child by his father and tried to live by the New Testament, he was not a particularly churchgoing man. Taylor's views were, at a young age, informed by his preacher father's politics: "Of the type that stressed the Golden Rule, brotherly love, and a modified Christian socialism," he wrote.

At the age of twelve, in 1916, he quit school to work to help his family. He managed two movie theaters, one in Kooskia and one in Stites, for twelve dollars a week. At seventeen, he took to the road, acting and singing. After meeting and marrying Dora Pike, Glen, with Dora and other family members, formed the Glendora Ranch Gang. His sister Lee Morse, several years older than he, went on to become one of America's best-known jazz singers in the 1920s and 1930s.

Two events in Glen Taylor's young life led him to politics. In 1932, an almost penniless Taylor was invited to the Arco, Idaho, home of his cousin, a "doggedly faithful Republican precinct committeeman." Leafing through a barely touched volume on his cousin's bookshelf, Taylor recounts in his autobiography, *The Way It Was with Me*, the future senator asked if he could borrow it. "You can have the goddamned thing if you want it," his cousin said. "It's written by a bol-she-veeck."

The "bol-she-veeck" was King Camp Gillette, the multimillionaire inventor of the safety razor. The book, written with the silent collaboration of the Pulitzer Prize–winner Upton Sinclair, was *The People's Corporation*. "Each citizen, as his birthright, should receive one share of voting stock in 'The People's Corporation,'" wrote Gillette, who referred to himself as "a Utopian Socialist." "The whole nation and its economy should be run much in the same manner as The Gillette Razor Co." Gillette, who dedicated his 1924 book "to Mankind," proposed an annual minimum wage and cooperatives along the lines of the Farmers Union and the Grange, senior-citizen pensions and a full employment policy, national health insurance, and help for small business by controlling monopolies and the huge trusts.

Up until that moment, the autodidactic Taylor recalled, "I had accepted the status quo. I had accepted the economic system, starvation in the midst of plenty, and my own desperate struggle to live as practically preordained, inevitable, and unchangeable. A man doesn't think of change when he is ignorant of any alternative."

And he had seen so much pain all around him. "Nearly every community had its Hooverville, a collection of shanties made from packing boxes, scraps of sheet metal, and cardboard cartons." He told the *Inside USA* author John Gunther, "Kids didn't have proper clothes in winter. People came up to us, half-starving and miserable, and offered us chickens in ex-change for tickets [to Taylor's traveling show] . . . And when folks were sick with hunger in the towns, we saw other fields still producing food or pota-toes lying out to rot. I began to brood over how things could be so wrong."

Thus began a self-education in economics that lasted for years—voracious reading, incessant discussions, constant self-reflection. Taylor, who had only six years of formal education, began by his mid-thirties to impress people with his understanding of economics, especially with his ability to explain the causes of the Great Depression and to propose solu-tions to pull America out of it.

The second incident brought Taylor directly into the political arena. On a crisp fall day in 1936 in Driggs, Idaho, Taylor was scouting out a place for the Glendora Ranch Gang to perform. Less than forty miles from Jackson, Wyoming, in some of the most beautiful terrain in the country, Driggs had only one theater in town to serve its population of a few hundred people. As he entered the small theater, what Taylor saw stunned him. The governor, C. Ben Ross, and the Idaho secretary of state were campaigning in this little town five miles from the Wyoming bor-der. But to Taylor, the professional actor, it looked almost like a rehearsed vaudeville act. And the Democrat Ross, elected three times as gover-nor and now challenging five-term Senator William Borah, was a pretty good actor.

To Taylor it was a revelation. Recalling this incident forty years later, he wrote,

> If he can do this and get elected to office, so can I . . . But I can
> do it better than C. Ben Ross because he is an amateur and I am
> a professional. This depression, this crime of people starving
> while food was deliberately destroyed, could be corrected only by
> electing men to office who were determined to make needed
> changes, who had suited the problem and knew what should be
> done . . . My seven years of study had not been wasted. This
> afternoon was part of the scheme of things. If the object of all
> knowledge was action, then here was my opportunity to take
> action.

On the drive back from Driggs, he made up his mind. He would be a candidate for Congress in 1938. When he arrived at his house-truck parked in Jackson, Dora was asleep. In his autobiography published in 1979, he recounts the episode.

TAYLOR: Dora, wake up, I'm going to run for Congress.

She probably thought she had heard incorrectly in the struggle to extricate herself from the arms of Morpheus.

TAYLOR: I'm going to run for Congress.
DORA: Well, what do you know about politics? You don't even know a precinct committeeman.
TAYLOR: I learned a lot this afternoon.
DORA: And it takes money to run for Congress, doesn't it?
TAYLOR: Well, we've got $1,200 we've saved up.
DORA: You can't run for office because we have no home. You've got to be a resident of some place before you run for office. We don't even have a permanent address.

They took up residence in Pocatello.

For the next nineteen years, up through 1956 and his fifty-second birthday, Glen Taylor was a candidate. He won one and lost seven. Or five, if you only count Senate races. But his impact on progressive government and on our country may have been greater than that of almost any one-term United States senator in the twentieth century.

His low-budget campaign style consisted of singing, glad-handing, and talking progressive economics. His son Arod (Dora spelled backward) put it this way: "We bought a small boat from the Kalamazoo Boat Company which we used sometimes at Yellowstone National Park. We put it on top of our old Ford, put our luggage in the boat and covered it with a canvass, and sat on it when we were singing . . . I entertained them, Daddy spoke to them, and Mother collected the money. We did that about five or six times a day." During the 1940 Senate race, Glen Taylor wrote, five-year-old Arod sang more than two thousand times.

Sixty-eight years later, Arod—a retired dentist living in California—told me, "I sang at least that many times."

In his 1940 race for the Senate, Taylor ran against the more conservative Democratic Party establishment. He erased any doubt about his outspokenness and his progressive principles: "To me there is only one issue, and that was how to end the absurd situation of artificial scarcity in the midst of plenty. Solve that problem, and all the other issues would cease to have any meaning."

The Democratic establishment had its hands full with Taylor. He beat them in 1940 and 1942 in the Democratic primary but was unable to win the November election when the Democratic Party sat on its hands. Party insiders were willing to help if Taylor renounced his "wild ideas" and "semi-socialist" views. But Taylor saw it another way: "The object of the machine was to keep a tight rein on Idaho politics so the big corporations could have access on favorable terms to the state's resources of timber, metal, hydroelectric dam sites, enjoy ridiculously low taxes . . ." Besides, Taylor said, "The corporations had learned that it was much cheaper to elect senators, congressmen, and governors in small states than in large states."

Today, we would call Taylor a maverick. But, as the nation observed during the 2008 presidential race, those candidates who call themselves mavericks usually aren't.

The original maverick was Samuel Augustus Maverick, who stood out for refusing to brand his cattle. Those animals with no mark were considered to be Maverick's cattle. Sam Maverick's grandson was Fontaine Maury Maverick, a "fiery radical" who "defended communist party organizers" in Texas, according to the historian and biographer Robert Caro. Once labeled "the Robespierre of the Rio Grande," Maverick, with the help of young Capitol Hill staffer Lyndon Baines Johnson, was elected to the House of Representatives in 1934 and reelected in 1936. The young congressman, who could hardly walk because of a World War I injury inflicted at Argonne, assembled a group of young, progressive congressmen—they called themselves "the Mavericks"—who pushed progressive legislation as President Roosevelt urged them on. The reactionary vice president, John Nance Garner, a Texan with diminishing loyalty to his president, helped defeat Maverick in his 1938 reelection bid. Maury later became mayor of San Antonio, and was once again defeated for reelection when he was labeled a Communist.

More than thirty years ago, I saw firsthand how the family earned the title "maverick." In his San Antonio law office, Maury Maverick, Jr., ever a Maverick and always a maverick, described to me his break with longtime family friend Lyndon Baines Johnson over the war in Vietnam. After Maverick came out publicly against the war, the president never spoke to him again.

In the fall of 2008, I spoke with Maverick cousin Terrell McSweeny, who was Senator Joe Biden's deputy chief of staff at the time. As I rode the vice presidential candidate's campaign bus with her, and Biden, and longtime Biden friend and future senator Ted Kaufman, she told me: "We are proud progressives, and my family is not happy with McCain and Palin calling themselves mavericks."

Mavericks confronted authority, spoke out in the face of ridicule, and were prepared to risk their careers for their principles. Glen Taylor was all of that. Taylor was not self-congratulatory; nor did he try to be something that he was not. He simply fought for what he thought was right; whoever stood in his way—his own party leaders, timber and mining interests, Republicans, and later a president of the United States—was immaterial.

While campaigning, his sense of humor would show, usually with a serious, and often hard-hitting, message behind it. In his 1940 unsuccessful general-election run for the Senate, he held up a full-page newspaper advertisement for the Republican presidential nominee, Wendell Willkie. Pointing to the ad that read WENDELL WILLKIE: BORN TO WORK, Taylor said, "And Mr. Willkie is a hard worker all right. He works for big corporations and he works long hours, trying to find new loopholes in the tax laws so his bosses can pay less taxes and we can pay more." A different take, to be sure, on the dignity of work. He saved some of his best ammunition to expose Willkie's power-company allegiances. Applauding the FDR/Hugo Black legislation to regulate utility holding company excesses, Taylor, along with the progressive Republican George Norris, portrayed Willkie as a Power Trust Incarnate.

By 1944, Taylor had shed his cowboy outfit and was ready. In his successful Senate campaign that year, his progressive voice rang true. In comparing his philosophy with that of conservatives, Democrats with Republicans, he said, "When human values and property values clash, the Democrats would resolve the problem in terms of human beings, and the Republicans in terms of property . . . The Democrats say that the primary business of government is to safeguard and improve the conditions of life of all the people . . . The Republicans say that the first business of government is to safeguard and improve the conditions of property, private property."

Or, as Missouri Senator Thomas Hart Benton said in 1835, "There has never been but two parties, founded on the radical question whether people or property shall govern. Democracy implies government by the people. Aristocracy implies a government of the rich . . . and in those words are contained the sum of party distinction." For Idahoans in 1944, Taylor's words rang true. After three losses, it was his first electoral victory. For Taylor and his family, this six-year term must have seemed like the beginning of a long, distinguished career in government. When a freshman congressman or senator goes off to Washington with a young family, an observer might easily think of the almost last words of John Milton's *Paradise Lost*: "The world was all before them." In the heady days of a first congressional or Senate term, a family often looks to an unknown future with unrestrained optimism.

Taylor's first day as the Senate's presiding officer—freshmen senators in the majority party typically serve as acting president pro tempore—was, he said later, one of the most wonderful moments of his life: "As I took the gavel and gazed over that appealing sea of famous faces, I again had to pinch myself."

I remember so well my first day presiding over the United States Senate in January 2007. It was 2:30 in the afternoon, January 10, 2007. With my wife, Connie, in the gallery, with the swearing-in festivities only a few days earlier, I gazed out at the chamber as Vermont Democratic Senator Patrick Leahy was speaking. I looked down at the bill that we were debating, and wrote across the top of Senate Bill 1: "I can't believe I'm presiding over the United States Senate."

In the 1940s, a senator's maiden speech on the Senate floor was a celebratory moment. A senator would wait for months, sometimes more than a year, to make his debut. Taylor's first major speech to the Senate drew on his personal experiences as a sheet metal worker in a California defense plant during World War II. More than half of the ninety-six-member Senate came to the floor to listen, as was the custom. Taylor later recalled that he had never known a "greater personal satisfaction, or a more thrilling experience."

He outlined a lesson we need to relearn today. At the time, the defense plants operated under a 1940s version of the arrangement we now call "cost-plus": the government would pay the defense contractors a 10 percent profit on all costs. The bigger the defense contract, the bigger the payment from the government; the more that is spent, the more that is earned; the greater the waste, the more profit for the contractor; the more people hired, the greater the income for the boss. And of course the greater expense for taxpayers.

When Taylor worked in the plant, he saw too many workers with not enough work to do, a shortage of tools to work with, and a scarcity of materials. Workers and management were warned before inspectors arrived at the plant. Millions of taxpayer dollars were lost to greed, incompetence, and war profiteering.

In the Senate, he didn't always make friends with his colleagues. Early in his first year, he spoke out in support of Henry Wallace's confirmation for secretary of commerce, after Wallace had been dumped as FDR's vice president and been nominated for the cabinet: "I would rather have Henry Wallace, with all his idealism and love of mankind—which seems to be a crime in the eyes of some—than one of the fierce, troglodyte animals with tremendous power and no social brains."

Like so many progressives who sat at Desk 88, Glen Taylor was ahead of his time (a notion implied in the root of the word "progressive"). He joined Florida Senator Claude Pepper to fight against the Taft-Hartley Act and its attack on organized labor. On the Senate floor in June 1947, Taylor said, "I shall vote against it because I value human rights over property rights, and because I place the welfare of all the people above the narrower selfish interests of a few monopolies."

He warned of a powerful, much too expensive military more than a decade before President Dwight Eisenhower spoke out ominously about the military-industrial complex. From Desk 88 in the Senate chamber, he said, "Once it is saddled on us it will be impossible to get rid of it, because when a large segment of our industry is making guns, tanks, and planes, jobs will depend upon making guns, tanks, and planes, and profits will depend upon making guns, tanks, and planes."

He opposed a peacetime draft, partly because he thought it fed an already satiated military, but also because the armed services were segregated. "Once they have been inducted, we segregate them, and we discriminate against them," he told his Senate colleagues in 1948.

Taylor's positions on disarmament and peace, which would play prominently in the 1948 presidential race, were of course politically risky—especially coming from someone who did not serve in the military. He opposed Truman's efforts—notably in Turkey and Greece—to support authoritarian governments simply because they were anti-Communist. "The Greek government," he said, "bears no relationship whatever to democracy and it is not combating communism . . . Indeed, for every Greek who was converted to communism by Russian propaganda last week, 100 have been converted to it by the present Greek regime and by our State Department's insistence that the only alternative to that regime is communism."

Taylor opposed the Marshall Plan, believing it should be administered by the United Nations rather than the United States. He conceded that the European Recovery Act had done good things but added that it fell short. "Hungry people have been fed. Economies have been rehabilitated. But I do not feel that the good which has been accomplished can anywhere near off-set the harm which has been done the United Nations and the cause of world peace by our taking the ball unilaterally and running with it."

And in speeches in Cleveland, Grand Rapids, and Boise, he criticized the Truman Doctrine, contending that supporting anti-Communist dictatorships drove countries into the arms of the Communists, causing the United States to lose friends all over the world. In 1949, on the Senate

floor, he thundered that the American people "are tired of spending billions of dollars and having their taxes increased in order to send money
around the world—to Great Britain, for her imperialist ventures against
the Jews in Palestine; to the Dutch, for their imperialist ventures against the
Indonesians." France, Portugal, and other European powers were using
U.S. assistance and U.S. arms to help these colonial powers subjugate
their colonies in Africa and Asia.

In a speech delivered over a New York radio station in November 1947,
Taylor said, "The pathological fear and hatred of Russia . . . is leading
some of our more affluent citizens to risk the extinction of mankind in a
desperate effort to erase communism from the earth . . . Our militaristic,
Wall Street foreign policy is completely bankrupt. It has failed to make
friends of Russia, and by its arrogant manner has cost us the friendship of
practically every country on earth."

By early 1947, the former vice president (1941–1945) and commerce
secretary Henry Wallace was increasingly critical of what he considered
to be Truman's bellicose foreign policy and timid domestic policy, especially his treatment of organized labor. He believed that Truman had
betrayed the principles of Franklin Roosevelt.

Glen Taylor claimed Harry Truman as a friend. Even though, when
Taylor came to the Senate in early January 1945, Truman was already vice
president–elect and soon vice president, Truman kept his office in the
Senate Office Building. Taylor, in Room 244, often rode with Truman on
the Senate subway to the Capitol and always insisted his later criticism of
President Truman was never personal.

But the escalating rhetoric that Taylor used against Truman and the
harsh comments that Truman directed at Wallace made those early days
seem distant. A section in Taylor's autobiography is entitled "Truman
Sires McCarthyism." Truman's comment that Henry Wallace should "go
to the country he loves so well [the Soviet Union] and help them against
his own country" established, in Taylor's words, "the moral tone, or lack
of it, that encouraged Joe McCarthy [and] Richard Milhous Nixon to
launch one of the most vicious assaults in the history of our country
upon the constitutional rights of the people." Presciently, Taylor wrote

in *The Way It Was with Me*, "The Democratic Party would be pilloried for years as a result of the ruthless use the Republicans would make of the Pandora's box that Mr. Truman had recklessly opened."

TAYLOR WAS MOVING away from the more establishment Democratic Party view espoused by T. F. Green. Green was an internationalist who thought that America should lead in the postwar world; Taylor was surely troubled by American dominance of that world.

And as Senator Taylor escalated the criticisms of President Truman's methods of combating Communism, the likelihood of a third-party challenge to the Democratic president became more apparent. In December 1947 Wallace and his newly formed Progressive Party asked Taylor to be his vice presidential running mate.

The Progressive Party sounded not at all Communist, or even radical; to many, it sounded—well, American. Taylor wrote: "Our platform called for an end to racial discrimination and supported anti-lynching and anti-segregation legislation. Voting rights for eighteen-year-olds was also promised. We advocated a national health insurance program, a one-hundred-dollar-a-month old age pension, an increase in the minimum wage to one dollar an hour, and repeal of the recently enacted peacetime draft."

To Taylor—and to Dora and the family—the 1948 run for vice president did not seem that much different from the campaigns in Idaho. As Arod, by then the oldest of three children, told me six decades later, "we still got in the car, drove to the next event, sang a few songs, and then my dad spoke to the crowd."

It was only in the South, Arod recounted, that things were different. On several occasions, Dora and the children stayed in their hotel as Taylor challenged segregation. On a spring day in April 1948, as Taylor and his family arrived by train in Birmingham, they were greeted at the station by newsboys shouting, "Senator Taylor might be arrested." The front page of *The Birmingham Post* announced that, if Taylor spoke before the "nonsegregated gathering of whites and Negroes [at the Southern Negro Youth Congress] in violation of the Birmingham Code, the police will arrest him." The *Post* outlined the swaggering police commissioner Eugene "Bull" Connor's threat: "I have been elected three times by the people of this city as police commissioner to enforce the laws. I don't intend for the Youth Congress or any other similar organization to violate our segregation laws." Connor was quoted in *The New York Times*: "There's not enough room in this town for Bull and the Commies."

The local Chamber of Commerce liked to call their community the "Magic City," but beginning the year before Taylor's visit, terrorist attacks aimed at Birmingham's black citizens—from 1947 to 1965, there were fifty dynamite explosions, mostly bombings by the Ku Klux Klan—were beginning to earn Alabama's largest city a new name: Bombingham.

Later in the day, Taylor attempted to enter the "coloreds only" door of the church where the Youth Congress was being held. As a sitting United States senator and a candidate for vice president of the United States, he was arrested by Connor's Birmingham Police Department, driven around in a police car, and subjected to taunts and threats from Connor's men. Taylor, in his autobiography written thirty years later, remembered one of the officers: "I recall thinking that his eyes were glittering with malice and hatred, reminding me of the chilling glitter I had often seen as a boy in the eyes of cornered rattlesnakes, and he was ready to strike."

Yet Taylor remained calm, knowing anything confrontational or brash—whether he was a United States senator or not—could end very badly for him. "By swallowing my pride and playing it cool, I cheated Bull Connor out of a chance to be a genuine folk hero to more red-neck red haters, north and south, than you could ever imagine." After more than an hour, he was taken to the Birmingham jail.

"My dad," a proud Arod told me sixty years later, "was arrested and booked at the Birmingham jail while Martin Luther King was still in high school." It was more than a dozen years later that Dr. King wrote his famous letter from that jail.

In July 1948, a few months after Taylor's arrest, Bull Connor and other segregationist southerners led a walkout from the Democratic convention in Philadelphia to protest a civil rights plank in the party's platform. Soon after, in Birmingham, Strom Thurmond became the presidential nominee of the States' Rights Democratic Party, the Dixiecrats.

Later that month, at the Progressive Party convention in Phila-delphia in July 1948, Taylor was nominated for the vice presidency by the Progressive Party Senate candidate from Georgia, a black attorney named Larkin Marshall. Very few African Americans in that state, of course, would be able to register and vote for either Marshall or Taylor.

Two days after the Progressive Party Convention, Truman brought Congress back to Washington for a special session. He asked, or demanded, in essence, that the Republican Congress pass many of the planks of the Progressive Party platform: increase the minimum wage and expand So-cial Security, protect civil rights and provide less expensive electricity, expand the government's role in housing and education. Nothing much happened in the Capitol in the special session, but Truman's call began to marginalize the Progressive Party. While Truman had incorporated these plans in his Fair Deal platform, his new emphasis on them surely undermined public support for Progressives like Wallace and Taylor.

Earlier in 1948, before Wallace's official nomination by the Progres-sive Party, Truman sharpened his Red-baiting assaults: "I do not want and will not accept the political support of Henry Wallace and his Com-munists. If joining them or permitting them to join me is the price of victory, I recommend defeat. These are days of high prices for everything, but any price for Wallace and the Communists is too much for me to pay. I'm not buying." Those presidential comments—and their repetition by other leading Democrats—scared enough people that the Wallace-Taylor campaign never recovered. Surely Wallace's sometimes lame ex-cuses for Soviet behavior eroded his support for his candidacy and for a long-term progressive agenda. But there is little doubt that the fear of Communism—and candidates' and political operatives' enthusiasm in stoking those fears—kept the Progressive Party from being a real force in the middle of the twentieth century and helped set the stage for careers like Joseph McCarthy's and Richard Nixon's.

Taylor and Wallace, of course, lost their race in 1948; their percent-age shrunk to low single digits as the Red-baiting intensified. But their impact—especially when it came to civil rights and labor rights—on the Democratic platform and the Truman campaign, and ultimately on the government and the country, was significant. Wallace's candidacy and advocacy for civil rights and the national coalition of civil rights advocates, progressive New Dealers, and trade unionists set the stage for Truman, in July, to sign Executive Order 9981 to end the segregation in the United States military, declaring equal treatment for all who served in the armed services "without regard to race, color, religion or national origin." And while integration came more slowly to the armed forces than many hoped, the American military provided a huge opportunity for African American advancement, and was inarguably the biggest success story for integration in the second half of the twentieth century. In July 2008, to mark the six-tieth anniversary of Truman's order, I introduced legislation with Senator Barack Obama as the cosponsor, to memorialize that achievement. The legislation passed and was signed by President Bush.

And, almost surely, Wallace-Taylor's strong advocacy for civil rights provided impetus for the success of the Minneapolis mayor and Senate candidate Hubert Humphrey's efforts to include a strong voting rights plank in the Democratic Party's 1948 platform. Democratic Party bosses in large northern cities in crucial states knew that minority voters in their cities were attracted to the Progressive Party's commitment to civil rights and would be tempted to vote for Wallace-Taylor if the Democratic Party offered them so little, as it had in the past.

Why did Taylor—against the advice of his political advisors and con-trary to the wishes of his wife—decide to run as the Progressive Party's vice presidential candidate with Henry Wallace in a race with very little chance of success? Arod told me that his father came from a family of Texas Rangers and they always told Glen: "Be sure you're right . . . and then go ahead." And Taylor knew he was right in his criticism of Truman, especially on Cold War issues.

And of course, Taylor's decision to join Wallace's ticket, and in-stantly become a national figure, was too tempting for the forty-four-year-old Idaho senator to refuse. Taylor suffered from an affliction all too common to members of the United States Senate. *The New York Times* correspondent and future Democratic Senator Richard Neuberger (who, representing Oregon from 1955 until his death in 1960, also sat at Desk 88) thought that Taylor had incredible potential but lacked the humility and patience to be a great senator. There is an apocryphal story that has made the rounds in Washington for decades. A secret ballot was taken among the ninety-six members of the United States Senate, posing the question "Who should be the next president of the United States?" It was a ninety-six-way tie for first place. Taylor surely looked in the mirror many mornings and saw a future president of the United States.

On the campaign trail again and again, Taylor paid a price for his independence, his outspokenness, and his combative challenges to monied interests. For that, he was frequently and viciously Red-baited: in 1948 as he ran for vice president, and after he returned to the Senate in 1949. And then it got worse.

On February 9, 1950, Republican Senator Joseph McCarthy, the young ultraconservative from Wisconsin, spoke to the Ohio County Republican Women's Club in Wheeling, West Virginia. "While I cannot take the time to name all the men in the State Department who have been named as members of the Communist Party and members of a spy ring . . . I have here in my hand a list of 205 . . . names that were made known to the Secretary of State as being members of the Communist Party and who nevertheless are still working and shaping policy in the State Department," he told the Republican gathering in the Colonnade Room at the McLure Hotel. "The bright young men who are born with silver spoons in their mouths are the ones who have been most traitorous."

The next day at a press conference in Denver, McCarthy was asked to produce the list. He said it was in his other suit, which he had left on the plane. Then, the following day, in a letter to President Truman, McCarthy repeated much from his speech with the warning: "Failure on your part will label the Democratic Party of being the bedfellow of international Communism."

In June, the Korean War began, and it started badly for anti-Communist forces: Chinese forces invaded the Korean peninsula. The People's Republic of China—then a nation of 550 million people; the United States had about 150 million—had been formed only in 1949.

THE CONSERVATIVE ATTACKS on progressives intensified as the 1950 midterm elections approached—in Idaho, to be sure, but also in Florida,

Maryland, and California and across the country. In all four Senate races, the tone was particularly negative: Senator Glen Taylor challenged by D. Worth Clark in the Idaho Democratic primary; Democratic Senator Claude Pepper challenged by George Smathers in the Florida Democratic primary; Democratic Senator Millard Tydings challenged by Republican John Marshall Butler in Maryland; Democratic Congresswoman Helen Gahagan Douglass versus Republican Congressman Richard Milhous Nixon in California. President Truman himself showed his disfavor toward two of the Democratic senators. According to Truman's daughter, Margaret, Smathers told her, "Honey, the three most dangerous people in the world are Joe Stalin, Lenin, and Trotsky,* who are ably helped by their three close compatriots over here, Henry Wallace, Claude Pepper, and Glen Taylor."

Claude Pepper, the progressive three-term senator from Florida whom Hugo Black had recruited for his Senate Education and Labor Committee in 1937, had been an outspoken advocate for labor rights in a mostly non-union state, a supporter of civil rights in a mostly segregated region of the country, and a critic of his party's foreign policy in pro-military Florida. Pepper, who years later as a member of the House of Representatives wrote that he and President Roosevelt "were ideological soulmates," had no such relationship with President Truman. He thought Truman had betrayed the legacy of FDR on domestic and foreign policy, and made no secret of his feelings. Truman, in turn, summoned two-term Congressman George Smathers to the White House in late 1949 and said to him, "I want you to beat that son-of-a-bitch Claude Pepper!"

Pepper, labeled "Red Pepper" by his Democratic primary opponent Smathers, was attacked mercilessly by the business establishment and by Smathers himself, who said upon announcing his candidacy on January 12, 1950, "The leader of the radicals and extremists is now on trial in Florida . . . Florida will not allow herself to become entangled in the spiraling web of the Red network. The people of our state will no longer tolerate advocates of treason."

---

*Lenin had died in 1924, and Trotsky was assassinated in Mexico four years before Taylor was elected to the Senate.

Legend has it—perhaps only legend; there was no television, radio, or You Tube following Smathers in rural Florida—that Smathers said that Pepper "is known all over Washington as a shameless extrovert." And that he "practiced nepotism with his sister-in-law, he has a brother who is a known homo sapiens, and he has a sister who was once a thespian in wicked New York. Worst of all, it is an established fact that Mr. Pepper, before his marriage, habitually practiced celibacy." When I asked my colleague Florida Democrat Bill Nelson about this legend, he told me he is pretty certain that Smathers never said those words.

History does document that Smathers and his campaign accused Pepper of "treason," being part of a sinister "Red network," and calling his supporters "Communists and socialists." And in the last days before the primary election, an anonymous booklet—slick and sophisticated, with great detail—was distributed called "The Red Record of Senator Claude Pepper: A Documentary Case History from Official Government Records and Original Communist Documents." Like almost every other campaign—then and now—pitting an outspoken progressive against a candidate with establishment support, the newspapers overwhelmingly supported the conservative. Smathers, recalling the race in 1989, said that he was endorsed by thirty-six of Florida's thirty-eight daily newspapers.

In the end, Pepper lost in a landslide. The NBC newsman David Brinkley called the race "the dirtiest in the history of American politics."* Pepper, in his last speech to his Senate colleagues, discouraged by the racism, McCarthyism, and conservatism around him, proclaimed, "This is the darkest period of American history, if not human history."

Some of the same tactics were deployed in the 1950 race in Maryland, this time with Senator Joseph McCarthy personally involved. Mil-

---

*After his defeat in the 1950 Democratic primary, Pepper tried again for the Senate in 1958, lost, and then ran for Congress successfully from Dade County, Florida, in 1962. He served in the House until his death in 1989, at age eighty-eight. In 1987, the always opinionated Congressman Pepper, then eighty-seven years old, told *The New York Times*, "If the rich people of this country don't build a monument to Ronald Reagan higher than the Washington Monument, they'll be ingrates." Smathers, for his part, went on to serve three terms in the United States Senate, retiring voluntarily in 1969. Early in his tenure in the Senate, he did a toast for his friend JFK at the future president's wedding to Jacqueline Bouvier. He was a conservative senator who supported the creation of Medicare, but opposed the appointment of Thurgood Marshall to the United States Supreme Court and voted against the Civil Rights Act of 1964. He died in 2007 at the age of ninety-three.

lard Tydings, a four-term conservative Democrat from Maryland, was challenged by ultra-conservative attorney John Marshall Butler, a Republican who had never held public office. Tydings was not a particularly sympathetic character, and certainly not a progressive; aloof and distant, he had opposed anti-lynching and anti–poll tax legislation, voted against the creation of Social Security, and supported Taft-Hartley and other anti-labor initiatives. But, as chairman of the Senate Armed Services Committee, he had stood up to McCarthy and called his allegations "a fraud and a hoax" when the Wisconsin senator alleged Communist Party influence in the armed forces. The forty-two-year-old McCarthy drove across the District of Columbia city line and came to Maryland looking for revenge.

McCarthy and his friends—right-wing Texas oil men like Clint Murchison; Ruth McCormick Miller, editor and publisher of the Washington *Times Herald* and niece of Colonel Robert R. McCormick, one of the nation's leading ultraconservatives—took over Butler's campaign. The Wisconsin senator came into the state at least three times and directed his staff, in nearby Washington, to help run the campaign's day-to-day operations. And, as is typical of slash-and-burn campaign tactics, the candidate later tried to distance himself from those campaign tactics; Butler told *The Washington Post* after the election that he had asked McCarthy *not* to come into the state.

McCarthy himself called Tydings "Truman's whimpering lap dog" and said he was a member of the "Commiecrat Party" and the "whitewash committee." But it was the October surprise—the last-minute hate piece, the same kind of campaign brochure that helped to defeat Pepper—that inflicted the most damage on Tydings. Using the resources of the *Times Herald*, McCormick-Miller's photo and layout people created a composite picture of Tydings and Communist Party USA Secretary Earl Browder in the midst of intense conversation with the caption "Communist Leader Earl Browder, shown at left in this composite picture, was a star witness at the Tydings committee hearings, and was cajoled into saying Owen Lattimore and others accused of disloyalty were not Communists. Tydings (right) answered: 'Oh, thank you, sir.'" More than three hundred thousand copies were distributed a few days before the election and on Election Day itself. Tydings lost by forty-three thousand votes.

After the election, the Senate Rules Committee's Subcommittee on Privileges and Elections conducted a four-month investigation of McCarthy and Butler's role in the campaign. The bipartisan committee report decried the "despicable back street campaign" conducted by "outsiders" like McCarthy.

Standing outside the Senate chamber in March 2009, the NBC political director, and now host of *Meet the Press*, Chuck Todd commented to me: "The 1950 Senate races set the tone and the foreign policy strategy for Republican candidates for the next forty years."

The Idaho race was a combination of Butler-style attacks and Smathers-like tactics, with McCarthyism and Nixon antics thrown in for good measure. In fact, the Pepper-Smathers contest itself was, peculiarly, injected into the Idaho Senate race by Taylor's far-right detractors. The *Idaho Daily Statesman* published almost every day excerpts from "The Red Record of Senator Claude Pepper: A Documentary Case History from Official Government Records and Original Communist Documents" and editorialized about the alleged connections between their senator and the Florida senator. After incontrovertibly—in the editors' minds—establishing the link, the *Daily Statesman* aimed its guns directly at Taylor with a series entitled "The Red Record of Glen Taylor—As He Made It."

The paper claimed Taylor was "consorting with known Communists." The editors accused Taylor of "representing the Russians on the floor of the United States Senate with more words than all the other senators in history." When Taylor defended himself, the paper shot back, "it's the Communist line, because the Communists fear the free press."

One of Taylor's Democratic primary opponents said that he was "duped by communists into playing their game at the expense of anti-Americanism." Another opponent, Republican Herman Welker,* who was

---

*One Idaho historian, according to the Taylor biographer F. Ross Peterson, opined that Welker's only accomplishment in the United States Senate was to convince the Washington Senators owner Clark Griffith to sign the eighteen-year-old Idaho high school star Harmon Killebrew to a Major League Baseball contract. Killebrew went on to play twenty-two years for the Senators and then the Minnesota Twins when the franchise moved to the Twin Cities. He hit 573 home runs and was elected to the Hall of Fame in 1984. Baseball aficionados should note that Killebrew never laid down a sacrifice bunt.

the eventual winner, lumped Taylor into a group of "87 communists in Idaho . . . and radicals and stooges and crackpots who consistently follow the party line and play right into the hands of the communist cause."

Taylor lost the Democratic primary by fewer than one thousand votes; reporters estimated that four thousand to five thousand Republican voters had crossed over to vote in the Democratic primary against Taylor.

Taylor's political career came to an end in 1956. Since winning the Senate seat, he had lost his reelection primary in 1950, the 1954 general election when Vice President Nixon piled on by asserting that Taylor and other Democrats "belong to a left-wing clique in their party which has tolerated the Red conspiracy," and the 1956 Democratic primary to a young Frank Church, who went on to serve in the Senate for twenty-four years. Taylor had marginalized himself, with no small amount of assistance from Red-baiting newspapers, conservative hacks, and some fellow Democratic politicians.

But in so many ways, he was ahead of his time—on civil rights and on energy, on labor and on women's rights. Much of what Taylor—and Wallace in 1948—stood for was adopted by the Democratic platform— civil rights, most notably. Representing an almost all-white state, Taylor had never compromised on civil rights. His Disciples of Christ father, his own struggles, and the pain he saw in rural Idahoans gave him a sensitivity to human rights that is uncommon in politicians. And Truman's call to bring back the "Do-Nothing Congress" before the election to raise the minimum wage, pass housing legislation and aid for education and bring down electricity prices may have blunted the Progressive Party message, but led to a more progressive government and a stronger middle class in our country. Taylor's courage in promoting civil liberties and peace and standing up to McCarthyite hysteria likely cost him his seat.

In 1954, several months after the Battle of Dien Bien Phu, where the French were expelled from Indochina, including modern-day Vietnam, Taylor was campaigning to return to the Senate. He told an Idaho crowd: "We supported French colonialism, Dutch colonialism, British colonialism, any colonialism, and where there was no colonialism policy in the saddle, we found a cheap dictator to support instead of helping the aspirations of the common people, and we have reaped the harvest."

In 1957, General Douglas MacArthur said, "Our government has kept us in a perpetual state of fear—kept us in a continuous stampede of patriotic fever—with the cry of a grave national emergency . . . Yet, in retrospect, these disasters seem never to have happened, seem never to have been quite real."

Twenty-first-century America could learn some lessons from MacArthur—and from Glen Taylor.

THOUGHTS FROM DESK 88

I T'S ALWAYS BOTHERED ME when I hear politicians—even the good ones who want to raise the minimum wage and fight income inequality—say that they want to help "the least among us," as if low-income people are lesser creatures than we are. Yes, Jesus said it too, in Matthew 25. Or at least our modern-day translation of a writer of two millennia ago tells us that Jesus said it. On my 2018 election night victory speech, I told the crowd that I wanted to "dig a little deeper" and explain how I "see the world and the sisterhood and brotherhood of humanity."

Whether we are religious or not, Democrats seldom talk about our faith, or about our spirituality or what drives us. Maybe we should. In Matthew 25, Jesus tells us, "When I was hungry, you fed me. When I was thirsty, you gave me drink. When I was a stranger, you welcomed me. What you did for the least of these, you did for me."

I have a hard time believing that Jesus would have talked about "the least of these." Helping "the least among us" sounds paternalistic, like charity, not enough like justice: Reaching down to help. Giving away some of our largesse. Spreading good cheer. Good things to be sure, but not opportunity. And surely not justice.

The Contemporary English Version of the Poverty and Justice Bible, published by the American Bible Society in 1995, translates Matthew 25:40, quoting Jesus, this way: "The King will answer, 'Whenever you did it for any of my people, no matter how unimportant they seemed, you did it for me.'"

Or another translation for our times tells us this: "Whenever you failed to do one of these things to someone who was being overlooked or ignored, that was me—you failed to do it to me."

So let's start with this. The dignity of work means that every worker who puts in a full day should live above the poverty line. Or, as the workers at Culinary Local 226 in Las Vegas told me in February 2019, "One job should be enough." Martin Luther King, in a speech in 1968 to Local 1199 in New York, said, "You see, no labor is really menial unless you're not getting adequate wages." Every worker. No exceptions. Whether it means a higher minimum wage—which it does; or a strong, enforceable overtime rule—which it did, until President Trump, ensconced at Mar-a-Lago, threw in with his corporate allies; or an expanded Earned Income Tax Credit—which it should.

That's what started Idaho Senator Glen Taylor in politics, when he read King C. Gillette and Upton Sinclair's 1924 book *The People's Corporation*. And believing that an honest day's work should mean an honest day's pay. That's how it ought to be in this country, they believed.

How it would have angered Glen Taylor when Congress in 2016 and Congress and President Trump in 2017 and 2018 wouldn't do anything to help low-income workers—a Congress in thrall to the subcontractors and the non-union construction companies and the other powerful NRA, the National Restaurant Association. And how ebullient he would have been when the public went around Congress and did something about it.

The last time that Congress increased the federal minimum wage established by Hugo Black and FDR was more than a dozen years ago, in 2007, when a Democratic House and Senate and President Bush passed a bill raising it in increments to $7.25 an hour. Since then, every time we have tried, the Republicans filibustered our efforts. President Obama, in a State of the Union address and in a number of speeches around the country, asked for an increase to $9.50 an hour. Senator Tom Harkin—then the chairman of the Health, Education, Labor and Pensions Committee— and I introduced legislation to raise it to $10.10 an hour; again Republican opposition killed the bill.

Then Senator Patty Murray, now the senior Democrat on the Labor Committee, and a group of us offered a minimum wage of $12.00 an hour, pointing out that today's minimum wage has less buying power— one-third less in real buying power—than the minimum wage had thirty years ago. Again, no significant support from Republicans.

Then a few astonishing things happened. In 2012, two hundred fast-food workers in New York City walked off their jobs, demanding a minimum wage—a living wage—of $15 an hour. At first, they were— no surprise—ignored by official Washington. Then, as others across the country took up the banner, the effort was ridiculed by the United States Chamber of Commerce, the National Restaurant Association, a number of elected officials, and most of the national media—at least the "serious ones" on Sunday talk shows. As the saying goes: "First they ignore you, then they laugh at you, then they fight you, then you win."*

Most of these Washington lobbyists who were opposing the minimum wage, it would be fair to mention, don't know anyone who makes minimum wage—except for those who prepare their food and clean their offices, not that the corporate and Washington elite ever stop to ask them their names and inquire about their lives. And many of my

---

*While this quote has often been mistakenly attributed to Mahatma Gandhi, something similar was said by trade unionist Nicholas Klein in 1918 in remarks to a convention of the Amalgamated Clothing Workers of America.

colleagues in the House and Senate who oppose the minimum wage have voted to increase their own pay—often the same legislators who voted against Obamacare and who benefit from government health insurance for their families.

And those interest groups always—always—argue that raising the minimum wage would cause layoffs. We care about those low-income workers losing their jobs, they insist; but if Congress raised the minimum wage, it would force companies to raise prices, causing—here we go again—the products to be priced out-of-range for those same low-income workers that we care so much about. A funny thing, though. Whenever an executive gets eight-figure compensation, or is awarded a seven-figure bonus, we never hear those interest groups or those "very serious" Fox News or talk radio pundits or economics cognoscenti on *The Wall Street Journal* editorial pages rant about layoffs and higher prices. Economics is a complicated subject, they assure us.

How Washington shills for the privileged hate to play defense. When they are losing the argument—on minimum wage or tax cuts—they lob their class warfare accusations against their political opponents, and the editors at *The Wall Street Journal* and *The Washington Post*, the economists from the University of Chicago, and the megaphones on talk radio and Fox News cry out in unison: Why are the liberals trying to divide America?

But then, in the fall of 2012, a light shone on what the corporate Republican elite, and their representatives in Congress, really think about low-income workers, showing an utter disdain—make that "contempt"—for those "not like us." Earlier that year, on May 17 at a private home in Boca Raton, the GOP presidential candidate Mitt Romney told a group of his contributors at a lavishly catered fund-raiser that there are 47 percent of the people "who are dependent upon government, who believe that they are victims, who believe they are entitled to health care, to food, to housing, to you-name-it. These are people who pay no income tax . . . and so my job is not to worry about those people. I'll never convince them that they should take personal responsibility and care for their lives."

Whoever videotaped the former Massachusetts governor's remarks kept them to himself for several months. Whoever filmed it likely knew that Romney looked down on low-wage workers who didn't have to pay income tax because they earned so little, but do pay sales tax and property tax and Social Security and Medicare taxes. He knew that Republicans condescended to the disabled, to veterans receiving benefits they earned, to struggling retirees who might have worked for forty years in difficult jobs.

In October, less than a month before the 2012 general election, my wife, Connie, and I were waiting backstage at an AFL-CIO convention in Columbus for a "surprise guest" to join us on the stage. When President Obama arrived, he informed us—the news had broken only minutes before—about Governor Romney's 47 percent remark, that almost half of America are "takers." Although I assume we all knew that the video would do significant damage to the GOP, the president seemed taken aback. He seemed disappointed that a major party candidate for president disregarded, ignored, rejected almost half the country he wanted to lead. As the video swept the country, we could all picture what had happened that night in Boca Raton: as the invisible waitstaff responded to every grunt and call of the privileged partygoers, Governor Romney told his superrich supporters that those who work so hard for so little don't really count. He really didn't even want to be *their* president.

Then, in 2013, something else amazing happened. The voters in SeaTac, Washington, a ten-square-mile, incorporated city of twenty-seven thousand people encompassing the Seattle-Tacoma (SEATAC) airport, voted to raise the minimum wage to $15.00 an hour. SeaTac was once a middle-class town where airport workers—baggage handlers, ramp workers, jet fuelers, mostly but not always union members—could make a pretty good living. The voters' action would mean that more than 5,500 workers— airport employees and those working in airport-related businesses—were to get significant raises. Other cities followed suit: Seattle, San Francisco, Los Angeles. And dozens of other American cities were considering substantial minimum wage increases.

At this point, Alaska Airlines, headquartered in Seattle, sued the city of SeaTac. The SEATAC initiative was a direct threat to their business model.

After all, Alaska Airlines, like airlines everywhere, had laid off hundreds of workers, then subcontracted those jobs—ramp workers, cargo handlers, custodians, the people who push the wheelchairs and drive the carts—to Menzies Aviation, a Scottish company that specialized in mostly low-wage airport jobs. Menzies could do what Alaska Airlines with its concern for its public image could not afford to do—pay less, take away benefits, and bust the union when necessary. No one even knew what Menzies Aviation was; a little bad publicity would not matter so much to them; consumers didn't buy *their* products, didn't ride *their* airplanes. With Menzies's help, Alaska Airlines could significantly cut its personnel costs and wash its hands of any public responsibility for these low-wage workers.

It was a successful business model but not a necessary one. After Alaska's lawsuit failed and the SeaTac wage increase went into effect, the airline continued to do very well. In the early spring of 2016, the flush company paid $2.6 billion in cash for Virgin Airlines. And the company did later return much of the work it had outsourced to Menzies to its own employees. At any rate, the cost to a large profitable corporation of raising wages for their lowest-paid workers rarely has much impact on the bottom line. And the workers and citizens of that Seattle suburb learned a good lesson about citizenship; their victory, said the University of Washington professor Michael W. McCann, gave them an incredible sense of agency. "They changed the world in which they are a part. They participated in democracy in action."

Meanwhile, in another Washington, on the other side of the country, food service workers—mostly women and people of color—were taking notice of the $15-an-hour movement sweeping the country. Like food workers and janitors and hotel workers and security guards everywhere, they were mostly invisible, ignored, and underpaid. The people whose food they served, whose offices they cleaned, whose safety they protected—they rarely even knew their names. Early in 2015, an article appeared in a Capitol Hill newspaper about a middle-aged man who worked in the Senate cafeteria's kitchen but, because of low pay and an unpredictable, uneven work schedule, was living in a homeless shelter. He was preparing food for United States senators, their staffs, and visitors to our nation's capital.

The workers were not optimistic that things would get better; the contract between the United States Senate and Restaurant Associates, a private company based in Great Britain, was set to expire at the end of the year. Now that the GOP had taken control of the Senate, Republican leadership—all opposed to a higher minimum wage; a number of GOP senators think there should be no minimum wage whatsoever— would negotiate directly with Restaurant Associates. Further, the 160 food workers in the Senate did not have a union; their starting wage was about $10 an hour. In the House, where the workers were represented by the union UNITE HERE, the beginning wage was upwards of $13 an hour with decent benefits.

In early August 2015, I sent a letter to Senator Roy Blunt, a Republican from Missouri, asking him to negotiate a significantly higher wage and better working conditions for these employees, and asking him and the company to recognize a union if more than 50 percent of the workers signed cards requesting union representation.* Every single member of the Senate Democratic caucus signed our letter; no Republican cared to join us.

In October Pope Francis addressed a joint session of Congress and then chose to have lunch with homeless Washingtonians instead of congressmen and senators. That same week my labor assistant Nora Todd and other Senate staff launched a weekly boycott of the Dirksen cafeteria, the major Senate cafeteria operated by Restaurant Associates: their demand was a $15-an-hour living wage and a union for the workers. Every Wednesday, several dozen staff people brought food from home or bought it from a different vendor and sat in the Dirksen cafeteria; each week, a few Democratic senators would stop in to give the staff moral support and to personally tell employees that we were there for them.

In the end, Senator Blunt was able to do better than any of us expected: he raised everyone's pay by three dollars an hour, he promised more predictable scheduling for the employees, and he promised to call Restaurant Associates executives and ask them to be neutral in a union

---

*Roy and I first met when he was secretary of state of Missouri and I was secretary of state of Ohio; "I've known Sherrod Brown for thirty years," he once told a friend; "we've agreed on five issues, and all five are now federal law."

election. I thanked Roy profusely and announced at the Senate Democratic caucus lunch what he had done; a number of my colleagues also thanked him. (One of the great things about being a United States senator is what you can do outside of the legislative process; more than one hundred families—directly and immediately—would have a better life because of our efforts.)

But the victory was not as complete as it first appeared. We discovered from a number of the cafeteria workers that Restaurant Associates was misclassifying dozens of its employees, a violation of federal law, allowing them to pay these workers substantially lower wages. Upon discovery, Restaurant Associates, which has more than a dozen large federal food service contracts, agreed to pay $1 million in back wages to more than one hundred Capitol cafeteria employees. Joined by a dozen colleagues, I have asked the Department of Labor to audit Restaurant Associates' other federal contracts to find out if they owe similar back wages to many of their other low-wage employees.

As the movement for a living wage gathered steam, something was happening in official Washington—over at President Obama's Department of Labor. It illustrates why the election of a president really can matter for millions of low-income Americans. As we've seen, Hugo Black's Fair Labor Standards Act established both a minimum wage and rules for overtime pay. But the threshold over which salaried workers must be paid overtime had been raised only once in the last forty years—a minor adjustment a decade earlier to $23,660. If a night shift manager at a fast-food restaurant were classified as management and earned a salary—not an hourly wage—of $30,000, and she was working forty-five hours each week, she would receive no overtime, no time and a half; in fact, she received no compensation for the extra five hours. Of course those rules—no overtime pay for an employee on salary working longer than forty hours in a professional or executive job—make sense for a corporate executive making $3 million, or a lawyer making $190,000, or a doctor making $260,000 or a senator making $180,000; we should expect to work more than forty hours and we should not expect compensation for the fiftieth or the sixtieth hour.

In 2014 the labor committee chairman, Tom Harkin, and a group of us introduced legislation to almost triple the threshold. Anyone making up to $69,000 a year, we believed, should be receiving overtime—this rule would apply to the same proportion of the workforce that was covered by overtime rules in 1975. We knew that GOP opposition to changing the threshold would stop the legislation. It did.

In early 2015 Senators Patty Murray, Bernie Sanders, and I circulated a letter—signed by twenty-three other Senate Democrats; no Republican wanted to join us—asking the Department of Labor to issue a rule raising the threshold to $56,000. We knew that President Obama's Labor Secretary, Tom Perez, wanted to "go high" on this number, to include millions of workers who had earned, but been denied, overtime pay. We also knew that the White House, always cautious and always far too sensitive to criticism from the Chamber of Commerce and from Mitch McConnell, wanted to compromise, and might "split the difference" and come in with a much lower figure. Progressives in the Senate knew we had to keep the pressure on the Department of Labor and especially on the White House.

When Perez and the Labor Department issued the rule in May 2015—a $47,476 threshold with an annual increase to keep up with inflation—the congressional response was mixed. Progressive Democrats were exultant: close to five million Americans would get raises. Some moderate Democrats were silent; Republicans were furious. And of course business wrath, mostly from those companies who had avoided paying their workers overtime for decades, rained down on those of us who publicly supported the Labor Department rule. The same twenty-six of us immediately sent a letter to Secretary Perez in support of the new rule; we knew that the pressure to lower the number, denying millions of workers the overtime that they had earned, would be intense from the Chamber of Commerce and other Washington interest groups.

And then it happened: outside of the births of my seven grandchildren, May 18 was the best day of my Senate career. Vice President Biden, Secretary Perez, and I flew on Air Force Two to Columbus to visit Jeni's Ice Cream, to announce that the rule bringing the threshold to $47,476 was finalized; more than four million Americans would get raises; in many cases, they would now earn thousands of dollars more for working overtime. In my state of Ohio, 134,000 workers would see larger pay-checks, or work fewer hours and have more time off with their families, for the same pay. The Trump administration, at the behest of business lobbyists, has since taken overtime pay away from more than half those workers.

Whatever the challenges, our efforts continue. On April 17, 2013, I joined a few of my colleagues in the Capitol Rotunda as Nobel Peace Prize Laureate Muhammad Yunus was awarded the Congressional Gold Medal for his pioneering work with microcredit and microfinance in some of the poorest countries in the world. Our mission, he told us? "Let us put poverty in a museum."

What better reason to serve in the United States Senate?

4.

Herbert H. Lehman

PURSUING A DIFFERENT
FAMILY BUSINESS

SERVED IN THE UNITED STATES SENATE 1949–1957

*The purpose of government is not only to protect the lives and
prosperity of the people, but also to bring increased happiness,
contentment, and security into the homes of its people.*

—Senator Herbert H. Lehman of New York

I F THE VIRGINIAN THOMAS JEFFERSON could have returned to
1930s America, he might have found something he liked about New
York State. When New York Governor Franklin Delano Roosevelt
ascended to the presidency of our nation in 1933, his friend and lieutenant governor, Herbert Lehman, became New York's governor. Lehman,
although a "dull and austere campaigner," was prepared. Lehman—with
a nimble mind, an activist past, and a progressive philosophy—wanted
his state to play a role Jefferson would have admired; he wanted it to be

(in Louis Brandeis's phrase) a laboratory for democracy. Thus was born the Little New Deal.

Lehman had been New York's lieutenant governor for two terms, was a noted philanthropist and businessman, and had served as former New York Governor Al Smith's campaign chairman. He followed FDR's lead; and thanks to an even more propitious political environment than his mentor enjoyed in Washington, he in some ways exceeded President Roosevelt's domestic achievements. Lehman convinced the New York Assembly to enact a comprehensive program of social and economic reform. He pushed through legislation establishing old-age benefits, public housing, regulation of utilities, an unemployment insurance system, minimum wage, and a state labor relations board. Like Theodore Green, he overcame the common prejudices of his class—and did so with confidence and conviction. The worst kind of politician, other than a crook, is someone born to privilege who uses his political office to help his social class attain more privilege; Green and Lehman were certainly not that.

Herbert Lehman was the son of Babette Newgas and Mayer Lehman, Bavarian Jewish immigrants who settled in Alabama in 1849, started a general merchandise store, and later entered the cotton business. Immediately after the Civil War, the senior Lehman had either sold his half-dozen slaves or released them—history does not make it clear—and moved his operation from Alabama to New York, where he set up a cotton brokerage firm and investment banking house. Mayer became a trustee of Mount Sinai Hospital, establishing a one-hundred-year tradition of Lehman family members sitting on that hospital's board. His brother Emanuel, with whom he established Lehman Brothers, was elected president of his New York temple; their upbringing was informed by the German Reform-Jewish tradition of "to whom much is given, much is expected."

A half century after the Lehman brothers came to the United States, Mary Antin wrote in *The Promised Land* about Jews coming from a different part of Europe: "Even in my father's house, I did not feel safe." Life in the Pale, where Russian Jews were forced to live, was unrelentingly uncertain. "My father was inspired by a vision. He saw something—he promised us something. It was this 'America.' And 'America' became my dream." Mary Antin's *The Promised Land* and William Bradford's *Of*

Plymouth Plantation explain perhaps better than any other immigrant memoirs the magnet that was America for families like the Lehmans who sought an opportunity to begin life again.

Born on March 28, 1878, Herbert Henry Lehman was a child of privilege, went to the best schools, was successful in business, and—like so many other progressives who love their country—served his nation, as a captain in the United States Army. He joined the family business in 1908, and then, at the age of thirty-nine, left the firm to serve in World War I.

Before Herbert Lehman ever ran for office, he was a philanthropist, an activist, and a progressive. Late in his Senate service, he recalled that, during the 1920s, "We were called radicals and dreamers, but we were willing to wage seemingly hopeless fights. In the same way, we will get complete school desegregation and Negroes will get the right to vote in the South. These things are coming."

As a businessman, Lehman was a civic booster and a committed Democrat. But it was not until he met the New York politician Al Smith in 1924 that the successful banker became a political activist. By 1926, he was Smith's campaign chairman and largest contributor for governor. Then in 1928 Lehman served as finance chairman when Smith was the first Roman Catholic to be nominated as a major party presidential candidate.

Smith was desperate to get Roosevelt to run for governor, believing it would help him carry New York in his quest for the White House. FDR was spending most of his time in Warm Springs, Georgia, undergoing polio treatment. The future president continued to demur, avoiding Smith's calls from the New York State Democratic convention. Smith convinced Lehman to offer himself to FDR as his lieutenant governor running mate, and assured Roosevelt that Lehman—whom Roosevelt trusted—would run the state in FDR's absence. As history tells us, Roosevelt spent little time in Warm Springs after the election; he obviously wanted to run the state government. FDR later called Lehman "that good right arm of mine."

Four years later, Roosevelt ran for president, and Lehman was a candidate for governor of New York. FDR won in a landslide against the incumbent, President Herbert Hoover, the first Democrat since Franklin Pierce in 1852 to win a majority of the popular vote, and Lehman handily defeated "Wild Bill" Donovan, the World War I Congressional Medal of Honor winner who went on to lead the OSS (later to become the CIA) during World War II. While Donovan called for some government intervention to combat Great Depression suffering in New York, Democrats there reminded voters of the 1926 New York State Republican platform that extolled "the administration of President Coolidge as a model to restore economy, efficiency, and businesslike methods to Albany."

Lehman, who was sworn in as governor of New York two months before Roosevelt became president, faced a very troubled state. One-fourth of adult males—some 1.5 million New Yorkers—were unemployed. Another one-fourth of male wage-earners worked only part-time. And wages, already abysmally low for many New York workers, were being pushed down even further by unscrupulous businessmen and by the laws of supply and demand, as available workers were plentiful. New York City had one-half the state's factory workers, and 40 percent of them had lost their jobs. One government study estimated that almost 20 percent of the city's schoolchildren suffered from malnutrition.

A week after taking office, in his first fireside chat, President Roosevelt told the American people, "We have had a bad banking situation. Some of our bankers had shown themselves either incompetent or dishonest in the handling of people's funds. They had used the money entrusted to them in speculations and unwise loans . . . It became the government's job to straighten out this situation and do it as quickly as possible."

The morning of March 4, 1933, the day of President Franklin Delano Roosevelt's inauguration, Governor Lehman issued an order to close all banks and stock exchanges in his state, the forty-eighth governor to do so. Lehman called for emergency, temporary aid for New York's unemployed. The relief rolls continued to grow, and few people could find jobs. New Yorkers wanted something more. The stigma attached to relief was mostly gone. People no longer believed that the jobs were coming back. Wayne W. Parrish, in a report to the Federal Emergency Relief Administration chief, Harry Hopkins, declared that "the word 'emergency' disappeared out of the relief picture." Even the conservative *Buffalo Evening News* editorialized, "Relief shifted from the character of a stigmatized public service to an essential public service."

Lorena Hickok, the Federal Emergency Relief Agency's chief investigator, said with only a little hyperbole that New York, our most populous state in those days, was faced "with the biggest community relief job on earth—the biggest job of its kind ever undertaken by any city since the world began."

One of the most important components of Roosevelt's New Deal and Lehman's Little New Deal was unemployment insurance. When a worker lost his job, more often than not, the family's income evaporated. In June 1934 Roosevelt told Congress that government must provide "security against several of the great disturbing factors in life—especially those which relate to unemployment and old age." Roosevelt thought that unemployment insurance would be easier to pass than social security, old-age assistance, and other safety net legislation.

A few prescient legislators had tried before. Prior to the Great Depression, legislation establishing a compulsory system for unemployment insurance had been introduced in seven states—Massachusetts in 1916, New York and Wisconsin in 1921, and then Minnesota, Pennsylvania, South Carolina, and Connecticut. None had passed. Legislation introduced in Congress also stalled.

Around that time, Raymond B. Fosdick, John D. Rockefeller Jr.'s attorney, wrote a letter in which he suggested to his boss that he create and fund an organization to collect not only "current information as to industrial conditions, but [to] find out, on the basis of expert information, how these policies can best be promoted among the executives of your industries."

The son of the founder of Standard Oil, Rockefeller Jr. sat on the family's holding company board when, in 1913, one of the most protracted and contentious coal strikes in the nation's history took place in Ludlow, a small town outside of Trinidad in southwestern Colorado. The strike was aimed primarily at three Rockefeller-owned companies. Workers endured terrible work conditions and extremely low wages with the threat of even lower-wage immigrant workers ready to take their place. And they resented the distant and hard-edged Rockefeller management style.

When a strikebreaker was found dead, the governor and Colorado National Guard, at the behest of Rockefeller company management, attacked—literally. Nineteen people died, half of them children of miners. Rockefeller Jr. felt a heavy responsibility for his family's role in the Ludlow Massacre. With MacKenzie King, the respected labor minister of Canada, and armed with the advice of the future FDR presidential advisor Harold Ickes, Rockefeller went to Ludlow and "got to know the families and danced with the widows," West Virginia Democratic Senator John D. "Jay" Rockefeller told me. Standing outside the Senate chamber on the night the Senate voted on the $700 billion economic stabilization legislation in October 2008, Rockefeller told me, "Ludlow changed my grandfather's life."

In 1922 Rockefeller helped fund a section of Princeton University's Economics Department that popularized the terms "industrial relations" and "employee relations." Industrial Relations programs were established, also with Rockefeller financing, at the University of Michigan, Stanford, MIT, and California Tech.

The oil tycoon set up a small office to monitor working conditions, employee relations, and employee benefits. They found, for example, one company in which Rockefeller had financial interests that operated on a twelve-hour, seven-day week; Rockefeller fixed it. The office grew into Industrial Relations Counselors, Inc., which was incorporated in 1926 with Rockefeller funding it almost entirely. It began an exhaustive study of unemployment benefits and pensions in the United States: four books on unemployment insurance were published, including detailed information on industrial pensions and trade union plans. Legislators and administrators, in Washington and the states, consulted with IRC staff to develop unemployment insurance and pension programs.

While no one ever credited John D. Rockefeller, Jr., with being the father of American unemployment insurance, it is safe to say that Rockefeller—whose family was reviled by labor in the first quarter of the twentieth century—played a positive role in the legislative creation of Social Security and unemployment insurance.

But even after the collapse of the stock market in 1929, and the ensuing devastation of the economy in the early 1930s, neither the Hoover Administration nor the Congress—the Republican Senate nor the just-turned-Democratic House of Representatives*—passed unemployment insurance legislation.

Then came the elections of 1932 and Roosevelt's landslide win over the feckless Hoover. Democrats took huge majorities in both houses of Congress. Democrats were successful in statehouses across the country. In 1933 sixty-five unemployment insurance bills were introduced in twenty-four states. In the first half of 1935, unemployment insurance programs became law in New York, New Hampshire, California, and Massachusetts. A federal program was poised to follow.

BUT BEFORE CONGRESS acted, and as the New York Assembly considered adopting unemployment insurance, the opposition rallied. The Chamber of Commerce believed unemployment insurance "objectionable for social, political, and economic reasons." The benefits, the New York business group claimed, would "lessen the interest of the worker in keeping his job or getting other work."

Nonetheless, the New York Assembly passed it, the governor signed it, and New York became the second state in the nation to adopt unemployment insurance in 1935. Lehman called it "the most progressive and enlightened piece of social legislation enacted in this state in many decades." Labor Secretary Frances Perkins predicted that New York's new law would serve as a model for other states. And in the next few months, eighteen states—emboldened by federal actions—followed with unemployment programs of their own. Unemployment insurance would also be incorporated into the Social Security Act passed by Congress in 1935.

Most of the time, the progressive movement and its programs serve

---

*The November 1930 election produced a Republican majority with a very slim margin. In those days, the Congress did not begin its proceedings until the following December, a full thirteen months after the election. During those thirteen months, several incumbent congressmen died, and the Democrats won enough of the special elections to replace them that the majority flipped to the Democrats. The Democrats controlled the House uninterrupted until January 1947.

two functions—helping people individually and providing a significant benefit to society at large. Illinois Senator Paul Douglas thought unemployment insurance did just that: providing crucial help for the worker and his family; and, on a larger societal scale, helping to lift the economy out of its recessionary doldrums through increasing the nation's purchasing power.

Over the next seven decades, economists have overwhelmingly accepted Douglas's views. During the deep recession of the later George W. Bush years and early Obama administration, the extension of unemployment compensation was at the top of our list for alleviating suffering for workers and their families, and for generating economic growth in the affected communities; it was the quickest and most effective stimulus for the national economy. Many conservative Republicans resisted, to be sure; many ideologues on the right, especially the dominant southern wing of the Republican Party in the House of Representatives, have never been able to accept that workers who lost their jobs through no fault of their own should get checks from the government when they were not working.

Perhaps the best example of how assistance for individual members of society can work toward the greater good is the GI Bill, enacted by a progressive president and Congress in 1944. Before World War II, home ownership and a college education were only a dream, if even that, for most Americans. But as the war came to an end—and government officials, business leaders, and economists worried about millions of GIs returning to an economy with too few jobs—the GI Bill sent them to colleges and universities in all forty-eight states. In 1947, at the program's height, 49 percent of applicants admitted to college were veterans. And by the expiration of the original GI Bill in July 1956, almost ten million of our nation's sixteen million World War II veterans had participated in an education or training program.

And millions benefited from the GI Bill's loan guaranty program. The Veterans Administration supported almost 2.4 million loans for veterans of the Second World War. The postwar years are believed by many economists and historians to be our nation's best economic times ever. Economic growth, much of it brought on by home construction, brought prosperity to people in America who had never experienced it, helping to create an exploding middle class. Perhaps no government program, with the exception of the Homestead Act, provided such opportunity to so many individuals and, at the same time, created so much prosperity for the country at large.

But it should be noted that, to people of color, the GI Bill, like most government programs, was not what was advertised. In order to get the bill through Congress, President Roosevelt made concessions to segregationists like Mississippi Congressman John Rankin. As a result, the benefits were set up in ways that would continue segregated, discriminatory education and home loan policies, in both the North and the South. Black veterans were often steered to segregated, inferior trade schools, while white veterans went to four-year colleges; as a result, by 1950 only 6 percent of African American veterans had earned a four-year college degree.

In housing it may have been worse. In Mississippi—a state where almost half the population was black—three thousand Veterans Administration home loans were issued in 1947; only two went to black veterans. Ten years after enactment of the GI Bill, home ownership nationally climbed to two out of three white families; African American home ownership was less than 40 percent.

In the years immediately after World War II, with the Great Migration of black families to the North in search of better jobs, the GI Bill and federal housing policy conspired to create segregated housing in the North, with African Americans shoehorned into substandard housing in defined neighborhoods. In short, federal government policies robbed generations of black families of the opportunity to live where they chose and build family wealth that white families have enjoyed for decades. And millions of African Americans were sentenced to big-city ghettos.

IT WAS NO easier to establish a minimum wage than to enact unemployment insurance—though once again Lehman did not give up. In 1923 the very pro-business United States Supreme Court had overturned a federal minimum wage law, striking down minimum wage statutes in fourteen states, and essentially killing any state or federal initiative to put a floor under workers' wages. Only today's Roberts court seems to have decided more consistently with the most affluent over the least privileged in society—our present-day court has almost always "sided with the prosecution over the defendant, the state over the condemned, the executive branch over the legislative, and the corporate defendant over the individual plaintiff," as Rhode Island Democratic Senator Sheldon Whitehouse put it during Sonia Sotomayor's 2009 confirmation hearings, quoting the journalist Jeffrey Toobin.

In 1933, Governor Lehman was ready to try again. Pushed by the New York Consumers League—a grassroots progressive organization made up of reformers, labor union members, and outspoken Roman Catholic and Jewish activists—the New York Assembly passed what turned out to be a thirty-one-cents-an-hour minimum wage. On April 23, 1933, Lehman was presented with two bills passed by the Assembly, one increasing the minimum wage for most workers (farmers and some service workers were excepted), the other an increase only for women and children. Lehman, with his eye on the Supreme Court and its conservative majority, chose to sign only the increase for women and children.

President Roosevelt urged other states to follow New York's lead; seven others did in 1933 alone. But New York's law was struck down by the New York Court of Appeals (the state's highest court). The case was then argued in the United States Supreme Court, with future Secretary of State Dean Acheson supporting the state. But even with supporting briefs from the state of Ohio and New York City, the Supreme Court affirmed the lower court's decision, dealing another blow to low-wage workers.

The precedent did not last, however. FDR's plan to overcome judicial resistance by packing the court with new judges did not go over well in Congress, but it did likely push some conservative justices to reconsider their resistance to the New Deal. In 1936 the United States Supreme Court voted 5–4 to uphold a Washington State minimum wage law covering women when Justice Owen Roberts changed his vote. New York Industrial Commissioner Elmer Andrews commented: "Now that the United States Supreme Court has changed its mind, or at least one-ninth of its mind, New York can enact a minimum wage law."

Two years earlier, in 1934, Lehman had been reelected by more than eight hundred thousand votes, the largest numerical margin in the history of any state's elections, defeating Republican Robert Moses, one of the most powerful figures in twentieth-century New York politics. But the Democrats lost the majority in the New York Assembly, which could have dealt a death blow to Governor Lehman's ambitious progressive agenda. It was not until 2009 that the Democrats would again control all of state government: the governor's office, the New York Assembly, and the Senate.

Still, Lehman was able to work well with members of both parties in the Assembly. In 1936, after the Supreme Court upheld the Washington State statute, the New York Assembly quickly enacted a minimum wage.

THE BATTLE TO eradicate child labor had raged for decades. At the turn of the century, an estimated four hundred thousand New York State children, ages five to seventeen, were employed, mostly for very low wages in sweatshops or dirty tenement houses—making toys, sewing clothes, delivering packages. Tens of thousands of children were engaged in "industrial homework," where they took their work home with them, and were paid as little as fifty or seventy-five cents—not per hour, but for a full fourteen-hour workday.

Defenders of child labor, most notably industry groups like the National Association of Manufacturers, dug in. An arbitrary age limit for children should not be set by the legislature or Congress "any more than you can tell when a pig becomes a hog," stated W. W. Kitchin, the legal counsel for the Cotton Manufacturers in 1916. Yes, he actually said that. That same year, a company doctor testified, "Eleven hours' work a day is not excessive for a twelve-year-old girl."

In the face of that opposition, progressives had pushed through the New York Assembly some restrictions during the first two decades of the twentieth century, but enforcement was lackadaisical and loopholes were plentiful. Child labor opponents in New York and other states turned to the Wilson administration for help. Reformers were victorious, they thought, when Congress passed and Wilson signed a ban on the interstate sale of goods manufactured by children. But the conservative, business-dominated United States Supreme Court struck down the ban.

Then in 1924, progressives in the United States House and Senate passed a constitutional amendment to specifically allow the states to legislate a ban on child labor. Thirty-six states had to ratify it to attach it to the United States Constitution.

But progress was very slow. Only six states ratified the amendment in the first two years. Powerful New York business interests blocked it from even coming to a vote. But the Depression—with its scarcity of jobs for adult male workers—led to a renewed interest among the states. In 1933 fourteen states joined the original six in ratifying the amendment. And in New York, although bills calling for ratification were introduced in every session since 1925, it was not until 1935 that a child labor ban even passed out of committee.

Lined up against Governor Lehman, progressive members of the Assembly, and New York reformers were farm groups, some prominent news organizations, the president of Columbia University, and New York's Roman Catholic Church—all against a "minimum school-leaving age." Each opponent, as outlined by Robert P. Ingalls in *Herbert H. Lehman and New York's Little New Deal*, had its reasons to continue the practice of child labor.

The very conservative New York Farm Bureau Federation had polled its members and found less than 10 percent supporting a ban on child labor, even though farm labor had been exempted in almost every child labor proposal all over the country.

Newspaper publishers were overwhelmingly opposed to the ban, and increasingly so once it became clear that very young boys would no longer be allowed to deliver their papers. But, as always, newspaper editorialists wrapped themselves in the cloak of freedom of the press when criticizing the ban. One outspoken dissenter, the New York *Daily News*, retorted, "When our fellow publishers talk of freedom of the press, they mean freedom to hire children to deliver newspapers before light on winter mornings, because children are cheaper."

Opponents lined up prominent national spokesmen to promote their cause and buttress their case. Nicholas Murray Butler, the president of

Columbia University and the former GOP candidate for vice president with President Taft, said that the amendment had "revolutionary implications," an especially serious charge in the troubled 1930s. "Every Communist gathering which has recently met has endorsed it with unanimous enthusiasm . . . The effect of this proposal [is] not upon child labor, for that would be quite negligible, but upon our American form of government, upon the home, the family, the school, and the church." It was maybe the most disingenuous comment ever uttered by a university president.

Clarence E. Martin, president of the American Bar Association, weighed in that a prohibition on child labor is a "communistic effort to nationalize children, making them primarily responsible to the government instead of to their parents. It strikes at the home. It appears to be a definite positive plan to destroy the Republic and substitute a social democracy."

The most powerful, and by far most effective, opponents were the Roman Catholic Church and its leaders. Forgetting Pope Leo XIII and *Rerum Novarum*, and perhaps conveniently oblivious to the first four or five books of the New Testament, senior church officials worried aloud that the child labor ban might lead to federal controls over parochial education. Some Roman Catholic leaders warned that a minimum school-leaving age would place too heavy a financial burden on Catholic schools, requiring new buildings and more teachers and additional books to educate those students who would now be attending schools rather than working in factories.

The Most Reverend Edmund F. Gibbons, the bishop of Albany, testified in the New York Assembly in 1937 in opposition to the child labor ban: It would "seriously endanger the rights of parents . . . Menaces of alarming proportion to religion and morality, the family, the home, the child, the workingman, the capitalist, the businessman, and the lawfully constituted government itself, demand that we clergy be conservative." So said the Church.

The following year, as the tightly conservative Supreme Court began to unwind, an emboldened Congress passed the Fair Labor Standards Act of 1938, stipulating that children under sixteen could no longer be involved in businesses engaged in interstate commerce. By then, New York State had banned most child factory labor under the age of sixteen.

More than seven decades later, at the Ministry of Foreign Affairs in Islamabad, Pakistani Minister of State for Foreign Affairs Malik Amad Khan was discussing the issue of child labor. These families have many mouths to feed, and often the father cannot find work, he told us, sitting in a wood-paneled conference room with a stunningly colorful flower arrangement between us. "A son who is working benefits the whole family." But doesn't the child displace an adult worker who is trying to feed his family? I asked.

"It's one of those modalities that you need to understand," chimed in Foreign Secretary Salman Bashir. Not only that, "it's part of our anti-terrorism campaign," that children are working instead of being drawn to the Taliban. Even the most conservative estimates show that at least two million Pakistani children are working, most of them for less than a dollar a day.

In neighboring Afghanistan, a 2009 UNICEF report estimates that one out of four children between the ages of seven and fourteen is subject to the worst forms of child labor. Enforceable—and enforced—prohibitions on child labor would go a long way to end abusive practices that so many children in poor countries endure.

ONE OF THE most important victories for progressives in the 1930s was the passage of the National Labor Relations Act of 1935—and here too Lehman helped advance the cause. The act established the National Labor Relations Board, which supervised the elections process for workers to choose to join a union. The opposition to the bill came, of course, from the nation's major business organizations. The United States Chamber of Commerce argued that labor unions would harm the economy and distort relations between employers and employees. And Charles R. Hook, vice president of the National Association of Manufacturers, said, "This bill would utterly destroy the equality of bargaining power on the part of the employer, place unnecessary expense on the shoulders of employees and subject them to a coercion and abuse the like of which this country has never known."

Not to be outdone, the Liberty League, an ultraright national organization, attacked the New Deal's "ravenous madness." And—as conservatives always do—they accused the Democrats and Roosevelt of class warfare: "The dragon teeth of class warfare are being sown with a vengeance." Many years later, I saw these tactics up close. As a member of the House of Representatives in the late 1990s, I watched as Republican after Republican—advocating tax cuts for the wealthy and spending cuts for the poor and middle class—cried out that Democrats were engaging in class warfare. Actually, *they* were engaging in class warfare against the middle class and against less privileged Americans; *we* were simply pointing it out. Sometimes it's the only argument they have. One afternoon in the late 1990s, during a debate in the House of Representatives, when the ultraconservative Republican J. D. Hayworth of Arizona accused me by name of fomenting class warfare, I knew I was doing something right.

The labor bill's sponsor, New York Senator Robert Wagner, had come to New York City with his family from Prussia in 1885. Remembering his childhood, he said that unless you lived in the tenements, "you cannot know the haunting sense of insecurity which hangs over the home of the worker." A tenacious legislator, Wagner was cautious about his bill's reach because of the Supreme Court's noted hostility to labor. The Wagner Act was narrowly constructed, including only workers specifically defined as engaged in interstate commerce. About one million workers in New York State were covered, but hundreds of thousands of hotel workers, waiters and waitresses, construction trades, and other service workers were excluded. Many of the excluded workers were people of color, a restriction that southerners had insisted be part of the bill. Wagner's original National Labor Relations Act shamefully prohibited government certification of unions that did not grant African Americans membership. The American Federation of Labor lobbied to take it out; Wagner complied. The New Deal far too often was a Raw Deal or no deal at all for people of color.

In New York, Lehman attempted to pass a Little Wagner Act but faced a protracted struggle in the face of huge employer opposition. Then on April 12, 1937, the United States Supreme Court ruled that the Wagner Act was, in its entirety, constitutional. Wagner wired his home state governor, "The time is ripe to afford the same advantages to local industries in New York."

And New York's senior senator was right. Although one conservative Albany lobbyist claimed that the Little Wagner Act "would literally Sovietize the State of New York," the bill passed easily with overwhelming support from both parties.

Public housing, like much of the government's response to Depression-era suffering, was a temporary program that evolved into an ongoing public commitment. Lehman and New York State again led the way. While Washington had begun some public construction through the Works Progress Administration, it was not until 1937 that Congress passed and FDR signed legislation that created the United States Housing Authority. New York established municipal corporations to build and operate privately financed public housing. Now the challenge was for other states and the federal government to emulate the Little New Deal's housing efforts.

The 1937 session was perhaps Lehman's best. The Assembly reenacted a minimum wage, cut the maximum hours for women workers, established the right to collective bargaining, adopted a state social security program, and expanded the state's unemployment insurance benefits— truly a little New Deal in our nation's largest state.

Sometimes Governor Lehman and New York State led the way for other states to follow; other times New York followed what progressives in Washington and other states had accomplished; and on occasion New York blazed a trail for the federal government.

After Lehman defeated New York District Attorney Thomas Dewey in the governor's race in 1938, things began to change. He knew that across the country, voters in the 1938 midterms had cooled toward Roosevelt, the New Deal, and the Democrats. He rightly assumed that a time of progressive victories was drawing to a close, and that he would have to fight a mostly Republican state assembly to preserve them. And he knew that the storm clouds gathering in Europe would overwhelm his work in New York. He devoted his entire 1939 inaugural address to impending threats from Europe, urging unity and calling on New Yorkers and all Americans to be prepared.

After Roosevelt's reelection for an unprecedented third term in November 1940, Lehman was urged by some prominent New Yorkers to consider a presidential bid if President Roosevelt chose not to run in 1944; after all, a governor or former governor of New York had been a major party nominee for president in twelve of the nineteen presidential elections since the Civil War. But Governor Lehman expressed no interest and announced his retirement from electoral politics in 1942; ten years as governor, he believed, were enough. Under Lehman's leadership, New York had provided unemployment insurance and public assistance for the jobless, banned child labor and industrial homework, enacted farm price supports and a minimum wage, strengthened regulation of public utilities, and provided public housing for those most ignored in our society.

On December 3, 1942, Governor Herbert Lehman resigned, a month before his term ended, to become the director of Foreign Relief and Rehabilitation Operations in the United States Department of State, during which time his son was killed in a World War II practice exercise. Lehman was later selected as director general of the United Nations Relief and Rehabilitation Administration, where he served for three years.

A little while later, Lehman decided to try electoral politics again. In 1946 he lost a race for the United States Senate to Irving M. Ives by 250,000 votes, but ran almost 400,000 votes ahead of his party's gubernatorial nominee in a very bad year—nationally and in New York—for Democrats. Three years later, he won the 1949 special election, defeating John Foster Dulles, who had been appointed to the Senate only four months earlier. Dulles, a Republican attorney and diplomat, was to become president Dwight D. Eisenhower's secretary of state. The seat had been vacated by Robert Wagner, the author of the National Labor Relations Act, who resigned because of his health.

The United States Senate was never easy for the septuagenarian Lehman. The job of senator from New York brought a particular prestige. In Lehman's time, New York was the largest and by far the dominant state in the United States; today it is fourth in population. One out of ten Americans lived in New York State; today about one out of eight lives in California. New York boasted of its ethnic diversity and its wide range of interest groups. Lehman, as a resident of New York City, received more mail than anyone in Washington other than the president of the United States. His workload was simply too heavy to be accommodated by the government employees he had hired; he was allotted about $65,000 a year of federal funds to pay his staff of about a dozen. He used his own money to hire sixteen more assistants and secretaries—some in New York, others in Washington. Holed up in Suite 455 in the Senate Office Building—the same office I occupied in my first two years in the Senate in what is now called the Russell Building—Lehman had the largest staff of any legislator on Capitol Hill.

He often tilted at windmills, introducing legislation that he knew wouldn't pass, but believing that the issues needed to be placed in the public record and debated in the public forum. A member of the Senate Labor and Public Welfare Committee and eventually chairman of the Subcommittee on Health, Lehman had a tendency to "spread himself too thin," according to columnist Marquis Childs.

The Senate Labor and Public Welfare Committee—later the Education and Labor Committee and now the Health, Education, Labor, and Pensions (HELP) Committee—had a proud history and notable future. Chairman Hugo Black helped to create the middle class from that committee with the FLSA. All three Kennedy brothers served on the committee; for years Edward Kennedy chaired it, with great accomplishments on all four jurisdictions.

After I was elected, I asked Harry Reid and Edward Kennedy to be assigned to the HELP Committee. In December, 2008, when the number of slots for Democrats was expanded, Reid placed third-year Senator Barack Obama and first-year Senators Bernie Sanders and me on the committee. At a dinner of the eleven Democrats on the committee in December at Senator Kennedy's Georgetown home, I was seated at the far end of the table next to Sanders. As we looked around and saw Kennedy, Hillary Clinton, and Barack Obama, I said to Bernie, "What in the hell are *we* doing here?"

Interestingly, as my colleagues and I conversed, it occurred to me how many members of this committee have had presidential aspirations: Kennedy and Harkin had run for president; Dodd, Clinton, and Obama were getting ready to announce their candidacies; and, of course, seven years later, Bernie Sanders was a candidate.

Lehman was especially active in promoting civil rights legislation. "A fight is worthwhile," Lehman said, "even if you know you're going to lose it. It's the only way to crystallize attitudes, educate people. And in the end, I've seen many hopeless causes win out." He, along with other civil rights supporters in the Senate, was referred to by some as "the sons of the wild jackasses." He would convene meetings of like-minded senators: Brien McMahon and William Benton of Connecticut; Warren Magnuson of Washington State; Paul Douglas of Illinois; Hubert Humphrey of Minnesota; and Theodore Francis Green and John Pastore of Rhode Island.

EARLY IN HIS Senate career, even during his first two years, Lehman had earned the enmity of his southern colleagues because of his fervor for civil rights legislation, his support for government action to help the poor, and perhaps too because of anti-Semitism. When Majority Leader Scott Lucas, an Illinois Democrat, was asked what southern Democratic senators thought about Lehman, he answered simply, "They loathe him."

But Lehman was never cowed. Southerners, who pretty much controlled the inner workings of the Senate institution, had consigned Lehman, early in his Washington career, to the Senate Interior Committee, as punishment for his liberalism and independence. And Johnson, who ostracized Lehman, did not make it easy on him. Johnson told his aide Bobby Baker, "I don't see any profit in calling up bills so that [the Mississippi segregationist] Jim Eastland and Herbert Lehman can insult each other, or so that Paul Douglas and Albert Gore can exercise their lungs. Why should we cut ourselves up and then lose?"

JULIUS CAIUS CAESAR EDELSTEIN, Lehman's top assistant during his years in the Senate, recalled accompanying Lehman to the Senate floor after the New York senator had fallen into disfavor with LBJ: "You'd walk into the cloakroom. People would fall silent. You'd walk down the hall, and there would be an averting of eyes so that they wouldn't have to say hello. Lehman would begin making a speech, and if Johnson was on the floor he would walk out to the cloakroom, just ostentatiously enough so you knew it was deliberate. And other people would drift—leave—the floor."

No matter how badly Lehman was treated by Lyndon Johnson and his southern Democratic colleagues, the New York senator was always a gentleman, and never appeared to hold a grudge. Lehman's graciousness showed when he asked the Senate to stand for a moment of silent prayer for Johnson on the first day it met after the majority leader's heart attack.

His tenacity and mettle were on display not just on civil rights, but also on civil liberties. It is hard to imagine the fear instilled among politicians by Wisconsin Senator Joe McCarthy, and the courage required to stand up to him. Senators had seen what happened to their colleague, the former Senator Joseph Tydings of Maryland, who was certainly no progressive but was a Democrat who dared to disagree with the Red-baiting McCarthy. McCarthy had also played a major role in the defeat of Florida's Claude Pepper and Idaho's Glen Taylor and Education and Labor Chairman Elbert Thomas of Utah. In January 1951, less than three months after the defeat of Tydings, Taylor, Pepper, and Thomas, the Democrats' fear of McCarthy may have been at its peak. William White, author of *Citadel*, called McCarthy "the most politically powerful first-term Senator in this Congress, by any standards."

McCarthy took full advantage of his power and the fear he created. One day, on the floor of the United States Senate, the Wisconsin Republican again railed against Communist influence in the top echelons of the United States government. Standing with stacks of papers at his Senate desk, he claimed the documents in front of him proved his case, and challenged anyone to examine the evidence.

Only Lehman, in but his second year in the Senate, answered the call. He walked over to McCarthy's desk, put his hand out, and asked for the documents. Here is how the columnist Stewart Alsop described the scene:

> The two men stared at each other, and McCarthy giggled his
> strange, rather terrifying little giggle. Lehman looked around
> the crowded Senate, obviously appealing for support. Not a man
> rose. "Go back to your seat, old man," the 42-year-old McCarthy
> growled at the 72-year-old Lehman. The words do not appear in
> the Congressional Record, but they were clearly audible in the
> press gallery. Once more, Lehman looked all around the chamber,

appealing for support. He was met with silence and lowered eyes. Slowly, he turned and walked back [to his seat]. The silence of the Senate that evening was a measure of the fear which McCarthy inspired in almost all politicians . . . Old Senator Lehman's back, waddling off in retreat, seemed to symbolize the final defeat of decency.

Lehman's fight for civil rights continued unabated. He convened meetings in his office to figure out how to blunt segregationist obstruction, change Senate rules, and pass a civil rights bill. Typically fifteen or twenty senators came to these strategy sessions.

But by 1956 Lehman saw much of that energy dissipate. In January only twelve senators showed up in Lehman's office to plot strategy to reform Senate cloture rules, which could have brought a civil rights bill to the Senate floor. Lehman, by then in his late seventies, was tired and ready to leave the Senate. Robert Caro wrote that Lehman and Illinois Democratic Senator Paul Douglas were "uncompromising on their principles" and that Lehman was now "an old man who for years had stood shoulder to shoulder with Douglas, and who had left the senate battlefield because he was afraid he could no longer be effective on it."

In January 1957 he retired from the United States Senate, ending his elective office career at the age of seventy-eight. He won more statewide elections—for lieutenant governor, for governor, for the United States Senate, eight in all—than anyone in New York's history. In 1934 he set a record in New York in gubernatorial politics, winning the election by eight hundred thousand votes. He defeated a number of national and New York heavyweights—the war hero "Wild Bill" Donovan; Robert Moses, one of New York State's most powerful politicians of the twentieth century; the future presidential candidate and New York Governor Thomas Dewey; the incumbent Senator and future Secretary of State John Foster Dulles.

His success was never about charisma; some, in fact, said his strength was his awkwardness, his blandness, his humorlessness, his monotonic speaking voice. To New York voters, Lehman's courage and honesty shone through. Herbert Lehman, the labor official George Meany wrote, "was the ideal public servant . . . He had none of the average politician's guile, the average diplomat's evasiveness, the average banker's greed, or the average statesman's aloofness."

For Herbert Lehman, life was always about public service. The seventy-eight-year-old Lehman had spent the last three decades in elective office, had served his country in the military, had lost his son in war, and had been one of New York's leading philanthropists. Reflecting on his personal and professional career in 1962, Lehman estimated that during his lifetime, he had donated seven million dollars to charity.

Back home, working alongside Eleanor Roosevelt—he in his eighties, she in her late seventies—Lehman devoted his life to the reform movement in New York City politics. He was about as busy as he had always been, always lending his voice and his name to those with less privilege. *The New York Times* wrote that, even after his eightieth birthday, "he could be found in rain and cold carrying on his crusade for political decency in every section of this city."

In July 1963 President John F. Kennedy announced that Herbert H. Lehman would receive the Presidential Medal of Freedom, the highest honor a president can bestow for peacetime service to the nation, on December 6, 1963. Neither man lived to that day; President Kennedy was assassinated on November 22, and Herbert Lehman died at home of a heart attack as he prepared for his trip to Washington to receive the medal. He was eighty-five; he had lived a full life, for his community and for his nation.

He was, Republican Senator Jacob Javits said of Lehman on the Senate floor three days after his death, "a rich man who, throughout his political career, was the champion of those who had no money, no status, and virtually no chance of gaining either."

THOUGHTS FROM DESK 88

I WILL NEVER FORGET THE DAY—September 18, 2008—in Zanesville, Ohio, meeting with constituents. I got a call from Majority Leader Reid's office, instructing me to be on a conference call with Senate Banking Committee members, Bush Treasury Secretary Henry Paulson, and Federal Reserve Chairman Ben Bernanke. Only three days earlier, the New York investment bank Lehman Brothers had filed for bankruptcy.

The Lehman Brothers of 2008 would have been unrecognizable—and embarrassing—to Herbert Lehman. Lehman Brothers, cofounded in

the 1860s by Herbert's father, Mayer, and Mayer's older brother Emanuel, was one of America's most successful investment banks. A conservative institution, it was well run and usually quite profitable for decades.
But late in the twentieth century, Lehman Brothers became something
very different.

When markets are deregulated and rules are relaxed, even a company
with a reputation as good as Lehman Brothers is vulnerable to excessive
risk-taking and overreach. Lehman, like much of Wall Street, had an
almost religious belief in the infallibility of the market. The firm bor-
rowed huge sums of money, leveraging itself at a ratio of more than thirty
to one, which brought enormous profits in good times. Its bankers bet
heavily on investments in overheated real estate, leveraged huge amounts
of money to make even more money on these investments, and were slow
to recognize their losses. Its top management refused to believe—until it
was too late—that it could fail. In the fall of 2008, Richard S. Fuld, Jr.,
its longtime CEO, pleaded with regulators, begging taxpayers to buy
some of its billions in troubled assets. Bush Treasury Secretary Henry
Paulson, who was formerly CEO of the Lehman rival Goldman Sachs
and who had "rescued" other financial institutions in previous weeks, said
no this time.

At 2:00, with a dozen or so Treasury and Fed officials and senators
on the call, a chagrined, anxious Bernanke laid out for us the most serious economic problems our country had seen since the Great Depression.
He warned us that bank failures and panic among financial institutions
would lead to a depression. A collapse on Wall Street would devastate
Main Street. Paulson told us he needed $700 billion from Congress, with
no strings attached. He had a three-page bill ready to pass early the following week.

Senators in both parties knew that panic on Wall Street and multiple
bank failures would push our country into an even bigger recession than
we already were in. When the country realized that the Bush administration was asking Congress to "bail out the banks," the letters and calls and
emails were overwhelming, nothing like I had ever seen. Initially, calls
and letters and emails were one hundred to one against the bailout. By
the time of the vote, as people realized that alternatives were maybe even

worse—with maybe forty thousand people weighing in—the numbers were maybe three to one against. Politically I knew a yes vote could be career-ending. I voted yes.

In the end, the Democrats did what we had to do—the responsible thing for our country. Most Senate Republicans did the right thing too for our country. House Republicans did the right *political* thing (no surprise there), opposing their own president to play to legitimate public anger. President Bush's bill passed the Senate but was voted down in the House when the overwhelming majority of his party voted no. Immediately, the stock market tanked, dropping more than 770 points; bankers all over the country, including community bankers with whom I was speaking in Ohio, pleaded with their federal officials to vote for the rescue. Enough responsible Republicans in the House reconsidered and did the right thing. President Bush signed the bill immediately.

The following Tuesday, on September 23, 2008, in the Russell Caucus Room (now named the Kennedy Caucus Room—the room where the *Titanic*, McCarthy, and Watergate hearings were held; where the Affordable Care Act was written the following year; and where JFK and RFK announced for president), the Banking Committee heard from the see-no-evil-hear-no-evil Bush regulators: Treasury Secretary Paulson; Chairman Bernanke, the best among them and a good public servant; and Securities and Exchange Commission Chairman Chris Cox, the blindest and deafest of them all. The discussion was about the $700 billion TARP bill, and how to unfreeze capital so businesses could operate; to some of us, it was also about keeping in their homes the millions of people facing foreclosure, and it was about limits on executive compensation for those who had brought the financial system to its knees. To Cox and Paulson and most Republicans in the House and Senate, it was about protecting Wall Street.

Republicans could take care of bankers, but autoworkers? Not so much. We failed, because of GOP opposition, to rein in bankers' outrageous compensation; yet unionized autoworkers, they told us, make too much money . . . and there are all those "legacy costs." Fundamentally, special-interest Washington does not understand—or care to understand—collective bargaining: that workers give up wages today so that they can provide for their health care and a secure retirement; those were the legacy costs that Republican senator after Republican senator criticized.

For decades, risk and fear and regulation constrained the natural excesses of Wall Street investors. But in the late 1990s and early in the next decade, Wall Street financiers figured out how to minimize risk and overcome fear, or so they thought. And government regulators—in the first decade of this century, an era when untrammeled capitalism was believed morally superior to even the hint of government regulation—sleepwalked through the Bush 43 years leading up to Lehman's demise. New financial instruments—credit default swaps and other derivatives, most notably—were created by young Ivy League MBAs, bringing massive wealth to a relative few, but leaving behind the wreckage for others—taxpayers and homeowners and retirees, as it turned out—to clean up.

Alan Greenspan, whom many believe had more to do with the collapse of the financial system than any other single person, warbled at a House Banking and Financial Services Committee hearing in 1998, "Regulation of derivatives transactions that are privately negotiated by professionals is unnecessary. Regulation that serves no useful purpose hinders the efficiency of markets to enlarge standards of living."

Almost a decade later, when unbeknownst to him the economy was on the precipice of collapse, Greenspan noted in his 2007 autobiography, *The Age of Turbulence*, "From 1995 forward, the largely unregulated global markets, with some notable exceptions, appeared to be moving smoothly from one state of equilibrium to another.

"There is nothing involved in federal regulation per se which makes it superior to market regulation," he had pronounced. But he could not explain the fact that decades of regulation kept the financial system stable, and the deregulation of the last couple of years of Clinton and the entire Bush presidency pushed the financial system to totter and almost collapse.

Like many economists who favor the wealthy, Greenspan credited much of his economic worldview to his years-long association with the libertarian author-philosopher Ayn Rand. Rand, whose four novels have sold many millions of copies, assembled in her Manhattan salon a small group of ultraconservative New York intellectuals in the 1950s, including a young Alan Greenspan; with no small irony, they called themselves, according to the Rand biographer Anne Heller, "The Collective."

Rand, Greenspan often said, convinced them of the moral basis of capitalism. In a 1963 essay for Rand's newsletter, Greenspan asserted, "It is precisely the 'greed' of the businessman, or more appropriately his profit-seeking, which is the unexcelled protector of the consumer." That same year, in her lecture "The Fascist New Frontier," Rand compared President Kennedy's New Frontier and his economic policies, most notably an increase in the minimum wage, to the fascism of the 1930s.

Throughout his entire career, including and most importantly his years as chairman of the Federal Reserve, Greenspan shared the antiregulatory zeal and unbending certainty of his intellectual mentor. Watching Greenspan testify to House Financial Services and listening to his pronouncements about banking and our economy, I often thought of the always-knows-best British scholar Thomas Babington Macaulay. A British prime minister said of the young historian, "I wish that I were as certain about anything as Lord Macaulay is about everything."

It was only in October 2008 that the former Federal Reserve chairman affirmed the bankruptcy of that Randian-Greenspan philosophy. In a dramatic exchange with California Democrat Henry Waxman, the chairman of the House Committee on Oversight and Government Reform, Greenspan acknowledged: "Those of us who have looked to the self-interest of the lending institutions to protect shareholders' equity, myself included, are in a state of shocked disbelief." Yes, Mr. Chairman, as Gretchen Morgenson of *The New York Times* wrote, there was gambling going on at the casino.

IN *THE GREAT CRASH, 1929*, John Kenneth Galbraith described what happens to government regulatory bodies and the people who staff them. At first, like young people, they are aggressive and idealistic, sometimes even "evangelist and intolerant." They mellow with age, and in a space of fifteen or twenty years, they are—with some exceptions—either "senile" or "captive of the industry which they are supposed to regulate."

One of the first examples of "regulatory capture," as pointed out by the writer Thomas Frank, came after the establishment of the Interstate Commerce Commission, which was created in the 1880s to regulate railroad freight rates. President Grover Cleveland's Attorney General Richard Olney, a former railroad lawyer, was asked by his former employer to find a way to kill off the hated commission. Not so fast, he retorted: "The Commission . . . is, or can be made, of great use to the railroads. It satisfies the popular clamor for a government supervision of the railroads, at the same time that that supervision is almost entirely nominal. Further, the older such a commission gets to be, the more inclined it will be found to take the business and railroad view of things . . . The part of wisdom is not to destroy the Commission, but to utilize it."

But in the early 1900s things began to change. Theodore Roosevelt, the original trustbuster, was never afraid to take on powerful forces that he believed undercut the public interest, especially Wall Street and the steel and oil trusts. But the three GOP presidents between the World Wars—Warren Harding, Calvin Coolidge, and Herbert Hoover—saw a very different country, and set the tone for the next many decades. They cut taxes, mostly on the wealthiest citizens, weakened antitrust laws, and pledged not to interfere with Wall Street practices and profits.

Decades later, President George W. Bush and then Donald Trump perfected the art of regulatory capture. With a heavy-handed push from top political appointees in the White House, Wall Street had become fearless, and greed and recklessness had their way. The Bush administration hired banking regulators who did not really believe in regulation. In fact, except for the privatization of Social Security, Wall Street bankers got virtually everything they wanted from Congress and the Bush White House.

In Washington's ornate agency hearing rooms in an earlier day when the future looked rosy, it was almost a carnival-like atmosphere. Government regulators, ostensibly there to protect investors and safeguard the public, seemed not to worry too much about the future. Reported by *The New York Times*, Securities and Exchange Commissioner Roel Campos, a Bush appointee and owner of a Houston broadcasting company, said of a deregulation proposal, "I'm very happy to support it. And I keep my fingers crossed for the future."

On that April day in 2004, the Securities and Exchange Commission hit into a game-ending double play with the bases loaded. Wall Street's major investment banks asked the regulators for relief from a long-standing rule limiting the amount of debt that they could acquire. The mandatory capital requirements—requiring banks to have a relatively low debt-to-capital ratio—had served the financial community and the public well, but stood in the way of even greater profits for Bear Stearns, Goldman Sachs, Lehman Brothers, Merrill Lynch, and the other big firms.

The SEC complied with the request. Combined with the regulatory body's decision to establish only a voluntary supervision program, this helped set the stage for the biggest financial crisis in seven decades. The always prescient Mark Twain, speaking of course in a different day but always an acute observer of human nature, remarked: "Beautiful credit! The foundation of a modern society. Who shall say that this is not the golden age of mutual trust, of unlimited reliance upon human promises?"

Brad Johnson, an analyst for Goldman Sachs, wrote in *American Banker* in late 2008: "Common sense tells us that the animal spirit of capitalism can periodically turn into a mob mentality that needs braking before anyone goes over a cliff." He called the 2004 SEC ruling "the final morphing of deregulation into unregulation." Johnson warned in 2008, "There should now be general recognition that a mechanism to govern the animal spirit of capitalism at highly leveraged financial institutions is needed to prevent them from getting out of control and crashing the economy, as they have now done."

"History—including recent history—shows that without regulation," the Yale professor Robert J. Shiller and the 2001 Nobel Laureate George A. Akerlof wrote in *The Wall Street Journal*, "animal spirits will drive economic activity to extremes."*

And then along came former California Congressman Christopher

---

*The term "animal spirit," apparently employed first by the Scottish philosopher David Hume in 1739, was defined by John Maynard Keynes in his seminal 1936 book *The General Theory of Employment, Interest, and Money*: "a spontaneous urge to action rather than inaction and not as the outcome of a weighted average of quantitative benefits by quantitative probabilities."

Cox, whom I observed on the House Energy and Commerce Committee for several years, preaching his free market philosophy and doing the bidding of almost every corporation that brought business to our committee. Blocked by California Democratic Senator Barbara Boxer from a federal court appointment—"because of his ultraconservative politics," she told me; "he's wrong on every issue"—Cox was appointed chairman of the Securities and Exchange Commission in 2005. Now, from his perch as Wall Street's top regulator, Cox could implement his political philosophy and prove to doubters (like me) that markets always know best and that regulation did nothing but stifle growth and kill jobs.

And implement his political philosophy he did. There were more than five hundred enforcement actions for securities fraud in 2002. But with cutbacks in SEC funding, coupled with an obviously more lax attitude toward corporate fraud from the White House, there were fewer than 150 enforcement actions in 2008. Perhaps even more telling, according to a study by Syracuse University, the Securities and Exchange Commission launched sixty-nine agency investigations in the last year of the Clinton administration that led to Department of Justice prosecutions. By 2007, in the midst of the greatest malfeasance on Wall Street in seventy-five years, the SEC launched only nine investigations that led to Department of Justice prosecutions.

As the *Washington Post* columnist Harold Meyerson wrote in early 2009, "The financial structure that emerged from the New Deal ensured that small investors, pensioners, and depositors wouldn't be exposed to high levels of risk, but the repeal of the Glass-Steagall Act and other follies of deregulation plunged everybody into the same high-risk pool."*

Even Ben Bernanke, the Bush-appointed chairman of the Federal Reserve, acknowledged that it was the accelerated deregulation of the financial system during the Bush administrations and the reign of his own predecessor Alan Greenspan that brought on the meltdown. In a speech to the American Economic Association in Atlanta in January 2010, Ber-

---

*Full disclosure: I voted against House passage of the repeal of Glass-Steagall, but then made a mistake when I voted for the conference report—the worst vote of my twenty-seven-year career in the House and Senate.

nanke said, "Surely, both the private sector and financial regulators must improve their ability to monitor and control risk-taking. The crisis revealed not only weaknesses in regulators' oversight of financial institutions, but also, more fundamentally, important gaps in the architecture of financial regulation around the world."

Cox, distant from his professional staff, had created "procedural handcuffs" and had focused, when there were investigations and prosecutions, on "less important violations" instead of major legal and ethical transgressions. Mostly, in the words of *The Wall Street Journal*'s David Wessel in his analysis of the financial crisis, "Cox was largely a bystander." In the summer of 2009 in my office, the new chairwoman of the SEC, Mary Schapiro, emphasized how difficult her predecessor had made the process to even launch an investigation; there was "not an enforcement mentality" in the Bush years, she said with a shrug.

OF COURSE, in the revisionist history propagated by corporate conservatives, the financial crisis was caused not by bankers or weak regulation but by something very different. It was government bureaucrats who brought the economy almost to its knees. Such thinking was impervious to facts.

Back to 2007. Cox and friends were getting lots of political support. At every opportunity, the Bush administration used the threat of international competition to advocate for deregulation of financial services. Throughout 2007, as America's most serious housing crisis deepened to its worst levels since the Great Depression, regulators as prominent as Treasury Secretary Paulson reassured the Congress and the public that things were about to get better. In those days, the nation's most serious economic problems were confined to places like Indiana, Ohio, and Michigan—states hard hit by manufacturing job loss—and apparently of little interest to the East Coast regulators and their allies on Wall Street. For a period of fourteen years, beginning in the late 1990s, Ohio had more foreclosures every year than the year before . . . every single year. And in my neighborhood in Cleveland, just south of Slavic Village, in 2007 during my first six months on Senate Banking, our zip code 44105 had more foreclosures than any other zip code in the United States of America. Washington did not much seem to care. The 2008 election was mostly—in the end—about the failure of conservative Republican economics. A political party had had its way for six years, enacting its conservative, free market agenda, deregulating almost at will, writing the economy's rules, dictating economic policy, enacting free trade agreements—all of which may have swollen corporate profits, but which too often cost jobs, hurt small business, and wreaked havoc on communities.

And even as the nation looked to a new president in the late fall of 2008, Wall Street corruption continued. On December 11, 2008, federal agents arrested the New York financier Bernard Madoff and charged him with securities fraud.

The Securities and Exchange Commission doing its job? The regulatory cop on the beat busting the bad guys? Well, not exactly. The SEC had missed another one . . . a really big one. On December 10, Madoff had told his two sons of his *$50 billion* scheme, and they, supposedly at his request, turned in their father to the authorities. Even though, according to committee testimony in the House Financial Services Committee six weeks later, they had been warned several times, Cox and the SEC, even though they had been warned several times, had missed the biggest Ponzi scheme in United States financial history.

Much else was happening with the new president. With Democrats in the majority in both Houses, we went to work to change Wall Street rules—from stronger regulations to encouraging the safety and soundness of the financial system to consumer protections to ending "Too Big to Fail." For most of us in the Senate, but probably not for most of us on Banking (just as farm interests have great influence on the Agriculture Committee and the defense industry has great influence on Armed Services), the Great Recession was caused by deregulation and the complicit regulations of the Bush administration, and the increased concentration and consolidation of the nation's largest banks. Only twenty years earlier, the largest six U.S. banks' combined assets were less than 20 percent of the country's gross domestic product. By 2009, the six largest—J.P. Morgan, Chase, Wells Fargo, Citi, Bank of America, Goldman Sachs, and

Morgan Stanley—represented more than 60 percent of GDP, which gave them immense economic and political power over our economy.

THE DODD-FRANK BILL, named after its prime sponsors, Barney Frank, a House Democrat from Massachusetts, and Chris Dodd, a Democratic senator from Connecticut, was the product of dozens of hearings, hundreds of meetings, and thousands of individual discussions. It set higher capital requirements for financial institutions, forced banks to undergo regular stress tests to see how they would perform in a troubled economy, and set up a consumer protection bureau. The bill was a good start, but of course it had almost no Republican support; after all, Obama was for it and Wall Street was against it. No surprise, with a Banking Committee far too dominated by banking interests, that it did not go far enough to end TBTF, which can be called too big to fail, too big to manage, too big to regulate. Senator Ted Kaufman, a Democrat from Delaware, and I offered an amendment on the Senate floor to break up the nation's six largest banks. Chairman Dodd opposed it. President Obama opposed it. We lost 33–61; at one point we had 39 votes, but for whatever reason a number of senators, including John McCain, changed their votes (if not their minds). Only three Republicans voted yes—Richard Shelby, the senior Republican on the Banking committee, Oklahoman Tom Coburn, and Nevadan John Ensign.

ON THE SUMMER DAY when President Obama signed Dodd-Frank in 2010, the chief lobbyist for the financial services industry pronounced, "It's halftime." Now they were really ready to go to work.

And work they did, every week from that day in July 2010 until banking interests had their man in the White House on January 20, 2017: inundating regulators with documents and appeals and protests to slow the work of implementation, challenging and diluting strong rules, undercutting the Consumer Financial Protection Bureau by endless requests and hearings, delaying, slow walking, whatever it took to advantage Wall Street.

There is no question that the banking system is considerably more stable because of Dodd-Frank. Capital requirements are stiffer; banks are stronger and preparing for stress tests properly.

But the fever of collective amnesia seems to have infected almost every Republican on the Banking Committee and most of the Senate Republican Conference. Of course, pro–Wall Street Republicans, which is pretty much all of them, have been infected for almost the last decade with such amnesia, forgetting that the almost-collapse of our economy was mostly caused by the animal spirits that ran rampant on Wall Street in the first decade of the twenty-first century.

It took only months for the White House and the Trump regulators to cave to the big banks. First they worked to emasculate the Consumer Financial Protection Bureau, choosing the interests of payday lenders over the interests of borrowers and others victimized by them. Dodd-Frank had required Wall Street's largest banks to go through annual "stress tests"—were they strong enough to withstand a recession without a government bailout? Trump regulators, or more precisely, Trump *de*-regulators will now conduct those tests only once during a four-year presidential term. These new rules will allow more-risky behavior by big banks, meaning more profits for Bank of America and Wells Fargo and JPMorgan Chase. It will also result in a much higher chance of economic disaster, meaning more exposure for taxpayers. And while this president never missed a chance to trumpet his support for the military, the White House stripped away consumer protections for military families.

Let us end this chapter on a couple of optimistic notes—while again celebrating the progressive career of Herbert Lehman and the Little New Deal—by returning to the thoughts of John Kenneth Galbraith. As many parallels as some might cite between the crash of 1929 with the ensuing Depression and the economic crisis of 2008–2009, the differences are much greater. Galbraith's words of some years ago still ring true: "The much maligned farm program provides a measure of security for farm income and therewith for spending by farmers. Unemployment compensation accomplishes the same result, if still inadequately for labor. The remainder of the social security system—pensions and public assistance—helps protect the income and consequently the expenditures of yet other segments of the population."

Or, as Ohio Governor Ted Strickland, who inherited a very difficult economic situation when he took office in 2007, reflected on how much worse it could have been if it were not for Franklin Roosevelt's New Deal and Lyndon Johnson's Great Society: "What if there were no Social Security checks for our senior citizens? What if there was no Medicare to take care of our older people and no Medicaid for our kids and our disabled citizens? What if there was no unemployment compensation, no checks going out to laid-off workers?" What if there were no farm programs that saved the rural areas of this country?

Of course, good jobs with good wages should always be our goal; that's what the auto rescue was all about. But we also know that, without the efforts of progressives—in our churches and our union halls and our veterans' groups, in the streets and in Washington and in state capitals— the suffering brought on by Wall Street overreach in the first decade of the twentieth century would have been catastrophically worse.

5.

Al Gore, Sr.

LEADING FROM THE SOUTH

SERVED IN THE UNITED STATES SENATE 1953–1971

The South's story has been largely, but not entirely, a story
of its betrayal by political and cultural leaders.

—Senator Al Gore, Sr., of Tennessee

I T HAPPENED NEAR DESK 88.
As first-term Senator Albert Gore, Sr., walked into the Senate
chamber on March 10, 1956, Strom Thurmond was ready. With a
copy of the Southern Manifesto in tow, the South Carolina senator strode
toward Gore. As the southern reporters whom Thurmond had alerted
leaned over the rail in the press gallery, the segregationist Democrat-
turned-Dixiecrat barked, "Albert, we'd like you to sign the Southern
Manifesto with the rest of us."

The Southern Manifesto, officially known as "A Declaration of

Constitutional Principles," was the Southern Caucus's reaction to the 1954 Supreme Court *Brown v. Board of Education of Topeka* ruling. It was not the first manifesto from angry and defiant Congressional southerners. Almost a hundred years earlier, in 1849, John Calhoun led several of his southern colleagues in penning the Southern Address, threatening to secede if Northerners did not back off their antislavery rhetoric.

The Southern Caucus—made up of segregationist senators like Eastland and Stennis of Mississippi; Thurmond; Robertson and Harry Byrd of Virginia; Richard Russell, the leader among the segregationists, and Talmadge, of Georgia; and North Carolina's Sam Ervin—had drawn up the Manifesto, the formal document outlining segregationist opposition to *Brown v. Board.* And it was endorsed with enthusiasm by those conservative senators.

All but three southern senators—Lyndon Johnson, Estes Kefauver, and Gore—had signed the notorious document. Russell had let LBJ off the hook; the southerners had plans for the Texas senator, and they knew that the rest of the country would never elect as its president someone who had signed the Southern Manifesto. And Johnson was, as his aide Harry McPherson said, "solid on oil and gas" at home. Kefauver was not considered much of a southerner, far too liberal for his Dixie colleagues in the Senate. He was ambitious; in fact, he was the Democratic nominee for vice president later that year. And he was neither liked nor trusted by the southerners.

So Strom Thurmond, the 1948 Dixiecrat candidate for president, and Richard Russell, one of the most respected members of the Senate, set their sights on the rookie senator from Tennessee.

At that moment on the floor of the United States Senate, when Thurmond confronted the Tennessee senator, Albert Gore knew everyone was watching—and evaluating him. Taken aback at Thurmond's combativeness and showiness, Gore hesitated a moment, looked the South Carolina senator in the eye, and loudly retorted, "Hell no."

Two days later, Georgia's Walter George, president pro tempore of the Senate and chairman of the Foreign Relations Committee, went to the floor to announce that twenty-one senators in eleven states and seventy-seven House members, all from the Old Confederacy, had signed the Declaration of Constitutional Principles, and commended "the motives of those States which have declared the intention to resist forced integration by any lawful means." Most of the signatories had opposed anti-lynching legislation, and virtually all had opposed voting rights for black citizens.

The Declaration reaffirmed the 1896 Supreme Court decision *Plessy v. Ferguson*, the "separate but equal doctrine," which, according to the Declaration, "restated time and again, became a part of the life of the people of many of the States and confirmed their habits, tradition, and way of life. It is founded on elemental humanity and common sense."

Brown v. Board, the Declaration claimed, was "destroying the amicable relations between the White and Negro races that have been created through ninety years of patient effort by the good people of both races. It had planted hatred and suspicion where there has been heretofore friendship and understanding." Several northern senators took to the floor during the next few days to attack the Manifesto. Interestingly, not one senator who had signed it rose to defend it.* Some senators and congressmen who signed the Manifesto disappointed northern liberal and southern moderates and African Americans all across the country: Arkansas Senator J. William Fulbright, who a decade later, as chairman of the Foreign Relations Committee, led the opposition to the Vietnam War; Alabama Senator Lister Hill, who had a long record of public health achievements; Arkansas Congressman Wilbur Mills, who as chairman of the House Ways and Means Committee, would be a key player in the creation of Medicare; freshman Florida Congressman Paul Rogers, later a progressive voice on health care as chairman of the Commerce Committee's Health Subcommittee (he was succeeded as the top Democrat of the Health Subcommittee by California's Henry Waxman, then me, then

---

*More than five decades later, a group of progressive senators stood on the floor and denounced a different kind of hate speech, attacks aimed at people who are gay or transgender; our bill to ban employment discrimination was scheduled for a vote. After the bill's sponsor, Iowa Democrat Tom Harkin, gave his closing arguments in support of ENDA, no opponent rose to speak. More than thirty Republicans voted no. But just like the supporters of the Southern Manifesto, they knew better, and they knew they were on the wrong side of history.

Frank Pallone of New Jersey); and Louisiana Congressman Hale Boggs, the future majority leader of the House and the father of NPR's Cokie Roberts.

There were other southern members who, under pressure from seg-regationist colleagues in Congress and from racists at home, refused to sign: freshman Congressman Dante Fascell of Florida, later chairman of the House Foreign Affairs Committee; Texas Congressman Jack Brooks, later chairman of the House Judiciary Committee; and Tennessee Repub-lican Congressman Howard Baker, Sr., whose son became Senate majority leader in the 1980s. In those days, the 1950s, southern Republicans, rare as they were, were usually better on civil rights issues than were southern Democrats. Among northern elected officials, the reverse was true.

Later, describing his opposition, Gore called the Southern Manifesto "the most unvarnished piece of demagoguery I had ever encountered" and "a dangerous deceptive propaganda move which encouraged south-erners to defy the government and disobey the law."

Born in rural central Tennessee in December 1907, Albert Gore—by his own account—had a happy childhood. "It was because we lived apart from the world, relatively isolated and therefore dependent entirely on one another. Although the chores were heavy and discipline absolute, there was love in our family and reverence for each other."

As a boy and as a young man, Gore loved school, where he excelled. Although his father wanted him to stay on the farm, young Albert knew he wanted to be a teacher or a lawyer, and the only way to do that was to leave Possum Hollow. After finishing Gordonsville High School ahead of schedule, he enrolled at Middle Tennessee State Teachers' College in Murfreesboro, where he earned a teaching certificate but not a university degree.

His struggles during the Depression—he was twenty-one when the stock market crashed in 1929—exposed him to the hardships that so many of his neighbors faced. Holding odd jobs, playing the fiddle in lo-cal bands, teaching school for $75 a month, even working as a principal enabled him to enroll for a few quarters at the University of Tennessee at Knoxville, and then to return to Murfreesboro and earn his degree from Middle Tennessee State.

He lost an election for Smith County school superintendent by only a few votes, but when the incumbent was stricken with cancer, he won the race for county superintendent in the next election.

Gore eventually went to night law school at Vanderbilt in Nashville, where he met Pauline LaFon, a law student and waitress at the Andrew Jackson Hotel who would become not only his wife but also an invaluable political partner. Pauline became only the tenth woman ever to graduate from Vanderbilt Law School. She and Albert passed the bar at the same time, and she went off to Texarkana, Arkansas, to set up a legal practice.

After helping Gordon Browning in his successful 1936 run for governor of Tennessee, Gore was named, at the age of twenty-nine, Tennessee's labor commissioner. It was an exciting time to be commissioner of labor, where he would be charged with setting up the state's new unemployment insurance program, making sure that Tennessee employers were complying with mine safety laws, and helping with the passage of President Roosevelt's Fair Labor Standards legislation with its minimum wage and forty-hour workweek.

The Tennessee Labor Commission's Office of Mine Inspection, which Labor Commissioner Gore supervised, was underfunded, replete with political hacks, and, for all intents and purposes, a captive of the industry it was supposed to regulate. Gore fired the political hacks, brought in engineers and former miners, and went into the mines himself to learn as much as he could about mining and mine safety.

Tennessee's unemployment insurance program, mandated by the recent passage of the Social Security Act and Unemployment Act, became a national model as dozens of states were moving quickly to follow the federal mandate. Washington allowed each state to tailor the federal insurance program to its individual and unique situation. Gore made frequent trips to the nation's capital, where he talked with administration officials and labor experts, and often clashed with the anti–New Deal, reactionary Senator Kenneth McKellar, a four-term Democrat from Memphis. Gore noticed that, by then, a number of southern Democratic senators had cooled on FDR and the New Deal, especially on the new laws on labor rights.

And Gore saw up close, in Washington and in Tennessee, the organized opposition to FDR's Fair Labor Standards legislation. National business interests warned of impending disaster if a minimum wage were enacted and if a forty-hour workweek were established. The National Association of Manufacturers, which is still one of Washington's most powerful special-interest groups, proclaimed that mandated overtime pay and minimum wage would take us "in the direction of Communism, Bolshevism, fascism, and Nazism." Opposition in the South—from the wealthy and those who represented the wealthy—was intensive, from the Southern States Industrial Council to reactionary congressmen. Texas Democrat Martin Dies, Jr.—who would become the Red-baiting chairman of the House Un-American Activities Committee—thought a minimum wage to be the end of America as we know it: "There is a racial question here. Under this measure what is prescribed for one race must be prescribed for the other. And you cannot prescribe the same wages for the black man as the white."

Gore's early years and then his tenure as labor commissioner shaped his thinking about what he called "the South's chronic poverty." Gore was especially distressed by the Southern States Industrial Council and its influence with southern senators, congressmen, governors, and state legislators. In 1934, in Birmingham at an SSIC conference, the *Chattanooga Times* reported: "Applause greeted Theodore Swann, a Birmingham chemical manufacturer, when he said, 'Sherman's march to the sea was no more destructive than the National Recovery Act is going to be to the South. Before it is over, we may have secession." The power of this collection of ultraconservative southern businessmen was especially apparent when, in 1937, only eighteen of ninety-nine southern legislators in Washington, representing the poorest section of America, voted for fellow southerner Hugo Black's minimum wage bill.

The betrayal of African Americans and working class and poor southerners began, Gore wrote in his autobiography, with the Compromise of 1877 (some called it the Redemption of 1877). The deadlocked presidential race of 1876 between Samuel Tilden and Rutherford B. Hayes was resolved when the Ohio Republican was installed in the White House and the South was "given back" to the conservative bankers and the planter class. "They came to be known as 'the Bourbons,'" Gore wrote, "after the royal house of Spain whose reactionary members 'learned nothing and forgot nothing.'"

On the wall of majority whip Jim Clyburn's Capitol Hill office, I noticed a row of eight framed black-and-white photographs, all of African American congressmen from South Carolina elected during Reconstruction. "I am the ninth," Clyburn told me in March 2019. Elected in 1992, Clyburn was the first African American congressman from South Carolina in a century. In December, we freshmen Democrats elected him our class co-president.

After the Civil War, South Carolina and Mississippi were the only states with a majority of black citizens. In 1868, South Carolina became the first state to elect a majority–African American legislature. Fewer than a dozen years later, the legislature was entirely white.*

With the withdrawal of federal troops, the Bourbons ousted the uneasy coalition of "mountain whites" and newly enfranchised black voters. The conservative Bourbons, representing the South's wealthiest citizens and most powerful business interests, took over the Democratic Party, a party that existed, in the words of Frederick Douglass, "to serve the great privileged class at the South," and, raising the specter of race mixing, "intensified the hatred and fear of 'the cause of it all'—the Negro." It was a strategy that worked for southern Democrats for decades, and then for the national Republican Party from 1980 into the twenty-first century: the most privileged people in society with their corporate allies instilling fear among the less privileged—almost always over labor unions and race, and often about eastern elites and, later, about cultural threats from Hollywood. For decades, it has been a winning formula on Election Day.

The Bourbons' "basic goal," Gore believed, "was to lure Northern capital and industry southward by promising what was to become a standard package: tax benefits; a large, docile, and non-union pool of cheap labor; minimal restrictions and regulations; and sympathetic local governments and police."

---

*In 1881, in the early days of the James Garfield presidency, Mississippi Senator Blanche Bruce, the lone African American in the United States Senate, left office. It was not until 1967, during the presidency of Lyndon Johnson, that another African American came to the Senate, Massachusetts Republican Edward Brooke.

And they succeeded for decades and decades. Some would argue that they are still succeeding—a conservative South out of step with the rest of the United States; controlled by the monied class, anti-union, yet still the poorest region of the nation. "The exploitation of labor, whether slave or free, has been one of the constants in orthodox 'Southern-conservative' psychology and philosophy throughout history," Gore wrote. The southern economy and social order were built entirely on cheap labor, and some will say it still is. As W. J. Cash put it in his landmark book of 1941, *The Mind of the South*, the South "rested finally upon one fact alone: cheap labor." Ads targeted to northern millowners made their point clearly: "cheap and contented, 99 percent pure Anglo-Saxon labor."

During Gore's time as labor commissioner, Pauline returned from Arkansas and, in May 1937, they were married. Their partnership lasted sixty-one years, until his death in 1998. She once said that there were two kinds of men. "One, the wife is in the background. Albert wanted me right up front."

Already as labor commissioner, the ambitious Gore had his sights set on a seat in Congress. But the Fourth Congressional District's sixty-year-old incumbent Democrat, J. Ridley Mitchell, was effective and respected, and generally well liked.

Then one day in 1938, Gore heard from a newspaper friend that Congressman Mitchell was going to give up his House seat to run for the Senate. Without even telling Pauline, Gore made a statement to the reporter, announcing his candidacy.

He resigned his position as labor commissioner, took out a mortgage on the farm in Carthage, and started his campaign against five Democratic primary opponents with $3000 and a few volunteers. He had something none of his competitors had: the support of Governor Browning.

Gore could not resist playing his fiddle at his campaign events, although Pauline and his closest supporters advised against it; they warned him that his opponents would compare his fiddling in the midst of so much economic hardship in rural Tennessee to Nero fiddling while Rome burned. Sure enough, *The Nashville Tennessean* ran a story in which his opponents made that accusation. But the response from the crowds— in this district of some three hundred thousand people sprawled across eighteen counties—encouraged the candidate. He would talk about the Tennessee Valley Authority, then play "Turkey in the Straw," then discuss his support for the New Deal, and play "Shake the Foot."

And his message of support for farmers, for workers, for the little guy always came through. His time at the Tennessee Department of Labor deepened his progressive views, as he fought for New Deal values and FDR's policies. It surely helped him better understand the needs of workers—union and non-union alike; few of Tennessee's workers were members of labor unions. And many miners and laid-off workers, struggling low-wage laborers and union members, saw Albert Gore as a candidate who was on their side.

Gore took an instructive lesson from primary election night in September 1938. When it became clear that he had won, "a benign old gentleman laid his hand on my arm," Gore said. Speaking to the *Collier's* writer George Morris in 1942, he recalled the elderly gentleman's words. "I have just come from the headquarters of [your opponent]. He is the picture of dejection. His wife is crying. He probably will never be a candidate again. It is the end of his ambition." Although his excited supporters were expecting a triumphant speech, perhaps even some gloating, they saw something very different. "I lost my sense of elation. I could think only of the defeated candidates and their wives, and how my wife and I would have felt had I been among them. I often wonder what sort of fool I should have made of myself except for the admonition of that gracious old gentleman."

Gore's primary election win, in the heavily Democratic Fourth District, allowed him an easy win in November 1938. He was elected in a very Republican year, after an unprecedented series of decisive Democratic victories in 1930, 1932, 1934, and 1936. Gore came to Washington a true believer—in the New Deal, and in progressive ideals.

Gore's political philosophy was informed by southern progressive populist tradition. The populist movement, mostly southern and rural-based, grew as farmers and then laborers in the 1880s and 1890s increasingly came to believe that both major political parties had abandoned them. As a student of the South and its political traditions, Gore knew the words of the nineteenth-century Populist Party leader Tom Watson as he spoke to his white and black followers: "The accident of color can make no difference in the interest of farmers, croppers, and laborers . . . You are kept apart that you may be separately fleeced of your earnings."*

But Gore also knew something else. "If Watson's coalition sounded like good economic sense, Bourbon appeals to racial solidarity made more psychological sense." And as he went off to start his congressional career at the age of thirty-one, he took with him that sense of economic justice, and a realism about southern politics.

Gore had a rather quiet first term in the House, as most congressmen who go on to accomplished, productive careers do. Reelected easily in 1940 as he campaigned too for Roosevelt's third election, Gore saw—as did most of Washington—an ominous time ahead as Nazi Germany and the Soviet Union expanded their empires.

But as a young congressman, Gore's interest was almost entirely Tennessee, starting with the Tennessee Valley Authority. He spoke persuasively as one of TVA's strongest and most vocal supporters, defending the region's most important economic development project, which brought electricity and prosperity to several states. Opponents called TVA socialist, as the right wing often labels successful government programs, and contended it undermined entrepreneurial spirit and individual initiative. Gore pointed out the thousands of jobs that TVA was creating for Tennessee workers and the affordable electricity it was providing for hundreds of thousands of farms, businesses, and residences. TVA, Gore pointed out, was also essential to power private defense industry production, such as steelmaking and aluminum processing.

Gore, FDR, and other progressives were right about TVA's future success. For seven decades, the Tennessee Valley Authority—at its creation the nation's most expensive government-funded project—has served and

---

*Tragically, after serving a term in the United States House of Representatives as a member of the Populist Party, and as the vice presidential candidate of the Populist Party in 1896 and the presidential candidate for the People's Party in 1904, Watson later turned on the populist movement, betraying the poor man's coalition—dividing poor black and poor white farmers, and throwing in with the Bourbons. As Michelle Alexander pointed out in *The New Jim Crow*, he persuaded poor farmers and working-class whites to choose their racial makeup over the economic interests they shared with African Americans. Watson's betrayal "earned" him a seat in the United States Senate, representing the state of Georgia during some of the worst times in Georgia's racial history; he died in 1922, at the age of sixty-six, after serving only eighteen months in the Senate.

enriched the nation's most conservative and anti-government region. Gargantuan public works like NASA in Huntsville, Alabama, and the federal energy laboratory at Oak Ridge, Tennessee, were powered by *public* electricity generation. The increased prosperity of much of the southeast is due to Washington and American taxpayer investment, even as the region has grown more and more anti-government, more and more conservative, more and more Republican. And to be sure, the poverty still far too common in rural South Carolina, Georgia, Alabama, and Mississippi has meant significantly more social spending coming to those states—federal taxpayer dollars, of course—than to any other region of the United States.

In September 1941, in his second term in the House, Gore began his version of FDR's fireside chats. Every Sunday he went to WSM, the Nashville radio station, home of the Grand Ole Opry, to speak to Tennesseans about events in Washington, D.C. For much of the ten years that Gore did his Sunday morning show, he was preceded by the Carter family's musical show. Some years later, according to the Gore biographer Kyle Longley, June Carter Cash said that her family members would wince when the congressman arrived early and joined in the singing.

After the attack on Pearl Harbor in December of that year, Gore was of course an early supporter of the war effort. He spoke out against war profiteering, testifying in front of the Naval Affairs Committee. War profiteering, Gore emphasized, was bad for soldier morale, damaging to the economy, and potentially disastrous to the war effort. He advocated for strict limits on profits on war contracts, and ceilings on executive salaries. He pushed, with limited success, for price controls for all industry during the war.

For a junior congressman, Gore shouldered some major responsibilities. Within a few months of U.S. entry into World War II, secret work began at Oak Ridge, Tennessee, a federal laboratory on the edge of Gore's Fourth District. The German-born Albert Einstein had warned President Roosevelt that Nazi scientists were attempting to develop an atomic bomb for the German government.

One day, as recounted by the biographer Longley, Speaker Sam Rayburn summoned Gore to his Capitol office. He asked the young Tennessee congressman and four other lawmakers to shepherd secret appropriations through Congress to fund atomic weapons research in Tennessee, Illinois, and New Mexico. Gore worked on this secret project until the end of the war.

In early 1943, he joined first-term Congressman J. William Fulbright in his call for an international peace organization. The Arkansas Democrat's nonbinding resolution would put Congress on record to create "appropriate machinery with power adequate to prevent future aggression and to maintain lasting peace." By fall, a war-weary nation and its representatives came to the same conclusion that Gore did: "United States participation in an international organization to keep peace might be one of the great victories of the war."

There was opposition, to be sure; the FDR antagonist Hamilton Fish III, whose district included the president's home of Hyde Park, huffed, "Let's win the war and then fight it out with our allies." But the Fulbright resolution, which was the first major step in the creation of the United Nations, passed the House of Representatives 360–29, and a similar resolution passed the Senate 85–5.

In the fall of 1943, the thirty-five-year-old Gore began to feel the tug of military service. He decided to enlist in the United States Army but keep his seat. He got his orders to report to Camp Shelby, in Mississippi; but after Attorney General Francis Biddle ruled that a federal legislator must resign his seat to join the military, President Roosevelt ordered Gore to stay in Congress.*

A year later, in December 1944, after he was reelected to his fourth term in the House of Representatives, Gore resigned from the 78th Congress, which expired later that month. He told Speaker Rayburn that he was moving from enlisted reserve to active duty, and that he would return at some time in the future to take up his responsibilities in the

---

*Ohio's Thirteenth District Republican Congressman Albert David Baumhart, Jr., who held the seat I occupied five decades later, was the first congressman to listen to FDR's December 8 "live in infamy" speech and leave Congress to join the military. The thirty-four-year-old legislator enlisted in the navy in 1942 and served until 1946. Baumhart returned to the House of Representatives in 1955 and retired after three full terms. In 1999, shortly before his death, at his apartment in Lorain, he told me that he was glad that he left for the service in World War II, but wished he had stayed in Congress instead of retiring in 1960.

79th Congress, as the duly elected congressman from Tennessee's Fourth Congressional District.

This time he was off to Europe to serve his country. After completing his training at Fort Meade, he was assigned the task of helping in the prosecution of suspected war criminals.

But he also was impressed with some things German. His observation of the Autobahn, the German highway system—its efficiency, its complexity, its effectiveness and usefulness in moving people and war matériel—stuck with him, and helped him later in the Senate to work with his colleagues in support of Eisenhower's construction of the interstate system.

Gore returned to Washington—and to Congress—in March. He had been on active duty for only three months. It was a useful sojourn for the country; his insight into transportation and defense, and his understanding of the importance of reconstruction in Europe and the lessons of the aftermath of both world wars, served him and the Congress well. And of course, Gore benefited too from his service; his colleagues looked to him for his insight gathered from his time in Europe, and his constituents in Tennessee were appreciative of his service in the army; they knew he left the comforts and safety of Washington and exposed himself to a sometimes dangerous environment in Europe.

But some had a more cynical view. Bryce Harlow, a military liaison during World War II and later a top advisor to President Richard M. Nixon, referred, during a 1979 interview, to the military service of Gore and Lyndon Johnson and some other elected officials as a "political charade." His job, the GOP lobbyist recalled thirty-five years later, was "to get them in for a special basic training, and in for a special little advanced training, and then for a special shipment to a combat area, and a special escort through a combat area, special return to the United States, and special discharge."

At the conclusion of World War II, Gore—like his countrymen and -women and like most of his colleagues—turned his eyes toward home and, in his case, back toward politics. Always critical of the hidebound reactionary forces of his day, Gore spoke of a "conservatism which clings to, if not longs for, the conditions of the past, which intrinsically opposed change, which is inherently timid and distrustful of the future, which is so basically overcautious that it finds it all too difficult to be constructive or visionary."

Speaking to Ohio Democratic Women in Akron in February 1946, he contrasted a conservatism that was "putting the brakes on progress" with the progressivism of Roosevelt and Truman. "Laws and institutions must go hand-in-hand with the progress of the human mind." He warned that Republicans were "settling ever deeper into the mold of conservatism."

Instead Gore wanted to look forward; his populism led him to be pro-worker, but he was ambivalent about labor unions, at least in the first decades of his federal legislative service. Of course, as with most representatives, his thinking on civil rights and labor was informed by the state and the district he represented. Tennessee was the whitest state in the Old Confederacy and, like all southern states, was home to few trade unionists. The mostly Scots-Irish population of the South, unlike the central and southern European descendants who populated much of the North, was culturally less disposed to joining a union. And the more agrarian South was harder to organize than the more industrial Midwest and New England.

By 1947, with the Democrats in the minority in Congress for the first time in sixteen years, Gore was more centrist and cautious. He believed strongly in a progressive economic policy, but as a Tennessean, was less sure-footed about race and about labor unions. "I based my appeal for black support upon a liberal economic record—full employment at decent wages, Social Security, TVA, health, housing—and let the sleeping dogs be as best I could."

Gore thought, as did most southern moderates and progressives, that African Americans suffered systemic, inhumane discrimination. But he believed that a slow, incremental approach was the only workable solution. Anything faster could encounter massive southern resistance and likely result in violence, he told himself. Political ambition surely must have influenced his thinking too. Gore joined his conservative southern brethren in opposing the Fair Employment Practices Commission and, in 1947, voted with America's largest corporations in overriding President

Truman's veto of the Taft-Hartley Act, the most anti-union legislation enacted in mid-twentieth-century America.

By 1948, Gore was thinking seriously of a Senate run. But Estes Kefauver—elected to the House a few months after Gore in 1939, and four years older than Gore—decided first to challenge the Democratic incumbent Tom Stewart in the 1948 primary. About that time, in March 1948, Gore's son, Albert Jr.—their second child; Nancy, his older sister, was then ten—was born.

Gore campaigned actively for Kefauver after he won the Democratic primary, and more aggressively for President Truman. He comfortably mimicked Truman's populist, combative rhetoric, returning to the historic roots of a Democratic Party that fought for the little guy. Running against the "do-nothing Republican Congress" that bestowed tax cuts on the rich, Truman spoke out against "gluttons of privilege" who wanted a "return of the Wall Street economic dictatorship." The president said that Republicans, when given the opportunity to govern, always lined up in support of the most privileged people in the country, at the expense of the middle class.

Some were not so enamored of the president's aggressive partisanship and use of colorful language. The first lady was always concerned about her husband's shoot-from-the-hip tendencies. One day, after the president had referred to a Republican speech as "a bunch of horse manure," Mrs. Truman was asked to soften her husband's language. She responded, "You don't know how many years it took me to tone it down to that."

Truman viewed his come-from-behind victory in 1948, by more than two million votes out of almost fifty million cast, as a ratification of the New Deal and a rejection of reactionary, trickle-down, Wall Street politics. To Gore, 1948 was a great year for the nation, for the South, and for progressive politics. The election was an endorsement of Social Security, TVA, housing programs, and the New Deal. In his autobiography, *Let the Glory Out*, Gore wrote that Strom Thurmond and the Dixiecrats were "nothing more or less than the old Bourbon leaders of the South who believed that by 'hollering nigger' and waving the flag they could once more control the Southern states." Gore had no use for Thurmond—that sentiment only grew when he got to know him more intimately in the Senate—and understood even then that the Dixiecrats would hasten a "regularized two-party system" in the South; Gore also understood what Lyndon Johnson would proclaim almost two decades later: southern whites would leave the Democratic Party in droves when the Democrats did the right thing and became recognized as the party of civil rights.

As Gore began to plan his 1952 challenge to six-term Democratic Senator Kenneth McKellar, he spoke out on international issues, including on policy questions on which House members had no vote. Strongly supportive of the North Atlantic Treaty Organization, he watched as the Senate ratified it by a vote of 82–13 in 1949.

He traveled with Vice President Alben Barkley to the Middle East in 1951, and saw an always troubled, fast-changing region of the world. Israel had just become a sovereign state, Egypt and Syria and Jordan had tried to stop this from happening, and some eight hundred thousand Palestinian refugees fled their homes. For the rest of his career, he was an internationalist who believed that the United States had a crucial role in the world, and was a strong supporter of Israel. He also had an acute interest in humanitarian issues, with special concern for refugees in all areas of the globe.

And unlike most southern House members who hid in the shadows, Gore publicly chastised Senator Joseph McCarthy, the Red-baiting Republican from Wisconsin, as he destroyed careers and ruined lives. In his Sunday morning radio broadcast on WSM, Gore intoned, "Senator McCarthy continues on his reckless and irresponsible way . . . The time for proving his many charges is overdue. He hasn't proven one yet."

PRIOR TO HIS 1952 announcement for the Senate, Gore lent his enthusiastic support to Kefauver's presidential campaign. While Gore in fact respected his progressive Tennessee colleague, he also knew that aligning himself with Kefauver would help his own Senate candidacy.

Gore announced his candidacy in February 1952; campaigns started much later and were shorter and much less expensive in those days. He promised a clean campaign and pledged not to attack his opponent.

Although he mostly lived up to that commitment, he said at his announcement of his candidacy against the eighty-three-year-old six-term incumbent: "Tennesseans have the right to elect a United States Senator for a six-year term. I am the candidate for that post."

John Gunther, in *Inside USA*, said that McKellar "is one of the angriest men alive," and that "his career personifies the evils and inconveniences of committee seniority." Of course, the forty-four-year-old challenger out-campaigned his older opponent all over Tennessee. Former Tennessee Democratic Congressman Bart Gordon told me that the incumbent senator put up yard signs that advised "Think like a smart feller, and vote for McKellar." His young challenger placed his placards nearby that read: "Think some more and vote for Gore."

McKellar was chairman of the Appropriations Committee and president pro tempore of the Senate (the title given the longest-serving member of the majority party, third in line to be president after the vice president and Speaker of the House); he ran a campaign touting his seniority and his ability to bring money to Tennessee. Anti-labor and anti–civil rights, he had turned on Roosevelt and the New Deal early in FDR's presidency. But the voters wanted something else. Gore defeated McKellar in the Democratic primary by almost twenty percentage points; *Time* magazine's caption "44 to 83" told the story. Gore went on to win a decisive general election victory with more than two-thirds of the vote. He would be joined in the United States Senate by freshmen colleagues Henry Jackson, Mike Mansfield, and John Fitzgerald Kennedy.

Soon after his arrival in the Senate in 1953, Gore compared the rambunctious House of Representatives with the staid upper chamber. In a letter to a friend, he wrote, "The crust is a little thicker over on the senate side and the breeze is a little colder."

His southern colleagues in the Senate wasted little time in testing him. Just fourteen months into his term, Strom Thurmond tried to humiliate Gore for his refusal to sign the Southern Manifesto. Gore dismissed it as "a bit of low doggerel" and "utterly incomprehensible and unsupportable."

In those days, Gore would be seen as a moderate on race issues—

surely not the crusaders that Lehman and Illinois's Paul Douglas and Minnesota's Hubert H. Humphrey were, but never a demagogue or race-baiter like Eastland and Robertson and Russell were. In 1957, two of Gore's ten candidates for the Air Force Academy were African American.

Gore was outspoken in his support for voting rights for African Americans, and he voted—albeit reluctantly—for the 1957 Civil Rights Act, although he thought it gave too much authority to the federal government to force southern compliance. "The customs and the mores of the people are not easily set aside," he thought. And forcing southerners to desegregate schools would create too much upheaval and even violence, he claimed.

But the next year, Gore crisscrossed Tennessee campaigning with and for segregationist Democrat Buford Ellington, who was opposed by a more moderate independent candidate, former Democratic Governor James Nance McCord. During that campaign, Ellington spoke of himself as "an old-fashioned segregationist." Always a loyal Democrat, Gore let his party and his ambitions—he was considering a run for president of the United States in 1960 and wanted the support of the governor—trump his beliefs.

But again—this time in October 1962—Gore showed some political courage in the face of racism and demagoguery by his fellow southern politicians. Mississippi Governor Ross Barnett had tried to block the entrance to the University of Mississippi of James Meredith, an African American veteran of the United States Air Force. Georgia Senator Richard Russell, after whom one of the three United States Senate office buildings is named, lauded the "great and courageous governor of Mississippi" and lamented: "It is regretful that we have no one on the Supreme Court that recognizes the fundamentals of democracy."

Although many in the South vilified President Kennedy and especially his brother, Attorney General Robert F. Kennedy, Gore stood with them, telling Tennesseans that citizens must respect and obey the laws of the land. Gore later said that the "incident at Oxford represented a turning point, signaling the end of an era in which the threat of mob violence and state interposition could actually prevent the enforcement of federal court orders."

In 1964, against the wishes of his children, twenty-six-year-old Nancy and sixteen-year-old Al, and contradicting his "moderate" reputation on civil rights, Gore voted against the Civil Rights Act, suggesting a more gradual approach instead. His vote spurred angry black leaders in Memphis to promote an "Ignore Gore in '64" campaign during the senator's reelection race. The next year he supported the Voting Rights Act and later acknowledged that his opposition to the Civil Rights Act was "the biggest mistake" of his life. Gore knew, as did President Johnson, that passage of civil rights and voting rights would mean the beginning of the end of Democratic Party domination in the South. The veteran columnist Mark Shields, who was on the staff of Wisconsin Democrat William Proxmire in the mid-1960s, told me, "The Civil Rights Act changed customs; the Voting Rights Act changed power."

Luci Baines Johnson remembers the scene vividly. Standing in her Austin condominium in front of framed letters from Hubert Humphrey, Richard Nixon, Harry Truman, and Jimmy Carter, she told me about the 1964 meeting in the president's living quarters between Georgia Senator Richard Russell and her father.

"'Uncle Dick,' as I called him—he was so good to my father [for] as long as I can remember—warned Daddy that the South will be lost forever and that he would lose the election if he moved forward on the civil rights and voting rights bills. Daddy looked at him and said, 'Well, if that's the price I have to pay, I'll gladly pay it.'"

On many other issues, Gore was perhaps the South's leading progressive, with the possible exception of his state's senior senator, Estes Kefauver. Larry Daugherty, an editorial writer for *The Nashville Tennessean* (young Al Gore would write for that paper many years later before beginning his political career), emphasized Gore Sr.'s courage: "Gore was one of the last of Tennessee's Roosevelt Democrats to hold office; men unafraid of the word liberal, if it meant they stood up against powerful corporations and political interest in favor of ordinary people."

Gore was unhappy with several of President Eisenhower's appointments from the start. He called Federal Reserve Chairman William McChesney Martin, Jr. "a big bankers' tool" and Treasury Secretary George Humphrey "a noted rightist" and a "modern Andrew Mellon." Gore feared that the Eisenhower economic team, enabled by a compliant Congress, would revert to the traditional Republican orthodoxy of trickle-down economics. He noted that the last time the Republicans controlled the White House and the Congress was 1930, and look what happened to the economy then. He warned his colleagues and the country about the "turn back faction" of the Republican Party, which he thought had learned nothing about American economic history.

Always in the 1950s conservatives' crosshairs was the Tennessee Valley Authority. Although it enjoyed some bipartisan support at its creation, TVA was "creeping socialism" or, to some, "galloping socialism." A government program as spectacularly successful as the Tennessee Valley Authority inevitably infuriated right-wing Republicans. Ultraconservative Senator William Jenner, a Republican from Indiana, labeled TVA "the great showpiece of the socialist economy." The *Oklahoma City Times* editorialized that "the Socialist party in the United States was the chief promoter of the TVA programs and related nationalized power programs." More than a few times did Gore have to take to the floor of the Senate to defend TVA.

In 1955, in Gore's third year in the Senate, from his perch on the unheralded Public Works Committee, he played a major role in shaping President Eisenhower's plan to build a national highway system. Gore's two months in Europe in 1945 had given him insight into how to construct an efficient, modern transportation system, one that served national defense needs, transportation in an increasingly mobile society, and economic development, especially in more rural areas. The auto industry in the United States had exploded: in 1943, when demand for weapons and military vehicles was at its height, only 139 cars were manufactured. Producing 69,532 cars in 1945, 2.1 million in 1946, and seven million in 1955, the automobile industry was changing the country. And the transportation system of course had to respond.

A limited access interstate system, Gore and its supporters believed, would be considerably safer for motorists. And they were right; there had been 37,000 highway deaths in the United States in 1955, in a nation of 165 million people. In 2006, 43,000 died on the nation's roads in a country of 300 million people, with about three times as many cars and trucks on the road. In the mid-1950s, the number of deaths per 100 million vehicle miles traveled was 6.1. Today—because of better-designed highways and motor vehicles, and government-imposed safety features like airbags and seatbelts—there are 1.1 deaths per 100 million vehicle miles traveled.

The Eisenhower administration wanted the states and local governments to provide most of the money for the new interstate system; the feds would provide less than 30 percent of the funds. Gore argued that the federal government should provide 70 percent of the cost of construction, with local and state governments contributing 30 percent. Federal funds would be generated mostly from a per gallon gasoline tax. Gore believed that the system would never develop fully without more substantial federal support, and that poor states especially would lag far behind wealthier ones; after all, they were proposing a *national*, *interstate* system.

Gore and the Congress won the argument; new construction for the interstate system would be funded with 90 percent federal funds; state and local governments would provide 10 percent of the construction dollars to attract the federal funds. Over the next several decades, almost the entire United States interstate system was built with that 90/10 formula.

Gore and other progressives believed—rightly, as it turned out—that national programs needed to be funded and directed by the federal government; when left to the states, as conservatives argued, little was accomplished. In the last half century, the federal model has worked to build a strong, vibrant middle class: the interstate highway system, Medicare, Medicaid, the Environmental Protection Agency—all successful, all federal, and all opposed in their day by conservative ideologues. It has been especially important in my part of the country—Ohio, Michigan, Pennsylvania, and New York, which borders Lake Erie, the shallowest and most vulnerable of the Great Lakes. Here and in the adjoining Great Lakes the federal government has worked in partnership with states and communities to clean up the most important body of fresh water in the world.

Of course, the interstate system Gore supported would produce mixed results. It helped to bring prosperity to our nation—more development, more automobiles, more jobs with middle-class wages. It helped to prepare our country for national emergencies—rushing assistance to hurricane and other natural disaster victims, and also protecting our national and civil defense.

The interstate system also led to more traffic congestion, more urban sprawl, more damaged neighborhoods especially in communities of color, crippled railroads, more pollution, and, we now know, a huge increase in global warming. And many communities—big cities and small remote towns—were bypassed and sent into an irreversible decline.

Gore's burning ambition, coupled with his enhanced national profile, made him a potential national candidate in 1956. He addressed Democratic gatherings around the country—he was tapped by the Democratic National Committee as one of its principal speakers—and he was becoming known as a different kind of southern politician: moderate on civil rights, acceptable to northerners.

After the presumptive presidential nominee, Adlai Stevenson, threw open the Democratic convention in Chicago to choose a vice presidential nominee, Gore saw his chance. In the end, although an early favorite, he was running a close third to Massachusetts Senator John F. Kennedy and his senior Tennessee colleague, Senator Kefauver. As his campaign stalled, he directed his substantial and crucial support to Kefauver, who was nominated by the delegates to be Stevenson's running mate.

The next year, Majority Leader Lyndon Johnson placed Gore on the Senate Finance Committee, the prestigious tax-writing panel. It gave Gore a more solid, visible platform from which to work. He tackled a number of progressive issues, arguing for a fairer tax structure, increasing funding for international family planning, and advocating for an international ban on atmospheric nuclear testing. And he always fought for TVA, jobs for Tennessee, and rural hospitals.

Like many progressives, Gore's plate was full. That there was so much to do caused Gore to succumb to the temptation of trying to do too much at once, a common affliction among activists who believe that government can be a positive force in our country. Progressive elected officials—true believers in the ability of government to do good—often find it difficult to limit themselves to a few issues. And Gore's work did sometimes suffer from his lack of focus. Fifteen years after Gore left the

Senate, Frank Valeo, a former staff member of the Senate Foreign Relations Committee, told Senate Historian Donald Ritchie that the Tennessee senator "had his own way of getting interested for a brief period of time, and posing, and displaying great erudition in regard to the problem, and then kind of dropping and leaving it."

He did concentrate, however, on economic policies that affected the everyday lives of Tennesseans. He was very critical of conservative politicians, even of his own party, who pushed for tax breaks for wealthy, corporate interests. He insisted throughout his career that government should pay for its programs with a progressive tax system, "taxation based on ability to pay." He was especially critical of breaks such as stock options, the oil depletion allowance, and foreign tax dodges.

One fall day in 1963, Gore was complaining to progressive Alaska Democrat Ernest Gruening that President Kennedy was "going conservative." Gruening responded that Kennedy was never as liberal as Gore thought—and apparently hoped—he was. According to Gruening's autobiography, Gore then observed, "When Democrats go conservative, voters go Republican."

Gore saved much of his venom for Washington lobbyists and Wall Street. Gore told a Michigan audience, according to *Time* magazine, that "if the Republican Party was ever reincarnated into a homing pigeon, no matter from where it was released into the universe, whether from a jet plane or in outer space, it would go directly home to Wall Street."

But he did not let his fellow Democrats—even a Democratic president—off the hook. According to the biographer Longley, Gore told Majority Leader Mike Mansfield during the Kennedy presidency: "the graduated income tax is a hallmark of a democratic society . . . That a Democratic Administration would seek to attack the graduated income tax by drastically lowering the top brackets and making the graduations less steep is unthinkable."

During a hearing in the Finance Committee in early 1964—only months after President Kennedy's assassination—Gore questioned Henry Ford II about the Kennedy-Johnson "tax reform," which gave a family of four with an $8,000 annual income an increase in take-home pay of about 5 percent. A Ford executive with $100,000 in income would get a 100 percent increase in take-home pay. Gore asked the Ford heir: "Do you think that's fair?"

Ford answered, "If a man worked his way up in the organization, the reductions will be greater than for a fellow with lower pay." Then he continued after further questioning, "There are always inequities in things and it's too bad, but that's the way things are."

Gore recounted the exchange in his 1972 autobiography, and then wrote: "As I studied him, the thought occurred to me that except for the ingenuity and fortune of one of his grandfathers this man might be a check-out clerk at a supermarket, or the manager of a small store after he had 'worked his way up.' Yet because of his gargantuan inheritance from one of American's richest fortunes, permissible by our faulty tax laws, there he sat as chairman of one of the world's largest industrial combines, a frequent guest of the White House, prating on as if his financial position somehow endowed him with a wisdom he must impart to Congress."

Gore opposed the tax cuts, always slanted toward the wealthiest Americans, because of the unmet spending needs of the United States— education, highways and bridges, health care, housing, water and sewer systems, and nutrition. He also thought that tax cuts were a less effective stimulus to the economy, while expanding the chasm between the most privileged and everyone else.

He cited the wrongheaded and dangerous approach of the banker Andrew Mellon, the Republican Secretary of the Treasury during the 1920s, whose economic policies helped to bring on the Great Depression: "A decrease in taxes causes an inspiration to trade and commerce which increases the prosperity of the country so that the revenues of the Government, even on a lower basis of tax, are increased." Gore showed how it never happens that way, and never will—in the 1920s, in the 1960s, or today.

MOST ECONOMISTS AGREED that the 1964 tax cuts—weighed heavily toward the wealthiest Americans—had little to do with the economic growth of the Johnson years. The huge expenditures for the Vietnam War, the longest war in American history, provided the stimulus—and the staying power—for the economic good times. And the budget deficits.

And just as in the George W. Bush years, war spending plus huge tax cuts conspired to produce gargantuan budget deficits.

And then . . . And then . . .

It happened again in 2017. Big tax cuts, they told us, would pay for themselves in huge revenues for the federal treasury. Slashing taxes for corporations will trickle down to the rest of us. Wages would go up, President Trump promised us in the White House Cabinet Room, at least $4,000 for each household we represent. And of course, companies would invest, expand, and hire millions of workers. But Trump's promised benefits evaporated: the budget deficit exploded, wages were mostly stagnant, there was little new private investment. As we predicted, corporate profits increased dramatically, and the inevitable corporate stock buybacks enriched corporate executives but did little for the economy.

History should teach us something.

Gore was favored to win his first reelection in 1958, but he knew he faced a potentially troublesome primary, in large part because of his views on civil rights. He knew he would have to answer for his refusal to sign the Southern Manifesto. He expected criticism for his 1957 vote for the Civil Rights Act. His increasing prominence on the national stage—and speechmaking around the country—had caused resentment among some Tennesseans.

Former two-term Democratic Governor Prentice Cooper—father of veteran Democratic Congressman Jim Cooper—used all those issues and more. Cooper pledged to sign the Manifesto, calling it "a sacred document," appealing to the segregationists in the Dixiecrat wing of the Tennessee Democratic Party. Gore's Democratic challenger called the incumbent anti-South and non-Tennessean, paying for billboards all over Tennessee with the slogan: "Tennessee needs a Senator FOR, not FROM Tennessee."

In the end, Prentice Cooper's appeals to race, to "Southern values," and to regional resentments came up short. Gore, who could claim success in defending TVA and helping to launch the interstate highway system, won decisively. His general election victory that year was even more clear-cut.

Coming off his own and his party's big midterm election wins in 1958, Gore thought a Democratic win in 1960 was probable. Like many—perhaps most—United States senators, Gore thought seriously about running for president. Gore was receiving more and more invitations to speak in other states. "What politician," he wrote, "is not enthralled by the sound of his own voice, especially when it is orchestrated with a crowd's applause and fired by the hope, however dim, of holding office?" He was succumbing to the presidential virus that Vermont Republican George Aiken called "an infection that can only be cured by embalming fluid."

When first mentioned as a potential candidate for president, Gore recalled, "My first reaction was an incredulous 'Who? Me?' But then I thought about all those other 'potentialities'—Jack, Lyndon, Stu, Hubert Horatio, Estes—and I must admit that I could do at least as well as any of them, or better." After all, he had "crossed verbal swords" with every single one of them "on equal terms": with Kennedy and Johnson and Symington and Humphrey and Kefauver. "So my pulse quickened."

Up close, the giants of the Senate never look that tall. Or, as baseball's greatest-ever shortstop, Honus Wagner, said more than one hundred years ago, "There ain't much to being a ballplayer—if you're a ballplayer."

Some of Gore's finest moments in the Senate came as his public opposition to the war in Vietnam intensified. An early skeptic of the war, he had suggested caution about Indochina to Presidents Eisenhower and Kennedy, and urged President Johnson to extricate the United States from Vietnam before the nation got bogged down in Southeast Asia.

On several occasions beginning in 1965, several members of the House and Senate were invited to the White House to be briefed on the Vietnam conflict. Gore had expressed his unhappiness with LBJ's announcement that he was sending more combat troops to Vietnam. At the briefings, President Johnson, Secretary of State Dean Rusk, and Secretary of Defense Robert McNamara would, according to Gore, "in turn, denounce any kind of a negotiated settlement: it would give aid and comfort to the enemy (how often I heard that!), [and] create divisiveness at home."

The setting was the historic and ornate Senate Caucus Room in the Old Senate Office Building (now the Russell Building), the site of hearings on the Teapot Dome Scandal and General MacArthur, the McCarthy hearings, and the site of Senator John F. Kennedy's presidential announcement in 1960. The date was January 28, 1966. Although the stated purpose of the hearing was to consider S2793, to authorize an additional $415 million in foreign economic aid for Southeast Asia, it was not an ordinary hearing of the Senate Foreign Relations Committee. An increasing number of senators, including Chairman J. William Fulbright, had strong misgivings about Johnson's war policies.

The day's most prominent witness was Secretary of State Dean Rusk, a Kennedy holdover then serving in the Johnson administration. When Fulbright asked Rusk whether congressional support for the supplemental appropriation would be seen by the administration as an endorsement of LBJ's war policies, Rusk refused to answer. Fulbright bristled. A run-of-the-mill hearing about a foreign aid bill was leading the news in millions of American living rooms. CBS's president, Fred Friendly, observed that the Fulbright-Rusk exchange was "the most dramatic film from Congress in years."

Three days later, Johnson resumed the bombing of North Vietnam, infuriating Fulbright and a score of other senators. The chairman went on national television, apologized for his vote for the Gulf of Tonkin Resolution, and then announced plans the next week for hearings to examine the war itself.

Johnson pressured network executives to restrict their coverage, and when CBS cut short the hearings to air *I Love Lucy* reruns, Friendly resigned. But during the month of February, all three networks aired hours and hours and hours of dramatic and contentious testimony.

Gore said at the hearings, "What we are seeking to do now is to go over the head of the president to the American people." And that they did. As the hearings drew millions of Americans to their TVs and radios, the overwhelming support for the Vietnam War began to erode; the consensus on the war was slowly breaking apart.

Fulbright, as Senate Historian Richard Baker told me, "viewed the hearings as the only suitable educational forum for informing the public about the dangers of the war's further escalation." And David Halberstam, perhaps the late twentieth century's foremost chronicler of American political, social, and economic life, wrote that the Fulbright hearings were a "constitutional confrontation of the first order."

More than forty years later, Massachusetts Senator Edward M. Kennedy—who, along with his brother Senator Robert F. Kennedy, paid close attention to the hearings and the public reaction to them—described their impact. "The hearings changed the public debate," he told me in his hideaway office on the third floor of the Capitol, less than a year before his death. And, coupled with the CBS News anchor Walter Cronkite's vivid newscasts over the next two years about the carnage in Vietnam, opposition to the war threatened the political establishment and roiled the social order.

But as millions of Americans began to look at the United States presence in Vietnam differently, and as dozens of senators and congressmen started to question U.S. involvement, Gore's Tennessee rallied around President Johnson and the war. Not one Tennessee congressman joined Gore in opposing the war. Few senators and congressmen in the South—with the notable and celebrated exception of Chairman Fulbright—were critical of the war. And strong support for the Vietnam War among Tennessee voters and citizens all across the South spelled political trouble for Gore in an election more than four years away. (Fulbright lost his nomination for a sixth term when he was beaten in the Democratic primary in 1974 by Dale Bumpers.)

Gore knew that his run for a fourth term was going to be difficult. Although 1970 was shaping up to be a Democratic year nationally, in large part due to Nixon's handling of the Vietnam War and the nation's economy, the South was moving in a very different direction, and after thirty-two years in the House and Senate, Gore had "gone Washington" a bit too much, many thought. Interestingly, or tragically, depending on one's viewpoint, Tennessee voters seemed to say the same thing a generation later about Al Gore, Jr. In his last Senate race in 1990 before becoming vice president, Gore collected more than 70 percent of the vote, but then lost Tennessee in his race for the White House in 2000, costing him the presidency. Had Vice President Gore won his home state, the United States Supreme Court's antics in Florida would not have mattered.

Albert Gore's courageous opposition to the Vietnam War in the very pro-military Tennessee, his principled if incomplete support of civil rights, and his fighting for the little guy in the face of an increasingly well-organized business community all spelled trouble for the state's senior senator. There should have been, of course, no question about the Gore family's patriotism. In the fall of 1969, after his graduation from college that spring, Albert Gore, Jr., enlisted in the United States Army. He was one of only a few of Harvard's twelve hundred graduates to join the armed forces. Young Al was sent to Vietnam the next year.

But to make matters worse for Senator Gore, an increasing number of voters, especially in the South, were making their electoral decisions based on a new set of issues: prayer in the schools, crime, court-ordered busing, gun control, and the defeat of two of Nixon's nominations to the United States Supreme Court; the second one of them, G. Harrold Carswell of Florida, especially rankled many white Tennessee voters.

Nixon himself put a target on Tennessee's senior senator—especially because of Gore's opposition to the war, to Carswell, and to the South Carolinian Clement Haynsworth, the other defeated Nixon Supreme Court nominee. Gore was the perfect candidate to test-drive Nixon's Southern Strategy: Gore had opposed Nixon on almost every major issue. Gore was ambitious and a leader in the Democratic Party. Racial tension in Tennessee was heightened since the civil rights leader Dr. Martin Luther King was killed in the state's largest city only two years earlier.

And there was no love lost between the president and the three-term senator. Gore wrote about Nixon, whom he had known for years, in 1972: "Deficient in grace or charm, unprepossessing in appearance, plebeian in intellect, and painfully humorless, his appeal was to me incomprehensible."

Gore's nondescript—and relatively unknown—Democratic primary opponent, Hudley Crockett, who was Governor Ellington's press secretary, appealed to conservative voters by playing to race and cultural issues. Gore, he insisted, was soft on crime, far too supportive of student radicals, against the war, pro–civil rights. In the end, the eighteen-year senator won the primary by less than 6 percent, signaling big trouble in November.

On paper, Tennessee was still a Democratic state. An overwhelming

majority of voters still were registered as Democrats, and the state legislature was solidly Democratic. But the Bourbon South, as Gore characterized his conservative rivals in Tennessee and the Old Confederacy, never
really went away. Earl Long, governor of Louisiana two decades after
his brother Huey Long, spoke derisively of the Bourbon appeals to race,
calling them "grass eaters." And when President Lyndon Johnson signed
the Voting Rights Act, he acknowledged that this law would lose the
South for the Democrats, driving white southerners out of the Democratic Party in droves. He of course was right.

In the fall of 1970, Albert Gore, Sr., was in the wrong place at the
wrong time. Gore's Republican opponent, Congressman William Brock,
took up where Gore's primary opponent left off, pounding the three-
term senator on the Vietnam War, school prayer, gun control, crime, and
big government—always, of course, with a racial overtone. The heir to
the Brock candy fortune, the Chattanooga Republican had considerable
help from the Nixon White House as it kicked off its Southern Strategy.
Nixon's goal was to turn the conservative South Republican. He believed
that voters in that region should vote for the party that best represented
them, and white southerners' views were surely represented better in the
Republican Party than they were in the Democratic Party. Nixon always
remembered that Wallace carried five southern states in 1968, and he
had finished third in three of them. By appealing to fear and bigotry, the
White House goal was to siphon off 1968 George Wallace voters and
blend them into a permanent coalition with southern Republicans.

Nixon's Southern Strategy was a bald appeal to southern prejudices—
Republicans and a compliant national media call them values: a hawkish
militarism, southern sectionalism, states' rights. Underneath all of these
appeals, of course, was a thinly veiled racism. The strategy polarized
voters; that was its goal and its modus operandi, similar to the strategy
employed three decades later by Karl Rove in the Bush White House. A
key Nixon strategist said, "The whole secret of politics is knowing who
hates whom." At least he was grammatically correct.

Nixon and his vice president, Spiro T. Agnew, seemed to take a special pleasure in attacking Gore. Labeling Gore "a radic-lib," Agnew came
to Memphis in September 1970 and called Gore the "Southern regional

chairman of the eastern establishment." No one executed the Southern Strategy with more venom and more invective than did Agnew, the former governor of a border state, Maryland.

Brock echoed Nixon's and Agnew's thinly veiled appeals to race and southern pride. And he skillfully, with adroit help from the Republican National Committee, wrapped several hot-button issues around Gore's votes against Nixon's picks. Gore's votes against the two southern nominees, the Republican Brock told *The New York Times*, "were cast despite the crisis facing America in law enforcement, drugs and crime and despite a record of abuse of our lower court decisions to force school busing of our children to achieve numerical and racial balance."

"I remember the ad like it was yesterday," Rick Jacobs, now an adviser to Los Angeles Mayor Eric Garcetti, told me in April 2009. Then twelve years old and growing up in Oak Ridge, Tennessee, Jacobs saw the incendiary words almost jump off the screen: "Albert Gore said yes to integration. Tennessee said no . . . Isn't it time to say NO to Albert Gore?"

The two southern nominees to the United States Supreme Court fit Nixon's Southern Strategy perfectly. If either had been confirmed, it would have given Nixon an ultraconservative justice on, in his mind, a far too liberal court. And if the Senate refused both of them, Nixon had his wedge issue: "It is not possible to get confirmation for a judge on the Supreme Court of any man who believes in the strict construction of the Constitution, as I do," the thirty-seventh president of the United States said after the Senate had turned down Carswell. "I understand the bitter feeling of millions of Americans who live in the South about the act of regional discrimination that took place in the Senate yesterday. They have my assurance that the day will come when men like Judges Carswell and Haynsworth will sit on the High Court."

The journalist David Halberstam covered that race. "This is the first time a [disreputable and scurrilous] campaign like this has been tied to the President, the Vice President, and the Attorney General of the United States."

Gore lost in 1970 for a multitude of reasons. He had lost touch with citizens of his state, a common illness that afflicts many an elected official. It is in some sense almost inevitable that the more important a senator's experience and seniority become, the more time he spends in Washington using the experience and skills he has developed, and the committee positions that seniority has provided him. And Tennessee was changing, to be sure, becoming more Republican as the South, with increasing frequency, voted its conservative ideology by lining up with the conservative party.

Mostly Gore lost because he was unwilling to sacrifice his principles for another term in the world's preeminent legislative body. His political courage—his opposition to ultraconservative southern Supreme Court nominees, his willingness to confront special interests on the Senate's tax-writing committee, and his early and sustained opposition to the Vietnam War—ultimately brought him down after thirty-two years on Capitol Hill: fourteen in the House of Representatives and eighteen in the Senate.

Gore, like many politicians, got braver later in his career. Long-serving senators develop a certain maturity about what really matters, presidential ambition tends to fade, there is often greater political security after several electoral victories, and a simple "Why am I here?" attitude begins to take over.

After his defeat, Gore wrote, "A senator can ill afford to forget he is a politician, but, above all else, he must always remember he is a senator. Unless he can meet this test he should never have been elected in the first place."

N EAR THE END OF THE FOURTEENTH DECADE after the Civil War, the Solid South was beginning to crack.

For the first time since the 1964 Lyndon Johnson landslide, Virginia voted for a Democratic president in 2008. That same year, North Carolina also voted for the Democrat Barack Obama. In 2012, Virginia elected its second Democratic senator, Tim Kaine, joining Mark Warner, both pro–civil rights moderate Democrats and former governors.

Political scientists and the media used the term "Solid South" because Democrats could, from the end of Reconstruction in 1877 until the Civil

Rights era, almost always count on the South to deliver its electoral votes and an almost unanimous congressional delegation. For example, Arkansas voted for the Democrat running for president in every single election between 1876 and 1964. And the delegations to Congress from the Old Confederacy, in those years, were almost all Democrats. Only in the year 1928, when the Democrats nominated New York Governor Al Smith, a Roman Catholic, did a handful of southern states vote Republican. The pope, a number of ultraconservative southerners believed, was plotting to seize the White House. Interestingly, there has been only one Roman Catholic nominee of a major party since John F. Kennedy in 1960.* And there have only been one Greek Orthodox and one Mormon nominee. All three lost.

Solid South meant more than delivering unanimous verdicts at election time. The Solid South, in the words of W. J. Cash in his 1941 masterpiece *The Mind of the South*, was a region of "a democratic country without an opposition party," empowering the elite to regard "the governmental machinery of the South as their private property." And southern politics was "a constant progress in demagoguery, in full gallop against the Yankee, and even more, the Negro."

It was—and still is, but maybe less so—a region like no other. Among white southerners, there was a uniformity of origin and background and thought, and of course two common enemies, the Yankee and the black man—"all co-operating to cut men to a single pattern." Writing in 1941, Cash emphasized, "Dissent and variety are completely suppressed and men became, in all their attitudes, professions, and action, virtual replicas of one another." And that meant, only half-jokingly, "quarantining Yankee thought at the Potomac."

In most of the 150 years since the Civil War, southern whites have been out of step with most of the country. From General Robert E. Lee's surrender at Appomattox on April 9, 1865, until the election of Frank-

---

*In Robert Slayton's *Empire Statesman: The Rise and Redemption of Al Smith*, we see the strong anti-Catholic sentiment in the South. The Daytona Beach, Florida, board of education sent home flyers with every student warning that, if Smith won, "you will not be allowed to have or read a Bible." One cartoon showed the pope, sitting at the head of the table, presiding over the president's cabinet in Washington. The Ku Klux Klan sent out postcards calling 1928 the "darkest hour in American history; the anti-Christ has won."

177 ||| AL GORE, SR.

lin Roosevelt in November 1932, the ultraconservative Democratic Solid South—with of course very few African Americans allowed to vote—saw the Democrats win the presidency only four times, and not once with a majority of the nation's popular vote. And now that the Solid South has become the ultraconservative Republican Solid South, the Democrats have been the popular vote winner in six of the last seven presidential elections.

My mother, born in a little town in rural Georgia in 1920, understood earlier than most that the Party of Lincoln no longer was. It was fifty years ago in South Carolina, while dozens of Republicans in Congress were backing civil rights, that private citizen Richard Nixon began to formulate a southern strategy centered on race that would shatter the Democrats' "solid South." George Packer, writing in *The New Yorker* in 2008, recounts the then-Nixon aide Pat Buchanan's recollections of traveling with the former vice president in the mid-1960s to South Carolina in the Heart of Dixie. Buchanan described the room full of "sweat, cigar smoke, and rage," relaying how Nixon whipped his audience into a frenzy with appeals to patriotism and law and order. His rhetoric and their reaction, Buchanan said, "burned the paint off the walls." As they left, Buchanan recalled, Nixon turned to him and said, "This is the future of this party, right here in the South."

The bronze medal for race-baiting would have to go to Ronald Reagan, the master of symbols, who kicked off his 1980 presidential general election campaign at the Neshoba County Fair in Philadelphia, Mississippi. It was about fifteen miles from where three young civil rights workers—Andrew Goodman, James Chaney, and Michael Schwerner—were murdered by racist thugs only sixteen years earlier. During the presidential debate in Cleveland, Reagan was either blissfully ignorant or wittingly whistling to his southern base when he said, "We've made great progress from the days when I was young and this country didn't even know it had a race problem." Reagan and his advisors knew the message that such visits and statements would send to white southerners. It worked, and Reagan carried more white southern voters than any Republican presidential candidate had before.

Soon after, the Republican operative Lee Atwater, George H. W.

Bush's campaign manager and Karl Rove's political mentor, insisted to his fellow Republicans that they should play the race card, but cautioned them that they needed a new, glossy deck. "By 1968 you can't say 'nigger'—that hurts you. Backfires. So you can say stuff like forced busing, states' rights, and all that stuff." Those appeals reached beyond working-class southerners.

But the Dixiecrat Strom Thurmond foreshadowed the future Republican decades before Nixon and Reagan and Atwater. Reflecting on the Reagan election of 1980, Thurmond said that his presidential campaign a quarter century earlier had married white supremacy with anti–New Deal big business interests, laying the foundation, with lots of corporate cash, for Goldwater's nomination and victory in the south. It was a straight white line to Nixon's "law 'n' order" campaign to suburban southern white voters, the 1980 Reagan landslide in the South, and the anti-labor policies in the Old Confederacy. Thurmond told the Jackson, Mississippi, *Clarion-Ledger*, "President Reagan ran on practically the same platform that I ran on in 1948: less federal intervention, less federal control, and less federal spending."

What Republican politicians had done, beginning with Thurmond and culminating in Reagan's victory, was prey on fear to convince much of the white South that "federal intervention" and "federal spending" serve only immigrants and minorities, at the expense of white working-class voters. They effectively sold the myth of the "welfare queen" as a scapegoat for their own policy agenda, which sold out the middle class to wealthy corporations and Wall Street billionaires.

Never mind the fact that trickle-down economics never quite seemed to trickle down to white working-class voters either—that tax cuts and trade agreements favored Wall Street and the Republican donor class, that the real welfare fraud is large U.S. corporations' fleeing overseas to hire cheap labor and avoid environmental rules, and then collecting a tax break from their allies in the White House and Congress.

Of course, many 2016 Donald Trump voters have real concerns—stagnant incomes, lost jobs, depleted retirement accounts. But the Republican establishment has offered no solutions to these problems, just groups to blame for them. So can they really be so shocked that their dog whistles are no longer enough? As Hosea 8:7 tells us: "For they have sown the wind, and they shall reap the whirlwind."

In the Solid South of 2019, there are only three Democrats in the U.S. Senate, Doug Jones from Alabama and two from a state that now has huge northern influence, Kaine and Warner of Virginia. The South's Republican elected officials are the most conservative on social issues and most pro-corporate on economic issues in the country.

It is the South today—still—that has the highest percentage of minimum-wage workers. It is the region where almost all of the governors refused to expand Medicaid even though the federal government pays the entire or almost the entire cost of the expansion. It is a region with one of the highest divorce rates, the most abject poverty, and state legislatures that have passed the most liberal gun laws—if "liberal" in this case means access to as many guns as you want—and the most restrictive regulations in our bedrooms. In Texas, the voter ID law denies the vote if you have a University of Texas student ID (we don't want *them* to vote) and gives you the ballot if you have a concealed weapon permit (we *do* want *them* to vote).

In the spring of 2019, the most extensive antiabortion laws in the country—with no exceptions for rape or incest—came cascading out of the Old Confederacy. And with the ultimate nod to hypocrisy, the crowd that believes in local control and states' rights forgets that principle when a local government passes legislation on gay rights or gun safety or drilling for oil inside city limits or passing a municipal minimum wage.

Of course, it was the southern Democrats who played to race from post–Civil War Jim Crow days until Senator Albert Gore, Sr.'s 1970 defeat. Gore's southern populism had mostly disappeared in the South by that year. In the next couple of decades, as millions of African Americans were empowered to vote, dozens of segregationist and ultraconservative southern Democrats in Congress and in state legislatures retired, lost, or switched parties. A number of moderate southern Democrats had won elections during those years, but one by one they either retired or were defeated. By the normal drip-drip measurement of history, the South's change was torrential. As late as 1950, there were only three Republicans among the 109 members of Congress from the South, and none in the Senate. And while

Gore's loss may have been the canary in the southern coal mine, there was not much that the national Democrats could do about it. The one-party Democratic Solid South of a half-century ago had become the one-party Republican Solid South of today. And now the Republican heirs to the Dixiecrats play an outsized role in the national Republican Party.

By most accounts, of course, the unraveling began in 1964 when LBJ signed the Civil Rights Act and told the presidential aide Bill Moyers that Democrats had lost the South forever. And of course Republicans saw the opportunity. The GOP nominee, Barry Goldwater, acknowledged, "We're not going to get the Negro vote in 1964 or 1968. Let's go hunting where the ducks are."* A few months later, the Arizona senator—the most conservative and anti–civil rights presidential candidate his party had nominated in decades—won only his home state and five states in the Old Confederacy. Many years later, at the Library of Congress, at an event marking voting rights and civil rights victories, the Reverend Jesse Jackson told me, "Jefferson Davis Democrats became Barry Goldwater Republicans."

Exactly right. Into the 1990s, when I came to Congress, conservative southern Democrats liked to represent themselves as centrists on the political spectrum. After the 1994 elections, when Republicans won the majority for the first time in forty years, my Democratic colleagues like Billy Tauzin of Louisiana and Nathan Deal of Georgia switched parties and immediately became right-wing Republicans, suggesting that they and their southern brethren may have not been comfortable in the Democratic Party for a long time—since LBJ signed voting rights, civil rights, Medicare, and Medicaid. Or maybe ever since FDR signed the law providing workers collective bargaining rights.

A few moderate white Democrats in the 1980s and 1990s won races in South Carolina or Mississippi or Alabama or Georgia. But by the second decade of the twenty-first century, they were mostly extinct. Virginia and Florida by many measures are no longer southern states, with northern migrations and Asian and Latin American immigration. But in the rest

---

*Goldwater's principal advisors on civil rights were the young attorneys William Rehnquist and Robert Bork.

of the Old Confederacy—Tennessee, South Carolina, North Carolina, Georgia, Alabama, Mississippi, Louisiana, Texas, and Arkansas—the Democratic cupboard is bare. Seventeen GOP senators, one Democrat. Eighteen state legislative chambers—all of them—controlled by Republicans. A handful of Democrats represented African American or university districts in the United States House of Representatives, but except for Texas, that was it. There are only two Democratic governors in the nine states: and Governor John Bel Edwards of Louisiana was elected in large part because of a scandal and the immense unpopularity of his opponent, Republican Senator David Vitter.

The white South did not just fall into the lap of the GOP patriarchy because President Johnson signed the Civil Rights Act and the national Democrats supported voting rights. The Republicans aggressively courted the Old South, and segregationist southern Democrats sensed their opportunity. When ultraconservative Republican John Tower came to the Senate in 1961, replacing the new vice president Lyndon Johnson, the Georgia Democrat Richard Russell greeted him, "I want to welcome Texas back into the Confederacy."

Strom Thurmond's run for president in 1948 was, of course, all about race. But he and other Dixiecrats understood that economic issues could play an important role in his efforts too: his monied supporters had hated Roosevelt and now despised Truman. They were the tobacco interests in North Carolina, the textile firms in South Carolina, the oil men in Louisiana and Texas, the Black Belt planters in Mississippi, the lumber interests in Georgia, the coal operators and steel magnates in Alabama—all rabidly anti–New Deal, all virulently anti-labor.

Joseph Crespino noted, in his book *Strom Thurmond's America*, that Thurmond's campaign was "the building block of the modern conservative GOP" and its "antipathy to labor rights one of their most enduring legacies." Since the Civil War, the South had used states' rights to safeguard segregation; states' rights continued to mean resistance to any expansion of federal power, especially labor and civil rights laws. It was not by accident that Martin Luther King, Jr., promoted labor rights as he fought for civil rights, that he saw labor unions and civil rights organizations as a powerful coalition.

The calls for lower taxes and less federal spending were good at election time, but were not the recipe southern politicians needed to bake their future. Southerners were very good at electing their congressmen at a young age, then reelecting them again and again until they were senior enough to matter—and to pull in massive amounts of federal dollars. The growing South was watered and powered by federal spending: the Tennessee Valley Authority, which provided low-cost reliable electricity in the rural South; major military installations in almost every state in the Old Confederacy; a gigantic space center in Houston and another in Florida; a fast-growing NASA in Huntsville, Alabama; major tax subsidies for oil production; and, every five years or so, an always tilting-South farm bill, with big gifts to wealthy cotton, peanut, sugar, and rice farmers.

By the 1990s, when I came to Congress, conservative Republican victories—there was hardly a moderate Republican in sight—were working their way down to Senate and House races. Since 1954, Democrats had enjoyed a majority in the House—a not particularly liberal majority most years because of the presence of so many conservative southern Democrats, but a majority nonetheless. With the takeover of the House of Representatives by Newt Gingrich and his acolytes in 1994, the Republican victory in the South was almost complete. All the top leaders of the House—the Speaker from Georgia, the majority leader and the majority whip from Texas, the chairman of Ways and Means from Texas, the chairman of Appropriations from Louisiana, the chairman of Energy and Commerce from Virginia—were white, male, ultraconservative southerners. Every single one.

WEALTHY BUSINESS INTERESTS dominated southern politics more than in any region of the country. In 1895 a Massachusetts company opened a factory in Alabama to escape strikes and other labor-management problems, but only after the Alabama legislature repealed its 1887 child labor law. In 1901, the Alabama legislature, in reaction to the resurgent Populist movement, rewrote its state constitution to make it harder for poor whites to vote and nearly impossible for blacks to vote.

But it started way earlier than that. When the Texas governor and

Senator Hugo
Black testifying
before the
Senate Judiciary
Committee during
hearings on the
thirty-hour-week
bill in 1933
(BETTMANN/GETTY
IMAGES)

Justice Hugo Black
(JAMES WHITMORE/
THE LIFE IMAGES
COLLECTION/GETTY
IMAGES)

Senator Theodore
Francis Green
(U.S. SENATE
HISTORICAL OFFICE)

Senator Lyndon Johnson gives T. F. Green "the treatment" in 1957.
(*THE NEW YORK TIMES* PHOTO ARCHIVE / REDUX)

Senator Glen Taylor gives an impromptu
concert on the steps of the Capitol before the
start of the 79th Congress on January 3, 1945.
With him, from right: son Paul Jon, age three;
wife, Dora; and son Arod, age nine
(U.S. SENATE HISTORICAL OFFICE)

Glen Taylor holding his union card in
1946, after threatening to sue the federal
government for demanding that he
renounce his union membership before
drawing his senatorial salary
(U.S. SENATE HISTORICAL OFFICE)

Glen Taylor (center), holding his son Gregory, and Henry A. Wallace (left)
at the 1948 Progressive Party convention in Philadelphia (AP PHOTO)

Senator Herbert H. Lehman (left), with Mayor Robert F. Wagner, Jr.,
of New York in 1956 (THE LIBRARY OF CONGRESS)

From left: Herbert Lehman, Eleanor Roosevelt, and Adlai Stevenson during
Senator John F. Kennedy's presidential campaign, October 1960
(JAN STUDIO / INTERNATIONAL CENTER OF PHOTOGRAPHY)

Senator Al Gore, Sr., rides the underground monorail between the Capitol and the Senate Office Building with his family in 1957. From left: daughter, Nancy; wife, Pauline; and son, Albert Jr.

(AP PHOTO)

From left: Senator John F. Kennedy, Dr. Alvin Weinberg, Al Gore, Sr., and Jackie Kennedy at the Oak Ridge National Laboratory

(OAK RIDGE NATIONAL LABORATORY / UNITED STATES DEPARTMENT OF ENERGY VIA WIKIMEDIA COMMONS)

Al Gore, Sr., with Vice President Al Gore, Jr., in 1993

(AP / THE WHITE HOUSE)

Senator William Proxmire (second from right) listens to Democratic majority
leader Lyndon Johnson on August 29, 1957. Proxmire was sworn in the day before,
replacing Senator Joseph McCarthy. From left: Senators John F. Kennedy,
George Smathers, and Hubert H. Humphrey (AP PHOTO)

William Proxmire appearing in the 1973 Old Milwaukee Days parade
(ENVIRONMENTAL PROTECTION AGENCY / NATIONAL ARCHIVES AND RECORDS ADMINISTRATION)

Senator Robert F. Kennedy with Marian Wright Edelman (second from right),
near Greenville, Mississippi, in April 1967 (AP PHOTO / JACK THORNELL)

Robert F. Kennedy eulogizes
Martin Luther King, Jr., at
the Cleveland City Club on
April 5, 1968, the day after
King's assassination.
(*THE PLAIN DEALER* FILE PHOTO)

From left: Arthur M. Schlesinger, Jr., George McGovern, and an
unidentified man at a school near Madras, India, in 1962

Senator George McGovern in 1972

two-time presidential candidate Rick Perry suggested that Texas might consider secession because of Obamacare, immigration policy, and other federal actions, he was tapping into a long southern tradition. The ideas of nullification and secession have been around the South almost as long as the nation has existed. The Tories—those loyal to Britain during the Revolutionary War—were overrepresented among southern business interests, especially the major plantation owners. Before the Civil War, a South Carolina state convention, influenced by their powerful senator John Calhoun, adopted a provision to nullify tariffs enacted by the United States Congress. To Calhoun and the nullifiers, their states' rights and their personal liberties would allow them to nullify any federal law with which they didn't agree; they could secede if necessary. If the South isn't protected by nullification, Calhoun argued, "they must in the end be forced to rebel, or submit to have their permanent interests sacrificed, their domestic institutions subverted." Therefore, the South Carolinian asserted, "The right of interposition . . . be it called what it may—State-right, veto, nullification, or by any other name—I conceive to be the fundamental principle of our system." Calhoun's philosophy, stripped of its intellectual veneer, was principally a defense of slavery and the southern planters.

The South's view that it should have special privileges began even earlier than Calhoun's intellectual gymnastics. The South has always had inordinate power in our federal government, beginning, not to put too fine a point on it, at the beginning. For fifty of the first seventy-two years of the United States Constitution—from George Washington's inauguration until the South seceded in 1861—the president of the United States was a southern slaveholder.*

Ensuring that our government—from the beginning—would speak with an upper-class accent, Virginia's James Madison argued for the creation of a more conservative Senate that could protect plantation owners and other elites. At the 1787 Constitutional Convention, he observed that our government should "be so constituted as to protect the minority of the opulent against the majority . . . If elections were open to all classes of people, the property of landed proprietors would be insecure."

---

*Among them, only President Washington freed all his slaves upon his death.

In 1800 Thomas Jefferson would have lost the electoral college to President John Adams if slaveholding states had not been rewarded for their chattel; we all remember from high school that our Founding Fathers had decided that slaves, who of course enjoyed few of the benefits of personhood and none of the benefits of citizenship, counted as three-fifths of a human being for the purposes of increasing the number of congressional districts and electoral votes for the slaveholding states. In short, our constitution incentivized and rewarded slavery and left us with the Electoral College, which has become increasingly anti-democratic; the popular-vote winner has lost two of the last five presidential elections.

Jefferson's election was likely enabled by the South's constitutional advantages, and he in turn reinforced them. Over the following four decades, the three states that were carved out of President Jefferson's 1803 Louisiana Purchase all entered the union as slave states.

Now, in our time, the tradition continues. After the Affordable Care Act was enacted in 2010, Tea Party Republicans resisted it by citing John Calhoun and the nullifiers, invoking the Tenth Amendment's stipulation that states hold all rights not explicitly delegated to the federal government; in some cases, they threatened secession. Southern governor after southern governor—egged on by their legislatures and their congressional delegations and Koch Brother–funded Tea Party interests—rejected Medicaid expansion. Even though their region has the lowest income, the most poverty, and the highest uninsured population in the country, and even though the federal government would have picked up the cost for almost all of the newly insured, wealthy interest groups and southern politicians said no. And the national Republican Party, driven mostly by its southern base and by its hundreds of millions of Koch brother dollars, moved further to the right.

With the treasure chest of Republican House districts, Senate seats, and dozens of presidential electoral votes came the baggage that the Solid South has always brought to national politics—secessionists, rigid right-wing politics, a fury of fear and resentments. And the rest of the country cannot help but notice.

It first began to show in the early 1990s when New Jersey and Illinois—once Republican-leaning swing states—became solidly Democratic in presidential races, in large part because suburban white women came to understand that their Republican Party had become a mostly southern white male–dominated party. The national Republican Party—intolerant and very conservative on issues like civil rights and abortion and guns and gay rights and the environment—made them feel unwelcome.

Its right-wing politics and segregationist past burned brightly in late 2002, when Republican Senate Majority Leader Trent Lott of Mississippi, speaking at a tribute to Strom Thurmond, intoned: "I want to say this about my state: When Strom Thurmond ran for president, we voted for him. We're proud of it. And if the rest of the country had followed our lead, we wouldn't have had all these problems over all these years, either." The Council of Conservative Citizens, which Trent Lott frequently addressed, had emerged out of the White Citizens Councils that were created in response to *Brown v. Board of Education* and were considered a highbrow, more socially acceptable version of the Ku Klux Klan. They were, as President Bush might have said, for the "kinder, gentler" segregationists.

As the segregationist southern Democrats did all they could to protect their beloved southern Democratic Party from change, the new Solid South Republicans did pretty much the same. After the conservative-dominated United States Supreme Court issued its 2013 *Shelby County v. Holder* decision, freeing the South to disenfranchise black voters (my view) or giving them the green light to lift the voting rights yoke from their necks (conservative southern politicians' view), the one-party South—at least for a while—became the even-more one-party South: Redistrict. Cut back on voting hours. Shrink the number of voter registration sites. Make voter identification laws most difficult for people of color and low-income voters.

Even putting social and religious issues aside, the South remains the most profoundly conservative region of the country. Conservative business interests seem to have greater influence on elected officials, Republicans and Democrats alike, in the Old Confederacy. Southern politicians are more inclined to protect wealth, voting in large numbers to repeal the estate tax, for example. Rare is the populist or progressive white southern elected official willing to take on the pharmaceutical industry or banks or insurance companies, or, God forbid, the gun lobby. And even harder to find is a southern white politician closely aligned with organized labor, the most reliably and consistently progressive force in our society.

Formalized or not, northern conservative Republicans and southern Democrats had an arrangement in the late 1940s and 1950s. Southern Democrats opposed unionism and wanted to attract anti-union northern businesses, and northern conservative Republicans were willing to oppose civil rights legislation if southern senators would vote to weaken labor unions. That coalition was successful in weakening the labor movement in the 1940s and delaying significant civil rights legislation until the 1960s, and in encouraging industry in the North to move to the anti-union South. To his later regret, Albert Gore, Sr., was a part of that coalition. Taft-Hartley dealt a blow to the labor movement from which it has never fully recovered.

THE LANDOWNERS, the tobacco companies, the millowners, the wealthiest and most powerful interest groups—once the core of the Democratic Solid South; and now in the last decades the core of the Republican Solid South—stood in the way of all kinds of progress for workers, the environment, the poor, and children. From the early days, southerners used race to promote an economic agenda for the elite. For decades it was tobacco in Virginia and North Carolina, cotton in Mississippi and Alabama, textiles in Georgia and South Carolina, oil and gas in Texas and Louisiana. Republicans now, of course, use race and also use the religious right to promote a corporate agenda. No longer are there populist southern politicians who fight for poor blacks or poor whites, who fight for working-class whites or blacks. Appeals to race divide the poor, white against black, and betray them both. For all but seven years over the past seven decades,* the party that held the South has held the congressional majority. The burst of progressive energy in the last 175 years always took place in spite of the South. Most of the progressive changes in this

---

*1953–1954, 2007–2010, and 2019

country—from civil rights to Medicare, from strong environmental laws to Obamacare—happened in the face of southern resistance, with few southern votes in the Congress. And history tells us that during the nation's bloodiest conflict, when the South, of course, had no representation in Congress, the United States House of Representatives and United States Senate had some of their most productive years: the founding of Gallaudet University, which serves the deaf, the only school of its kind in the world; President Lincoln signing the Homestead Act, which promised 160 acres of free public land in the West to settlers who agreed to farm it for five years; the Morrill Act, providing public lands to states for the establishment of land grant colleges; and the Pacific Railroad Act, which made the construction of a transcontinental railroad possible. And of course the Thirteenth and Fifteenth Amendments to outlaw slavery, establish the equal protection of the law, and enfranchise African Americans.

It's now been more than 150 years since the Civil War, and more than two hundred years since the invention of the cotton gin. But the white southerners of the past would probably still feel at home in today's electorate. After all, in 2008, Barack Obama got 58 percent of the white vote in Democratic Maine, 51 percent in swing-state Iowa, 42 percent in Republican North Dakota, and well over 40 percent in the Appalachian regions of Ohio. But in Louisiana in 2008, America's first black presidential nominee of a major party got 14 percent of the white vote, and in Mississippi 11 percent. In Alabama only 10 percent of white voters cast ballots for the first African American president.

Despite this, there has been a steady shift in election results that tracks with the changing demographics and voting practices of the United States as a whole. African Americans provide a substantial share of the Democratic votes in the South, but they do not exceed about 30 percent of the vote in any of the states of the Old Confederacy. As southern blacks began to vote in large numbers in the late 1960s, they voted increasingly Democratic, even, of course, as the white Democratic Solid South became the white Republican South. But these dynamics may be shifting at last. New people are moving into Georgia and North Carolina: young people who support marriage equality, Latinos who bristle at anti-immigrant hate speech, college-educated white women who find good ol' boy southern-style politics repugnant, Asian Americans who re-ject a political party that has rejected the science of climate change and wants to wall off immigrants.

And then came the 2018 Georgia governor race. Stacey Abrams, the Democratic leader in the Georgia House of Representatives and one of the smartest people I know in American politics, resoundingly won the Democratic primary and was facing off against the Georgia secretary of state, a right-wing politician known for his Trump-like positions on im-migration, race, and crime. Although he was declared the winner, there was little question that his years of voter suppression efforts as Georgia's chief elections official—and his use of his official office right up until Election Day—cost Abrams the race.

We may be approaching a time in our history where there is no Solid South.

6.

William Proxmire

A WORKHORSE AND A SHOW HORSE

SERVED IN THE UNITED STATES SENATE 1957–1988

A good politician leaves nothing to chance.

—Senator William Proxmire of Wisconsin

H E HAD LIVED IN WISCONSIN for only eight years. He had lost races for governor in 1952, 1954, and 1956. And now, on August 28, 1957, less than ten months after his last defeat, William Proxmire was coming to Washington, D.C., as Wisconsin's junior senator, symbolically shutting the door on the McCarthy era.

On November 11, 1915, Edward William Proxmire was born into privilege in Lake Forest, Illinois, the middle child of a prominent physician, from whom he learned about public service and public health. As commander of the hospital at Fort Sheridan during World War I,

Dr. Theodore Proxmire responded quickly to the influenza epidemic that would claim millions of lives around the world. Every man was quickly inoculated and ordered to sleep outside in pup tents even though it was winter. Fort Sheridan, unlike most bases all over the United States and the world, suffered no casualties. Later, when Bill was a boy, his father founded and was a director of the Lake County Tuberculosis Sanitarium.

Proxmire later told the story of sitting with his father in 1955 on a platform at the annual Lake Forest Day, dedicated that year to Dr. Proxmire, watching a parade of several hundred people—ages twelve days to fifty years—whom the elder Proxmire had delivered. Among his older patients in that affluent suburb were Jack Benny and Adlai Stevenson.

It was from his father that Bill Proxmire learned his extraordinary work ethic. "He always stressed hard work, pride in achievement. He appraised people on the basis of the work they did," Proxmire told his biographer Jay Sykes in 1972. It was morally wrong, as well as inefficient, to be awake and not at work. The Proxmire work ethic and incredible self-discipline took him to the United States Senate, kept him there for thirty years, and made him the most physically fit United States senator of his time. His obsession with work certainly damaged his two marriages, he acknowledged. "Politicians shouldn't be married," he told a friend years later.

One place that the paternal influence fell short was in young Bill's politics. "I didn't raise my boy to be a Democrat," Dr. Proxmire said later. "Harvard's where it happened."

After graduation from Yale and stints at Harvard Business School and then J.P. Morgan in New York, Proxmire joined the United States Army in early 1941. For most of the war, he was part of the Counter Intelligence Corps, first in Chicago and then in Fort Meyer, Virginia. In those days, unlike our day with rare exceptions, young men born into high society more often than not served their country in the military. In 1946 he married Elsie Rockefeller, a great-granddaughter of William Rockefeller (the brother and partner of the legendary John D. Rockefeller) and attended Harvard, where he earned a master's in public administration and then taught political science.

But he was impatient; he wanted a career in journalism first, which he hoped would lead to elective office, a path many would find curious. And he chose a few states—Oregon, Indiana, and Wisconsin—that he thought provided the best opportunity for an outsider, a progressive outsider, to build a political career. He sent letters to some fifty newspapers, requesting work as either an investigative reporter or an editorial writer.

The best offer came from *The Capital Times* of Madison, Wisconsin, a newspaper with a rich and interesting history. It was founded in 1917 to defend Robert M. La Follette, Sr., Wisconsin's senior senator, against attacks that he was a traitor because of his opposition to United States entry into the First World War. Many considered "Fighting Bob" La Follette the founder of the twentieth-century progressive movement, and *The Capital Times* took up—and still does after almost a century with its crusading and talented editor John Nichols—the cause of workers, human rights, civil rights, and peace. A crusading newspaper fit Bill Proxmire just perfectly.

He accepted the job as a political and labor reporter for forty dollars a week. In 1949 he and Elsie moved to Madison. A journalism career and a political career were born.*

Almost immediately, Proxmire's activism shone through. He worked to organize the paper; the reporters already belonged to a union, but most of the rest of the paper did not. He volunteered to help the Democratic

---

*At least one other time in mid-twentieth-century America, an ambitious young writer figured out how and where to capture a seat in Congress. And he got there a good bit faster.

Born on Long Island in 1914 and educated at Swarthmore and Columbia, Ken Hechler served in the United States Army during World War II, was a Truman speechwriter for four years, a staff assistant for a Colorado senator, and a political science professor at Princeton. As the assistant director of the American Political Science Association in the mid-1950s, he identified a district in West Virginia where he thought he could win a seat in Congress. With no apparent ties to that state, he got a job teaching political science at Marshall University in Huntington in 1957.

The next year—the sixth year of the Eisenhower administration, an almost inevitably bad year for the party of the president, every political scientist knows—Hechler challenged the eighty-three-year-old Republican incumbent for Congress and defeated him. It was the same year that Robert C. Byrd, after three terms in the House of Representatives, moved over to the Senate, where he served for more than five decades. Hechler represented West Virginia's Fourth Congressional District until 1976, when he lost to John D. (Jay) Rockefeller IV in the Democratic primary for governor. He was elected West Virginia secretary of state in 1984 when I got to know him.

caucus in the Wisconsin legislature, located not far from the paper. He helped organize a Democratic club in his community just outside Madison, again curious behavior for a journalist.

In early 1950 Proxmire announced his run for the Wisconsin House of Representatives, challenging the Democratic incumbent, who had lived in eastern Dane County for six decades, forty years on the same farm. Proxmire left *The Capital Times* and was hired by the *Union Labor News* as its business manager. He also wrote and broadcast a weekly radio program—*Labor Sounds Off*—for the local American Federation of Labor.

Proxmire's primary opponent in the 1950 race for the legislature, John Blaska, knew, of course, that the young upstart had lived in Wisconsin for less than a year and had no real job. But, as is often the case when young, ambitious candidates challenge long-term incumbents, hard work and the efforts of the challenger's family went mostly unnoticed by the incumbent. Proxmire, after months and months of full-time campaigning for a job that paid almost nothing, won by 211 votes out of some 3,500 cast. He went on to an easy general election victory in this overwhelmingly Democratic district.

The same week that Proxmire announced for the legislature—in February 1950—Wisconsin's forty-one-year-old junior senator, Joseph McCarthy, told the Republican Women's Club of Ohio County, West Virginia, that he had in his hand "a list of 205 names, known to the Secretary of State as being members of the Communist Party," but still working in the top echelons of our government. "McCarthyism" was born. The young Wisconsin senator, with his advisor and confidant Roy Cohn—who was brought to his attention by FBI Director J. Edgar Hoover—perfected what the novelist John le Carré would later call "militant simplicity"—name-calling, accusations, us-or-them kind of politics. After McCarthy's demise, Cohn went on to represent mob figures, the Roman Catholic Archdiocese of New York, the New York Yankees, and a number of prominent New Yorkers, and continued his hard-edged race- and gay-baiting. Later, in the 1970s and 1980s, as a member of the John Birch Society, Cohn represented and mentored a young Donald Trump, and counseled Trump in his longtime legal strategy and the art of politics—and, obviously, taught the future president something about militant simplicity.

McCarthy had been elected in 1946 by knocking out progressive Republican Senator Robert La Follette, Jr., in the Republican primary. La Follette had succeeded his father in 1925 after his death and had been reelected three times. He was a strong progressive, just like his father. But by the end of World War II, the progressive movement in Wisconsin had pretty much left the Republican Party; many of the state's Republican progressives were becoming Democrats and voting in Democratic Party primaries.

Young Bob's voting record, except for his disagreements on foreign policy, lined up with FDR and the Democrats. So surely his run for reelection in the 1946 Republican primary was going to be close. La Follette was leading McCarthy until the votes came in from Milwaukee, a heavily Catholic and largely working-class ethnic city. With no small irony, the Communist Party members within the labor movement went all out to beat La Follette because of the progressive's criticism of Stalin and the Soviet Union. "What beat Bob," John Gunther wrote in 1947, "was in short, strange as it may seem, a kind of Catholic, big business Communist coalition." McCarthy, who defeated La Follette by only 5,396 votes, commented on his narrow win and the strange bedfellows who had elected him: "They have a right to vote, haven't they?"

At the time of La Follette's defeat in 1946, he had served almost twenty-two years. He was the third-longest-serving member of the United States Senate, longer than anyone but eighty-seven-year-old Carter Glass of Virginia and seventy-seven-year-old Kenneth McKellar of Tennessee. Today's Senate, interestingly, is much older; when I came to the Senate in January 2007, the average age was sixty-two, more than a dozen senators were over seventy-five, and twenty-one senators had been serving longer than La Follette did.

The Pulitzer Prize–winning journalist Allen Drury, then a United Press International reporter, wrote about the fondness that La Follette's colleagues felt for him, his "dogged persistence with which he has gone on fighting for twenty years for things he had only rarely succeeded in attaining. It would have broken a less determined man long ago . . . But he sticks with it regardless, and by that fact alone contributes much to his country . . . La Follette comes as nearly as any to the ideal public servant— a man who works tirelessly and consistently and honestly, through many defeats, toward the goal of a better society for his fellow men."

Politics in Wisconsin in the first four or five decades of the twentieth century was mostly fights between the conservative stalwarts and the La Follette progressives in the Republican primaries—with Democrats playing only a bit part. For one six-year period in the 1920s, the Democrats held not one seat in the Wisconsin State Senate. Milwaukee, very different from the rest of the state, tended to elect socialists as mayors and as its representative to Congress.

Wisconsin's progressive tradition, launched when Robert La Follette, Sr., was elected governor in 1900, brought to Wisconsin the most progressive state government in the nation—direct primary elections, a nonpartisan civil service, the nation's first graduated income tax, the first prohibition on child labor, the first pure food law, the first unemployment insurance program, the first inheritance tax, the first constitutionally upheld workers' compensation law. Governor Philip La Follette, brother of Robert Jr., said in the 1930s, "It is not an accident that nearly every forward-looking concrete achievement in public affairs had its origin in Wisconsin."

Wisconsin, as pointed out by Jay Sykes in *Proxmire*, produced and exported twentieth-century progressives. They include Thomas Walsh from Twin Rivers, Wisconsin, a University of Wisconsin graduate who fought for worker rights for four terms as a United States senator from Montana; Wayne Morse, born in Dane County, Wisconsin, graduate of the University of Wisconsin, and four-term Republican and then Democratic senator from Oregon who warned against United States foreign entanglements, especially the Vietnam War; and Gerald Nye, born in Hortonville, Wisconsin, who served North Dakota for twenty years in the United States Senate as a progressive Republican and was "the scourge of Wall Street bankers and munitions manufacturers."

Tragically, in 1953 La Follette, Jr., killed himself, six years after leaving the United States Senate, at the age of fifty-eight. Many, including the newspaper columnist Jack Anderson, thought that La Follette suffered from depression brought on in part by his feeling that he let his father, and his progressive legacy, down—especially in light of the career of the notorious Joe McCarthy.

McCarthy cast a shadow over all things politics in Wisconsin in the first decade of Proxmire's career, when he served in the state legislature. By all accounts, the young Wisconsin transplant was an outstanding legislator, especially for a first-termer. The work ethic and focus that the nation would see two decades later was on display to the relatively small number of observers of a mid-twentieth-century state legislature in a medium-sized state. He learned more about issues than his opponents. He asked difficult and penetrating questions. He simply outworked, as a full-time legislator, all of his colleagues. But was it enough to warrant a race for governor for the thirty-six-year-old political neophyte?

Apparently, it was. In late 1951, freshman State Representative William Proxmire, probably the most liberal member of the Wisconsin House of Representatives, decided to challenge popular incumbent Governor Walter Kohler, a Republican whose father had also been governor. Proxmire told a campaign advisor: "I'm going to run and lose in 1952, and run and lose in 1954, then I'll win in 1956." The weakened state of the Wisconsin Democratic Party made the nomination a less than attractive prize. So Proxmire it was.

In the tradition of Wisconsin progressivism, Proxmire attacked the Republican legislature for corruption, wasting taxpayers' dollars, and selling out to special interests. He told friends and others that he would run against the reviled (at least among liberals around the country) McCarthy as much as against his opponent, Kohler, generating a few contributions from outside the state, including a check and a kind note from Eleanor Roosevelt. He linked Kohler to McCarthy, who was up for re-election that year, demanding—at least once every day, week after week after week—that the governor explain why he supported McCarthy. He stepped up his rhetoric, calling Kohler "McCarthy's official apologist."

He was generally ignored by Wisconsin's Republican-oriented media. The papers, like newspapers everywhere, were typically owned by conservative, anti-union businessmen; while reporters attempted to be fair and unbiased, conservative editors and publishers were free to show their

Republican and conservative leanings. So Proxmire went to the Democratic National Convention in Chicago to attract national media attention, rightfully figuring that Wisconsin voters would see and hear him. He inserted himself, as an alternate delegate, into a fight to seat a reformist Texas delegation over the ultraconservative, mostly segregationist party regulars, attracting national media attention. It was some of his best coverage of the campaign.

At the end of the campaign, Proxmire reported that he had driven thirty-five thousand miles and shaken hands with at least a quarter million people. He was a one-man show; he wrote his own speeches, he made his own decisions, he rarely consulted others. But 1952 was a horrible year for Democrats, as Eisenhower obliterated Stevenson almost everywhere. Proxmire lost to Kohler by more than four hundred thousand votes, earning only 37 percent of the vote.

The next morning at 6:00, Proxmire was campaigning at plant gates, thanking voters for their support. And beginning his 1954 race for governor.

Soon after the 1952 election, he purchased a half interest in the Artcraft Press Company in Waterloo, Wisconsin, which printed union publications, the *Wisconsin Law Review*, and *The Progressive*, which was founded by the senior La Follette decades earlier. But he never really stopped running; his father and Elsie's family provided enough financial assistance that he could devote most of his time and almost all of his energy to an ongoing statewide political campaign.

In 1952 Proxmire easily dispatched former Democratic State Chairman and Assistant United States Attorney James E. Doyle (and father of James Doyle, who was elected to two terms as Wisconsin governor fifty years later) in the Democratic primary.

And 1954 looked to be a much better year than 1952 had been. Budget problems had engulfed state government, and Kohler's popularity was lagging. Low farm prices turned rural voters, especially dairy farmers in this dairy state, against Eisenhower and Republican officials. And in September, Democrat Ed Muskie won the governor's race in Maine, the first Democrat since 1932 to be elected as that state's chief executive. As Maine goes . . .

Proxmire ran a progressive populist campaign, railing against monied interests and their corrupting influence on Kohler and the Republican legislature. He tied Kohler even more closely to McCarthy, repeatedly inviting the outspoken senator to come home to campaign for fellow Republicans. By then McCarthy's list of Americans with "Communist connections" had reached its tentacles into the Establishment's territory: Truman and Eisenhower, *The Saturday Evening Post* and the conservative *Milwaukee Journal*, even Protestant clergy. Candidate Proxmire supported the "Joe Must Go" campaign, which gathered 350,000 signatures, just short of the number to place the McCarthy recall on the ballot. And he tried to nationalize the campaign, with his attacks on Wisconsin's increasingly angry, embittered, and paranoid junior senator: "McCarthy has brought the moral squalor of brutal demagoguery to the once great Republican Party. He is a disgrace to the once great Republican Party. He is a disgrace to Wisconsin, to the Senate, and to America."

On Election Day 1954, the Associated Press called the upset for the thirty-eight-year-old insurgent Proxmire. Well past midnight, the vote totals indicated a Proxmire win. But late-arriving votes from Roman Catholic areas of the state, especially in Milwaukee County, were not as strongly Democratic as most observers had predicted, probably because of backlash and resentment among Irish Catholics who supported McCarthy. Proxmire lost by less than 1 percent of the vote. The next morning, he was up again at 6:00, thanking voters, handing out "We lost, but . . ." cards; he had prepared another set of cards in case he won. The 1956 campaign had begun.

His marriage to Elsie Rockefeller, with whom he had had two children, ended soon after the 1954 election. Democratic Party leaders, such as they were in a state where one party still dominated almost every election, thought Proxmire had had his chance and should have won in 1954—perhaps not a fair assessment, and surely not one the independent-minded Proxmire was willing to accept. Besides, no other Democrat was coming forward for the 1956 election, in large part because of Proxmire's thrashing of Doyle in 1954.

Governor Kohler chose not to run again, deciding instead to wait two years and challenge McCarthy in the 1958 Republican primary for the United States Senate. The Republicans turned to a candidate more conservative than Kohler, the sitting attorney general. Polling showed a slim Proxmire victory in October, but developments in the Middle East, and Eisenhower's strong response to them, caused a typical election year "rallying around the president." Eisenhower won decisively, Wisconsin's senior senator, Alexander Wiley, won handily, and Proxmire lost by a narrow fifty-nine thousand votes. He had run ahead of Democratic presidential candidate Adlai Stevenson by more than three hundred thousand votes, and the Democratic nominee for the United States Senate by more than two hundred thousand votes. But he had lost—for the third straight time.

Proxmire was—again—up at 6:00, visiting plant gates, handing out thank-you cards (and again, he had also prepared cards expressing his gratitude to Wisconsin for his victory): "We lost but your confidence and support is something I shall never forget. We may lose an election; but we are sure to win and sooner than you think because we are the party of all the people. Gratefully, Bill Proxmire."

His best friend in politics told him that he should not run again for at least ten years. But he had already decided that he would challenge McCarthy in 1958.

As early as 1950, in the early days of the Red Scare, dozens of gay men were fired from federal service, many of them from the State Department. To prove that there is always a political market for hate, McCarthy and fellow conservatives, and later Roy Cohn, continued the threats and attacks on gay public servants. Hundreds of qualified gay men and women—history has termed this parallel attack on human rights the Lavender Scare—were threatened or fired or blacklisted by the federal government. Leading up to the 1952 election, Illinois Senator Everett Dirksen said a vote for Republicans would keep "the lavender lads" out of the State Department.

One of the most sordid chapters in McCarthy's career took place in the summer of 1954. By then, the path of wanton destruction and character assassination and venom brought on by McCarthy had spread to the Senate itself.

Lester Hunt, a veteran of World War I and a dentist from Lander, Wyoming, gave up his dental practice after contributing multiple bone grafts to his son, which had compromised his own health. Deciding upon a political career, he was elected to the Wyoming state legislature and served as secretary of state, and then as governor for six years. In 1948 he joined Lyndon Johnson, Hubert Humphrey, Russell Long, and Margaret Chase Smith as freshmen senators.

A progressive Democrat, Hunt reacted quickly to McCarthy's witch hunts, watching the Red-baiting senator ruin lives with his often unfounded accusations. Hunt called the Wisconsin Republican "a liar and an opportunist."

In early 1954, an increasingly angry and paranoid McCarthy struck back. Hunt's son, long recovered from his childhood injury, had been convicted the year before for soliciting an undercover male police officer in Lafayette Square in Washington. McCarthy dispatched his lieutenants—Republican Senators Styles Bridges of New Hampshire and Herman Welker of Idaho—to let Hunt know that his son's homosexuality would become a major issue in his 1954 reelection campaign.

On June 8, the sixty-one-year-old Hunt surprised his colleagues and his friends and supporters when he announced that he would not be a candidate for reelection to the job he loved. Eleven days later, on a Saturday in his office on the third floor of the Senate Office Building, Senator Lester Hunt put a bullet in his head.

By 1957, Senator Joseph McCarthy—ostracized by most of his colleagues in the Senate, despised by increasing numbers of his constituents in Wisconsin, and in declining health because of alcoholism—had become a shadow of his Red-baiting self. In Robert Caro's *Master of the Senate*, the Johnson aide George Reedy recounted that he was standing on a Washington sidewalk when a mud-encrusted car drove up. "Something black and round and squiggly forced its way out the front door and rolled up to me . . . It took me about thirty seconds to realize that this was the remnant of Joe McCarthy—unshaven, needing a bath, bloated from too much booze, almost inarticulate."

McCarthy checked himself into the Bethesda Naval Hospital on April 28, 1957. He died four days later. The hospital bulletin announced that he succumbed to "acute hepatic infection." *Time* magazine reported that he died of cirrhosis of the liver. He was only forty-eight years old. But his influence lived on—from Roy Cohn to the far right of the Republican Party, even to the other side of the globe.

Qian Xuesen, born in 1911 in the eastern Chinese city of Hangzhou, went to the Massachusetts Institute of Technology in 1935 and then to California Institute of Technology as a teacher and researcher in rocket propulsion, quickly becoming known as one of the best young rocket scientists in the United States. Near the end of World War II, Qian was given the temporary rank of lieutenant colonel in the United States Air Force; he debriefed Wernher von Braun and became director of the Guggenheim Jet Propulsion Center at Caltech. He wrote a proposal for a winged space plane that inspired the research for NASA's space shuttle.

The next year he was accused of being a Communist; twelve years earlier, in 1938, he had apparently attended a social gathering that J. Edgar Hoover's FBI suspected was a meeting of the Pasadena Communist Party. University lawyers defended him, his fellow scientists vouched for him, but the United States government deported him. He went on to become "the Father of Chinese Aerospace" and China's "Rocket King," responsible for much of the progress of China's space, satellite, and defense programs. A former secretary of the United States Navy said years later that Qian's deportation was "the stupidest thing this country ever did."

"He was Joe McCarthy's present to the Chinese," John Logsdon, former director of the Space Policy Institute at George Washington University, told *The Wall Street Journal*. With no small irony, Qian Xuesen's contemporary the German scientist Wernher von Braun had helped the Nazis develop the V-2 missile; three thousand of those missiles were launched at Antwerp and London during the closing days of World War II. Von Braun, according to Wayne Biddle in *Dark Side of the Moon*, was not "just a scientist"; he was a member of the Nazi Party and the SS in the 1930s and 1940s. And when he came to the United States to join our missile program, he showed little remorse about his efforts on behalf of the Third Reich. McCarthy had nothing to say about that.

Even in death, the McCarthy accusations and name-calling continued. Showing he knew as much about the human body as he did American politics, the New Hampshire newspaperman William Loeb railed in a front page editorial in his *Manchester Union-Leader*: "A gang led by the stinking hypocrite in the White House"—Eisenhower, the general who led the United States to victory against Nazism in Europe only a dozen years earlier—"had worn down McCarthy's adrenalin and other glands." Not to be outdone by a Yankee editor, the Fort Worth *Southern Conservative* penned that McCarthy had been "slowly tortured to death by the pimps in the Kremlin." And the radio broadcaster Fulton Lewis, Jr.—the Rush Limbaugh of his day, always playing the victim—proposed a memorial fund for McCarthy for "those who believed in the fighting Senator who dared tackle the impossible and paid for it with his life."

More unexpected was the reaction of many of McCarthy's colleagues, showing the insipid senatorial courtesy that too often permeates serious Senate business. Even though McCarthy had been censured by the Senate 67–22 "for actions tending to bring the Senate into dishonor and disrepute," and even though one of their colleagues had committed suicide in response to McCarthy's attacks, dozens of senators seemed to put those seamy chapters in American history behind them. Only about a dozen times in Senate history, and not for a quarter of a century, had a senator been censured by his colleagues. Among Democrats, only Massachusetts Senator John F. Kennedy did not vote for or announce that he supported McCarthy's censure, perhaps because of his father's and brother Robert's ties to McCarthy. Kennedy, at the time of the vote, was in the hospital.

Yet, for the first time in seventeen years, since its tribute to the Idaho populist Republican William Borah, senators chose to honor one of its own with a funeral service in the chamber of the United States Senate.* Seventy of the Senate's ninety-five members were in attendance. Vice President Nixon and Speaker Rayburn were also there. With McCarthy's casket in the well of the Senate, Majority Leader Johnson, who had said only three years earlier that McCarthy's words belonged "on the walls of a men's room," praised him effusively. Rhode Island's John Pastore told his colleagues in the Senate chamber that the "courage of McCarthy's

---

*Only three times since that day in May 1957 has there been a funeral in the United States Senate: for William "Wild Bill" Langer of North Dakota in 1959, West Virginia's Robert C. Byrd in 2010, and New Jersey's Frank Lautenberg in 2013.

convictions had left its imprint on the American political scene." Nevada Republican George W. Malone stood to offer a unanimous consent request to expunge the censure of McCarthy and to wipe from history the 1954 action taken against Wisconsin's junior senator. Only the objection by Oregon's Wayne Morse saved the United States Senate from itself.

And it was not only his brethren in the upper chamber who suffered McCarthy amnesia. President Eisenhower ordered flags flown at half-staff. And the Wisconsin legislature—after a prayer from a Lutheran minister thanking God for giving America this "defender of free speech"—passed a resolution telling its descendants that "history will record him as the man who strove to awaken the public to the dangers and immediacy of Communism."

All the while—from Kenosha to Sheboygan—William Proxmire accelerated his campaign efforts, planning a 1957 campaign instead of a 1958 one. He had married again, to Ellen Sawall, a Phi Beta Kappa graduate of the University of Wisconsin who was serving as the executive secretary of the Wisconsin Democratic Party when she met Proxmire. The day after Governor Thompson called for a special election, Proxmire announced his candidacy, in the early summer of 1957.

He decisively defeated Milwaukee Congressman Clement Zablocki in the Democratic primary—after all, Democratic primary voters were now very accustomed to seeing Proxmire's name on the ballot. In a crowded Republican primary field, former Governor Kohler edged out conservative former Congressman Glenn Davis. So—for the third time—it was Proxmire versus Kohler. And as Republicans labeled Proxmire a "three-time loser," few thought Proxmire had much of a chance.

But Proxmire was ready. Again he shook every hand. He went every place. He outworked everyone. And he took on "the loser" issue directly. On a radio broadcast, as relayed by Proxmire's biographer, Sykes, he told listeners:

> Those pink tea boys who always get everything they want, don't know what it is to get into a fight where the other side has all the advantages big money can buy . . . Let my opponent have the support of the man who has never proposed to a girl and lost.

I'll take the losers. He can have the support of the man who has never owed a note he couldn't pay. I'll take the debtors. If all those who have ever lost in business, love, sports, or politics will vote for me as one who knows what it is to lose and fight back, I will be glad to give my opponent the support of those lucky voters who have never lost anything.

The Wisconsin special election took on an added significance because of the terminal illness of West Virginia Democrat Matthew Neely. After McCarthy's death, Lyndon Johnson and the Democrats had a 49–46 majority. The expected Republican victory—only once, in the FDR landslide of 1932, had a Democrat ever been elected by the people of Wisconsin—and the imminent death of Neely and predicted Republican appointment to the Senate by the Republican governor of West Virginia would yield a 48–48 deadlocked Senate, with Republican Vice President Richard M. Nixon giving the Republicans a majority.*

Something else was happening in the 1957 special election. As Election Day approached, conservative Republicans, who had tolerated Governor Kohler and his moderate policies in the governor's office, continued to grumble about Davis's loss in the primary. According to longtime Wisconsin Congressman James Sensenbrenner, who was just beginning his involvement as a teenager in Wisconsin Republican Party politics in 1957, many conservatives believed that a Proxmire win in the special election for a truncated Senate term of only a year would open the door to a conservative candidate who would easily knock off Proxmire the following year. "Many conservatives voted for Proxmire," Sensenbrenner—who has now served in Congress for more than forty years—told me in the spring of 2009. And many conservatives stayed home, unhappy with the choice between the liberal Proxmire and the moderate Kohler.

In a low-turnout special election, Proxmire won by 123,000 votes, attracting 56.5 percent of the vote. The next morning at 6:00, he was back at Milwaukee's plant gates, thanking the voters who had elected him.

---

*Neely died on January 18, 1958. The governor appointed Republican John D. Hoblitzell, Jr., who served for most of the year before he was defeated by Democrat Jennings Randolph in November 1958.

After Proxmire's upset win in the 1957 special election for the United States Senate, he had the good fortune to run for reelection in the most fortuitous cycle for a Democrat at any time in the twentieth century: in 1958, in the sixth year of Eisenhower's presidency when Democrats picked up fifteen Senate seats; in the LBJ landslide of 1964, when Proxmire won even after being selected by Washington insiders as America's least effective senator; in the Nixon midterm elections in 1970; during the Carter victory of 1976; and in the Reagan midterm elections of 1982. With the national Democratic wind at his back, he overwhelmingly won his elections with ever increasing margins. And nobody worked harder in ensuring electoral success than William Proxmire.

The day before Proxmire's victory was Lyndon Johnson's forty-ninth birthday. On election night, the new Wisconsin senator called Johnson and gushed, "I've got the biggest birthday present of them all for you: me." The fiftieth Democrat out of ninety-six, Proxmire with his victory had guaranteed Johnson's job as majority leader.

And how Johnson welcomed him to the Democratic caucus and to the United States Senate! He and five senators greeted him on the tarmac at National Airport when Ellen and he arrived in Washington to take his seat. The majority leader arranged a luncheon for his new senator in the Old Supreme Court chamber. He gave Proxmire the committee assignment he wanted: Banking and Currency. Then he sent Proxmire to represent him at the West German Bundestag in Bonn.

But the good feelings between the two did not last much beyond Proxmire's 1958 reelection for his full term. Johnson refused Proxmire's request to be placed on the Finance Committee. The Wisconsin senator bristled at Johnson's refusal to hold Democratic Party caucuses to discuss policy.

Then on February 23, 1959, Colorado Republican Senator Gordon Allott delivered the traditional George Washington Farewell Address, an annual Senate tradition going back to the Civil War where a relatively new senator delivers the speech that President Washington wrote as he departed the presidency. Washington never actually delivered the speech; he wrote it and had it published in a Philadelphia newspaper. On the day that Senator Allott delivered the President Washington speech, Proxmire gave a scathing speech attacking the majority leader's dictatorial ways of running the Senate: "There has never been a time when power has been as sharply concentrated as it is today in the Senate." A reporter in the press gallery commented, "There were two farewell addresses in the Senate today—Washington's and Proxmire's."

But Proxmire did not let up. He attacked the filibuster, saying it was a blatant violation of majority rule. He delivered a series of speeches attacking "one-man rule" by the two Texans—Rayburn as Speaker of the House and Johnson as majority leader of the Senate—and his colleagues' obeisance to them: "When you get these two men together with the power of making committee assignments, you see the obsequious bowing, scraping senators and congressmen around them."

While Proxmire was not the only senator who chafed under Johnson's leadership, he was the most outspoken and . . . er . . . irritating to the majority leader and many of his colleagues. Proxmire was exhibiting what his two most famous Senate predecessors were known for: an I-don't-give-a-damn-what-my-colleagues-think independence.

In early 1960, a *Washington Star* columnist opined that this David and Goliath drama did not work out so well for the Wisconsin senator: "It was David who was slain." Veteran Georgia Democrat Richard Russell summarized the views of many of Proxmire's colleagues: his "position reminded him of a bull who had charged a locomotive train . . . That was the bravest bull I ever saw, but I can't say a lot for his judgment."

But above all, Proxmire prized his independence. He liked to be called a maverick. He would become a progressive on civil rights, but a fiscal conservative in attacking government spending. He was very critical of Pentagon excesses but came late—very late for a northern Democrat—to opposing the Vietnam War. He opposed the anti-ballistic missile (ABM) and the military draft, but his bellicosity caused the leftist journalist I. F. Stone to write of Proxmire's "synthetic hair-on-the-chest foreign policy."

Meanwhile, no one worked harder. He cast more than ten thousand consecutive votes—not missing a roll call in more than two decades. No one in memory has compiled such a streak except Maine Republican Susan Collins, who, in her twenty-three-year Senate career, has never missed a vote. His frequent hard-charging, hand-shaking returns to Wisconsin—after the 1958 trip, he never traveled overseas at government expense—enabled him to win reelection in 1976 and 1982 without accepting *any* campaign contributions; he spent—out of his own pocket—$177.75 in 1976, and $145.10 in 1982, much of that for postage to send back contributions that people had sent him. By contrast, in that same year, 1976, North Carolina Republican Senator Jesse Helms spent $6 million to hold on to his seat. I spent $28 million in 2018. Proxmire estimated that he shook more than 150,000 hands a year through most of his career, making him, he thought, pretty much invulnerable to defeat. By 1970, his campaign bumper sticker read simply PROX. He was the first Wisconsin Senate candidate to ever win every county in the state, which he did twice.

Allen Drury, one of the most acute students of Capitol Hill in the twentieth century, observed, "I would say that on an average more back-slapping and handshaking are done in the United States Senate than in any other comparable area or body of men in the world." But nobody did it like Proxmire *outside* of the Capitol. Iowa Democrat Tom Harkin told me, as he prepared for his first reelection campaign in the late 1980s, about the time he visited Proxmire in his office to ask for political advice. How could he run like he did, spending virtually no money, and still be reelected handily? "You don't want to do that," Proxmire told Harkin. "I went home every weekend, spent every day on the road when we were in recess, never had a vacation, never traveled abroad. It's not a life you want if you have a family."

And that life he surely had. His successor Herb Kohl told me, "I think Proxmire shook the hand of everyone in Wisconsin." Before Kohl was involved in politics, he shook Proxmire's hand outside Milwaukee County Stadium after a Braves game. And the Jewish Kohl saw him at the Hob Nob restaurant in Racine, as the Protestant Wisconsin senator walked table to table introducing himself and shaking hands—on Easter Sunday. According to one of Proxmire's former aides, he would keep a clicker in his pocket when he visited state fairs to keep an accurate count of the number of hands he shook.

Even in an institution where ego and vanity were hardly in short supply, Proxmire stood out. He was almost obsessive in his fitness routine:

he ran five miles to and from work almost every day and did three hundred push-ups daily; he did not drink alcohol, kept a daily food journal, and wrote two books about physical fitness and diet. Unhappy with his baldness—while he did not seem to care what other senators thought about him, he seemed to care what everyone else did—he was one of the first public figures to undergo a hair transplant. After the surgery, he showed up on the Senate floor with two black eyes and his head bandaged. On that day he said to the media: "It will be a year and a half or more before the transplanted hair has grown out. And even then I will still be a semi-baldy, but a little more semi and a little less baldy . . . I expect humorous, critical, amused, outraged or even ridiculing reactions. But I will acknowledge none of them. This statement is it." And it was.

Along the way, Proxmire authored what we would today call a self-help book, *You Can Do It! Senator Proxmire's Exercise, Diet and Relaxation Plan*, in which he said, "Americans are a physical wreck. We are too fat, too soft, too tense."

In 1972, sometime after the transplants, George McGovern was campaigning in Wisconsin with Proxmire and Wisconsin's junior senator, the balding Gaylord Nelson. He told the crowd: "I've known both your senators for a long time. I knew Gaylord Nelson when he had hair, and I knew Bill Proxmire when he didn't." But perhaps no senator matched the vanity of one of my Ohio predecessors, the "handsome if vacuous John Bricker," in the words of Allen Drury. An ultraconservative Republican, then-Governor Bricker was Thomas Dewey's running mate in the 1944 presidential election. Surely the intellectual inferior of his senior senator, Robert Taft, but a strikingly handsome and regal man, the Ohio senator was described this way by the Senate scholar Robert Caro: Bricker "possessed a full head of meticulously waved senatorial white hair and a consciousness of his senatorial dignity so profound that it was said that he always walked as if someone was carrying a full-length mirror in front of him." Years later, future Ohio Senator Howard Metzenbaum said of Bricker: "He was a stately man. He looked like God had come down to earth. And he thought he was."

Ellen Proxmire, in her book *One Foot in Washington: The Perilous Life of a Senator's Wife*, tells a story of her husband's hurried trip to the airport.

Proxmire spotted a police officer on duty. She pulled up next to him, and Bill rolled down his window.

> SENATOR PROXMIRE: I'm Senator Bill Proxmire of Wisconsin. I'm in a hurry to catch a plane. Could you help me get to the airport?
>
> POLICE OFFICER: Sure I can help you get to the airport. Go straight ahead, turn left, cross the Fourteenth Street Bridge, and you'll be there in no time.

Occasionally, someone teaches a bit of humility to a United States senator.

Proxmire was best remembered for his Golden Fleece Award, his monthly "award to the biggest, most ridiculous or most ironic example of government spending." The first Golden Fleece Award, given in 1975, went to the National Science Foundation for its $84,000 study on why people fall in love.

Proxmire used his Golden Fleece awards to stop government spending that he found objectionable and wasteful, and discipline federal agencies that he thought profligate. It of course, likely of no matter to Proxmire, contributed to a public cynicism about government. And it undoubtedly helped to make him even more popular in Wisconsin. But scientists all over the country thought him demagogic, anti-science, and anti-intellectual. One researcher brought suit against Proxmire in 1976. The case went all the way to the United States Supreme Court over the question of congressional immunity; what a senator says on the Senate floor or in a congressional hearing might be protected on libel grounds, but not what he says at a news conference. Proxmire and the researcher Ronald Hutchinson settled out of court.

His dozen years of "presenting" Golden Fleece awards for "outrageous spending" brought him a national reputation that had eluded him in his first twenty years in the Senate. It also caused much of official Washington—and some number of scientists and researchers—to fear him. Wisconsin Democratic Congressman Ron Kind, who served as a college intern for Proxmire in the mid-1980s, told me a quarter century later, "I can't count the number of people who hung up on me when I said to them, "I'm calling from Senator Proxmire's office and I have a few questions to ask about your program."

And it certainly did not help him with his colleagues. Twenty years later, several senators who had served with Proxmire muttered terms like "those stupid Golden Fleece Awards" and "that damn Proxmire and the Golden Fleece" when I asked them about the Wisconsin senator. Ohio Democratic Senator John Glenn, whose heroics as an astronaut helped launch his successful political career, told me at dinner one night in 2009 that Proxmire's Golden Fleece awards "ridiculed the Senate."

Proxmire continued the Golden Fleece monthly until his retirement fourteen years later. He was bold in choosing his targets, and sometimes defensive in their aftermath; in 1978 a $405,000 National Science Foundation grant went to the Ohio State University for "a bionic bug." The best place for the bug, Proxmire cracked, would be the university's football team, where it could help Coach Woody Hayes produce "ten yards and a cloud of dust." In response, the chairman of the House Science Committee accused Proxmire of "semantic simplicities," NSF increased its grant, and other federal agencies rallied around NSF. According to Doug Stewart in *Omni* magazine, the research led directly "to the design of the first computer-controlled prosthetic knee joint."

Senators who served with Proxmire told me he had no real friends in the Senate, in part because he was never a team player, and in part because he simply didn't care if he was in the club. And it showed in the Appropriations process. When Proxmire funding requests came up in conference committees, Congressman Sensenbrenner told me, even when supported by the Wisconsin delegation, ranking Appropriations Republican Congressman Silvio Conte from Massachusetts would often object. Republican House and Senate colleagues disliked him. Democratic House and Senate colleagues didn't care to defend him. Often the Proxmire requests were stripped from the bill.

Idiosyncrasies aside, there was something very admirable about Bill Proxmire. Probably no elected official in the last half century could better take an ostensibly unwinnable issue—often obscure but very important— educate the public and his colleagues, and change the outcome. Proxmire almost singlehandedly killed the Supersonic Transport plane, a multi-billion-dollar boondoggle where taxpayers would have funded a private company's environmentally damaging airplane meant to fly wealthy passengers across the Atlantic Ocean. He exposed huge cost overruns on the C-5A transport plane, forcing Lockheed Aircraft to provide a much better deal for taxpayers.

But to Proxmire, it was bigger than one or two weapons systems. For more than a dozen years, he had seen the Pentagon—and its minions in Congress—stoke Americans' fears about Soviet power. In Boston in the spring of 1971, Proxmire told the Massachusetts Teachers Association:

"Every year when the crocuses push through the winter soil and forsythia and dogwood burst into bloom, one can predict a new round of speeches, based on selected intelligence data, telling us that the Russians are ten feet tall . . . But the real trigger for the Pentagon propaganda machine is that the hearings on the military budget are kicked off at this time. As the day follows night and spring follows winter, we get the same speeches, but with different selected intelligence every year . . ."

He told the audience to look past the fearmongers and listen to the facts: "We have over ten times the nuclear power needed to destroy the Soviet Union. They now have five times the nuclear power to destroy us. We can blow each other to smithereens. It is this action-reaction complex which increases our insecurity and destabilizes the Soviet–American balance. The way to security is to break this self-destructive chain."

Later that spring, Proxmire and liberal Republican Senator Charles Mathias attempted—unsuccessfully—to cut $8.6 billion from the bloated defense budget. "I am convinced," he once said after exposing Pentagon waste and military contractor abuse, "that this country would have a far greater military potential if instead of spending $80 billion on defense and $55 billion on education, we reverse that allocation."

No one in the United States Senate aimed more directly or more accurately at wasteful defense spending than Bill Proxmire. Progressives applauded him for the scrutiny and accountability he brought to the defense appropriations process. Conservatives applauded him for the Golden Fleece awards. That was the complexity, or perhaps consistency, of Bill Proxmire.

Lyndon Johnson liked to divide his fellow politicians into two camps: show horses and work horses. Wisconsin Democrat William Proxmire had a foot in each camp. He knew how to attract attention to his causes—and to himself—perhaps better than any senator of his day (at least those not running for president). The renowned national columnist Jack Anderson labeled him, in technology terms of the day, "master of the Mimeograph, the self-publicity mill." His power and authority were derived not from his seniority nor even his chairmanships—although they surely helped. He had an uncanny ability to focus public attention and outrage on a public problem, and to bring the American public to the congressional table.

And he had a major impact on several important issues in his long, storied career. He authored the Truth in Lending Act, which ensured that financial information is clearly and understandably disclosed to consumers, and that banks would have to compete on transparent and equal terms. He wrote the Fair Credit Reporting Act, one of the best consumer protection laws of the late twentieth century.

Perhaps his biggest victory began with a speech to his colleagues in the Senate chamber. On January 11, 1967, Proxmire rose on the Senate floor to speak in favor of the 1948 United Nations Genocide Convention. The Convention would have outlawed genocide, slavery, forced labor, and the denial of political rights to women. Signers of the Convention recognized that "genocide, whether committed in time of peace or in time of war, is a crime under international law which they undertake to prevent and to punish." The United States had helped to draft the Genocide Convention; the Truman Administration had signed it on December 11, 1948, but the United States Senate did not ratify it.

The United Nations had unanimously approved the treaty to outlaw genocide. And sixty-nine nations, Proxmire told his colleagues, had ratified this basic human rights convention. Of the major nations of the world, only apartheid South Africa and the United States had refused to ratify it. "The president favors its ratification," but "the Senate has failed again and again to act. The Senate's failure to act has become a national shame." Wisconsin's senior senator then pledged to speak "day after day in this body to remind the Senate of our failure to act and of the necessity for prompt action." And that he did . . . every day.

On the second day, Proxmire spoke proudly of America's place in the world, and faulted the Senate for its failure to live up to our nation's ideals.

"It is a cruel paradox as well as a national disgrace that the United States, which has proved conclusively to the world the practical effectiveness of our own Bill of Rights, must hang our national head in shame at our irresponsible unwillingness to lead the fight for the establishment of basic human rights for all men."

On day four, Proxmire gave his colleagues a history lesson:

"Genocide did not begin with the Third Reich. History recalls to us such atrocities as the sacking of Carthage by the Romans, the massacre of the Armenian Christians by the Turks, and the infamous Russian pogroms. The mass murder of eight million human beings—six million Jews and two million Poles—by the Nazi butchers emphasized to all mankind that the civilized society could not and would not tolerate such action ever again."

On the seventh day, Wisconsin's senior senator reminded his colleagues that he would not rest until the United States Senate did the right thing:

"America is conspicuous. We are conspicuous for our remarkable national record in the struggle for human rights. We are just as conspicuous for our international absence in the ratification of the United Nations Convention on Genocide . . . Almost seventy nations have recognized this elementary fact and chosen to ratify the Convention on Genocide."

In the days before liberal Republicans were extinct and moderate Republicans an endangered species, Proxmire had support from a small, bipartisan group of senators, notably Rhode Island Democrat Claiborne Pell and New York Republican Jacob Javits. The opposition at the beginning came principally from northern conservative Republicans and southern segregationist Democrats led by North Carolina Democrat Sam Ervin, and a bit later by North Carolina Republican Jesse Helms.

In 1970, trotting out the same arguments that he and his southern brethren had used against civil rights for two decades, Ervin told his colleagues: "We can reasonably expect that demands will be made that every homicide, every assault and battery inflicting serious injury and every kidnapping shall be tried in a Federal court, or in an international court to be established pursuant to the Convention." Furthermore, the

Convention if ratified "would make American soldiers fighting under the flag of their country in foreign lands triable and punishable in foreign courts—even in courts of our warring enemy—for killing and seriously wounding members of the military forces of our warring enemy." The Convention would "allow captured U.S. soldiers to be tried on charges of genocide . . . American soldiers who fall into the hands of the North Vietnamese are triable and punishable in the courts of north Vietnam."

And Ervin, showing the same appeals to fear that conservatives employ today in opposition to hate crimes legislation, asserted that a private individual could be "subject to prosecution and punishment for genocide if he intentionally destroys a single member of one of the specified groups."

Seven years—and more than fifteen hundred speeches in the Senate—later, Proxmire again took his crusade to the Senate Foreign Relations Committee. North Carolina Democrat Ervin was gone. North Carolina Republican Jesse Helms had arrived. Now the treaty's most vociferous opponent, Helms argued that ratification of the Convention was unconstitutional and would "undermine the most important right and duty of a State under international law, namely that of preserving and protecting its sovereignty . . . The treaty would provide enemy countries not only with a powerful propaganda but also with a psychological warfare weapon of unique effectiveness."

On May 24, 1977, Proxmire told Chairman John Sparkman, an Alabama Democrat who had been Adlai Stevenson's running mate in 1952, "a full quarter century" has passed since the treaty was sent to the Senate. "An entire generation has been born and grown to adulthood during these years, and still the Senate has not acted" to pass this treaty. "We are talking about the planned, premeditated murder or extermination of an entire group of people." And as we as a nation criticize human rights abuses around the world, "we are viewed as moral hypocrites."

And, Proxmire told his colleagues, support for ratification is growing. The American Bar Association, initially an opponent, has now endorsed it unanimously. President Carter had endorsed it. Jewish groups were overwhelmingly supportive. The late Chief Justice Earl Warren had said, "We as a nation should have been the first to ratify the Genocide Convention."

Yet a relatively small group of opponents—conservative, mostly southern—were able to muster up enough opposition to block the two-thirds majority necessary for ratification.

Still, Proxmire stood on the floor every day—usually during the Senate's Morning Business, almost always right after the chaplain had delivered his prayer—to make his case for the United States of America to join with every other industrial democracy in the world to ratify the Convention. And by the mid-1980s—nearly two decades after Proxmire first took the floor and almost four decades after Harry Truman sent the treaty to the Senate—the Genocide Convention appeared poised for ratification. Newspapers endorsed it in even larger numbers. Senators increasingly invoked national security and diplomacy in arguing for it. As the 1984 election approached, even conservative President Ronald Reagan announced his support for ratification, because, in the words of Connecticut Democratic Senator Christopher Dodd, "it would help him win support in the 1984 elections" from America's influential Jewish community.*

Nineteen years and more than three thousand Proxmire speeches later—3,211, to be exact—the Senate took action. On February 11, 1986, the United States Senate ratified the United Nations Genocide Convention, 83–11, the last major nation in the world to do it. The legislation that the Senate passed was watered down, but it was a victory for Proxmire, for our country, and for the world.

Few loved their job as much as William Proxmire. Several times he delivered addresses in the Senate chamber extolling the virtues of Senate service. Late in his career, as he announced his retirement, he said:

> Throughout American history, United States Senators have
> had this golden opportunity to live a life that makes a real
> difference . . . What an opportunity those of us who serve in this
> Congress have to help make this world a better place. Rarely do

---

*Twenty-five years later, Dodd told me a personal story about the Genocide Convention. The first civilian to testify in support of Senate ratification was his father, future Senator Thomas Dodd, who appeared before the Senate to push for ratification; Dodd had been a government lawyer at Nuremberg and knew all too much about Nazi war crimes and genocide.

those of us who enjoy this great privilege pause to think what a golden and rare opportunity we have . . . But just think of it, we are given a chance not just to play in the big leagues, but to work in the biggest league of them all—the policymaking body of the greatest country in the world. What we do for good or ill, or what we fail to do make a difference for this great country and beyond. For anyone looking for a career that offers the greatest prospect for a fulfilling life—how can you beat it? How lucky can you get?

You see some of us have a fear that our tombstone might read like this:

Here under the rocks lies Bill Prox
For him life held no terrors.
Prox became an observer, died an observer,
No hits, no runs, no errors.

I would prefer this instead:

Here under the rocks lies Bill Prox
For him life had its terrors.
Prox became a Senator, died a Senator,
Two scratch hits, one lucky run—a coffin full of errors.

THOUGHTS FROM DESK 88

I N 1970, a few weeks before my graduation from Mansfield Senior
High School, my dad and I were driving past the Beatty Clinic
near our home. The clinic, formerly a tuberculosis sanatorium, was
closing its doors. "TB isn't a problem in Mansfield anymore, son," my dad
said. By then, for the most part, TB was no longer a major public health
threat to our country. Neither was polio. Or diphtheria. Or smallpox. Or
malaria. Or tetanus. And I never really thought much about TB again.

Then, in 1998 in Washington, Joanne Carter from the public interest
group RESULTS came to my office to talk about international tubercu-

losis control. All I knew was that TB was pretty much nonexistent in the United States, that years before it had been called "consumption," and that the disease reportedly killed a number of historical figures: Eleanor Roosevelt, Fyodor Dostoyevsky, George Orwell, Charlotte Brontë, John Keats, B. F. Goodrich, Frédéric Chopin, Francis of Assisi, and dozens of others.

What I did *not* know was that eleven hundred Asian Indians were dying every day from TB, that two billion people in the world carried the inactive tuberculosis bacteria, including at least ten million Americans, and that the U.S. government was doing very little about it. Mostly, tuberculosis attacked the poorest people in the poorest countries in the world, and Americans were mostly unaware of its deadly reach. Over the next few years, from my position as the ranking Democrat on the House Health Subcommittee, I worked with the Centers for Disease Control, the National Institutes of Health, the World Health Organization, and Republican Congressman Tom Coburn, an Oklahoma physician, to scale up our nation's international efforts to combat tuberculosis.

Just as Senator Proxmire's father instructed his son, my dad taught me that millions of lives have been saved because of public health. There were reasons that Americans were living fifteen or twenty years longer than when *they* were born.

One of my proudest accomplishments in the House, when Republicans were in the majority and almost always rejected any new spending on health care, especially public health, was to engage—and to convince—my colleagues to tackle international TB. Better to fight it over there than to allow it to cross our borders, some Republican supporters argued. Others drew on their Christian faith as a reason. TB mortality began to fall as the United States government enlisted the support of other rich nations in helping developing countries in their efforts to combat this centuries-old scourge. When we began in 1999, the United States invested less than $1 million annually for TB control. More than two million people around the world were dying from tuberculosis every year.

A few years later, our efforts to combat international and domestic TB were expanded. Pushed by the part of the evangelical community that emphasizes the New Testament, President Bush announced his campaign to combat worldwide HIV/AIDS under his President's Emergency Plan for AIDS Relief (PEPFAR) in 2003, which also helped in the fight against TB and malaria. It was surely his greatest accomplishment. The effective diagnosis and treatment of TB have saved tens of millions of lives. And now, every year, some 2.7 million TB patients, including some sixty thousand infected by the much more virulent multi-drug-resistant version, are receiving effective treatment.

Although few Americans during my lifetime have paid much attention because TB and malaria had not been a serious domestic threat to our nation for decades, an infectious disease that Americans *did* dread was polio. "Apart from the atomic bomb," a PBS 2009 documentary stated, "America's greatest fear was polio." In 1952, the year I was born, America suffered its worst polio epidemic in the nation's history. Of nearly 58,000 cases reported that year, 3,145 people died and 21,269 were left with mild to disabling paralysis; most of its victims were children. Every summer, parents were terrified that the outbreak would come to their community and afflict their child.

But then in 1955, after a large clinical trial was completed, Dr. Jonas Salk's polio vaccine was declared "safe and effective." Physicians, nurses, and public health authorities recognized that parents' fears would keep people away from vaccination sites because health workers were injecting patients with polio, even though it was a dead form of the virus. To win public confidence, Salk injected himself, his wife, and his children, the first human beings to be vaccinated. My father and dozens of other family practitioners were asked by the federal government to vaccinate their young children in a public place with newspaper and television coverage. In 1955, Dr. Charles Brown—my father—vaccinated Brinkerhoff School first-grader Robert Brown, my oldest brother; their picture appeared the next day in the *Mansfield News-Journal*. The numbers of polio cases began to drop dramatically to only a few a year.

Soon after the introduction of the Salk vaccine, Dr. Albert Sabin developed a live-attenuated oral vaccination at the University of Cincinnati and the Children's Hospital Research Foundation at Cincinnati Children's Hospital. Public fears had not abated, even though Sabin and his researchers had swallowed live viruses. Around the same time, inmates at a prison in Chillicothe, Ohio, were given $25 and "some days off" their sentences to volunteer; the vaccine worked for all thirty prisoners with no lasting side effects. Collaborating with Soviet scientists, Sabin and his international colleagues tested the oral vaccine on more than a hundred million people in the USSR and parts of eastern and northern Europe and Mexico. On Sunday, April 24, 1960—and two succeeding Sabin Sundays—the oral vaccine was given to more than a hundred thousand Cincinnati schoolchildren, essentially eradicating polio in southwest Ohio.

Salk, whose vaccine required two or three booster shots, and Sabin, whose vaccine resulted in a very small—infinitesimal—number of mild polio cases, were successful. The last polio case in the United States originated in 1979. Rarely had such immense progress against a disease come so quickly; only thirty years earlier, more than twenty-five thousand people had been infected every single year.

In the summer of 2016, I had dinner on Capitol Hill with Dr. Thomas Frieden, then the director of the United States Centers for Disease Control and Prevention (CDC), the world's most prestigious public health agency. For the first time in human history, he told me, "more deaths occur among adults than children, more people are overweight than underweight, and non-communicable diseases such as heart disease and cancer kill more people around the world than infectious diseases." All unprecedented public health victories for humankind. All dramatically increasing life expectancy in the United States. All giving children a chance to live into adulthood throughout the developing world.

Across the globe in the last forty years, smallpox has been eradicated, polio has declined by 99 percent, cases of measles and diphtheria have declined by 95 percent, and tetanus and pertussis (whooping cough) have dropped by more than 90 percent. And in the United States, these diseases have been all but eradicated for years.

Public health, we have learned, is about clean water and sanitation, about vaccines and a safe blood supply, about well-baby care and access to modern contraception, about iodine sufficiency and insecticide-treated bed nets, about protecting children from tobacco and drug addiction, about community health workers educating and treating patients in their neighborhoods. Public health may be about having the best health care system in the world if you want a heart transplant (and we do), but also if you want a baby to survive to her first birthday (our country is not nearly as good at that). As Dr. Frieden told the Senate Democratic Caucus as we were strategizing how to convince our Republican colleagues to fund the CDC's efforts to combat the Zika virus, "Public health is prevention. Detection. Treatment."

Surely, public health's greatest victory ever was the eradication of smallpox, estimated to have killed at least three hundred million people in the twentieth century. Centuries earlier, it was brought by Europeans to the New World, wiping out much of the Native American population in North and Central America. The last outbreak in the United States was in 1949.

The World Health Organization kicked off its worldwide effort to attack smallpox in 1966. Under the leadership of Dr. D. A. Henderson of Lakewood, Ohio, joined later by Dr. William Foege of Decorah, Iowa, the World Health Organization marshaled some 150,000 workers and volunteers in some of the world's poorest and most inaccessible places. After initially attempting to vaccinate almost everyone, Foege instead suggested the concept of "ring vaccination," where health workers in essence surrounded infected populations. As a young man, Foege had learned the concept by the way he and his fellow forest rangers fought wildfires. The most difficult fight was in India, centered in the states of Bihar, Uttar Pradesh, and West Bengal; Dr. Foege called their efforts "a lot like the logistics of war." India had 65 percent of all the world's reported cases. But progress was faster than anyone expected. The last case of smallpox was found in the port town of Merca, Somalia, in late 1977. In 1980, the WHO declared smallpox eradicated.

Major U.S. government investment. Strong U.S. leadership around the world. Massive amounts of U.S. taxpayer dollars for medical research in government laboratories and great universities. The support of our European allies enlisted in our efforts. Young, idealistic physicians and nurses and health workers recruited. American-led efforts had paid huge dividends in health, quality of life, and life expectancy for the American people and made an even greater difference in poorer countries: smallpox, polio, diphtheria, tuberculosis, malaria, HIV-AIDS—all public health battles that Americans proudly led. While only smallpox was eradicated, there were magnificent victories against every other of these infectious diseases. Bill Proxmire may have sometimes been too quick to ridicule scientific research, but the physician's son might well have recognized that investments in public health are as efficient and beneficial as any use of taxpayers' funds can be.

And there was another very consequential but incomplete public health victory in the United States—the war against smoking, a very different kind of public health battle.

In 1942, my father, Captain Charles G. Brown, a young physician from Mansfield, Ohio, became addicted to tobacco—as so many in our armed forces did. It began as my father served our country in New Zealand, Egypt, and Persia, when the United States Army included cigarettes in his mess kit, and in the daily K-rations of millions of other soldiers. Every day, the United States Army provided every soldier in combat three separately boxed meals, each with four cigarettes. History is not clear whether taxpayers or tobacco companies paid for these cigarettes, most likely a combination of both. For most of the next six decades, my dad—like so many veterans—smoked at least a pack of cigarettes a day until he died of lung cancer at the age of eighty-nine.

Before the cigarette rolling machine was invented in the late nineteenth century, production of cigarettes was done by hand; a productive worker could roll about four a minute. Mass production soon increased that number to more than two hundred. Today these machines can produce several times that amount. With increased production and skillful marketing, American tobacco consumption exploded, and more Americans died.

I first saw Big Tobacco, up close, on April 14, 1994. Seven tobacco CEOs, each reaping millions personally from America's addiction to tobacco, stood behind a committee table at California Democrat Henry Waxman's Health and Environment Subcommittee of the Energy and Commerce Committee. Waxman asked them to raise their right hands. They swore they would "tell the truth, the whole truth, and nothing but the truth," and then proceeded, one after another, to tell us that nicotine, to their knowledge, was not addictive, and that they never—oh, gosh no, never—would add nicotine to their cigarettes.

The most important fact to know about Big Tobacco is this: every year, more than 480,000 Americans die of tobacco-related illnesses, more than 1,300 people every day. As with any business that is, shall we say, hemorrhaging customers, tobacco companies need to attract more than 9,000 new customers every week, fifty-two weeks a year, just to replace the customers they lost. Where to find them?

Surely not people my age—I'm a grandfather of seven. Not even people in their forties or thirties or even in their twenties are likely to start smoking. We all know, at our age, that smoking is dangerous, that it's not cool, that lots of people find it disgusting.

Big Tobacco aims at teenagers, including very young teens—as it has for decades. They use highly sophisticated marketing techniques developed by some of the most creative advertising minds in the world. Joe Camel? Good visual. Billboards next to your son's junior high? That will work. Camel No. 9, packaged like perfume, mailed to our daughter Caitlin? Sweet. Free samples handed out near schools and playgrounds? Why not? A million-dollar-a-year Madison Avenue marketing guru up against a fifteen-year-old high school sophomore with a few dollars in her wallet wins just about every time.

Big Tobacco has been doing this a long, long time. Former Oregon Senator Maurine Neuberger, an early and courageous critic of tobacco company practices, wrote in her 1963 book *Smoke Screen: Tobacco and the Public Welfare* that "the cigarette industry was a house that advertising built." Through the 1950s, 40 percent of college newspaper advertising was promoting cigarettes. College students smoked in very high numbers. Neuberger, a Democrat and at that point one of only two women in the United States Senate, spoke of the "fertile inventiveness of Madison Avenue"; it's how tobacco made some people fabulously rich.

The industry knew that the public, and maybe even some in Washington, were beginning to challenge its business model. In 1958 the companies formed the Tobacco Institute, the birth of Big Tobacco as a lobbying and public relations force. They suppressed and altered studies and stories outlining the harmfulness of smoking. They ran ads claiming "more doctors smoke Camels than any other cigarette." Neuberger called it "pseudoscientific guerilla warfare."

Then in 1962 the surgeon general of the Air Force, Dr. Oliver K. Niess, spoke out about the dangers of tobacco and declared there would be no more free cigarettes in flight lunches for its airmen. The next year, President Kennedy's surgeon general, Luther Terry, following the lead of the Royal College of Physicians in the United Kingdom, established the Surgeon General's Advisory Committee on Smoking and Health; in 1964, he released "Smoking and Health: Report of the Advisory Committee to the Surgeon General of the United States," concluding that smoking can cause lung cancer and chronic bronchitis and may contribute to emphysema, cardiovascular disease, and other types of cancer. By 1965 all cigarette packages and advertising were required to carry the label: "The Surgeon General Has Determined That Cigarette Smoking Is Dangerous to Your Health."

In the 1970s and 1980s the success of anti-smoking forces was still only intermittent and modest. The power that Big Tobacco wielded in Congress—especially in farm states, tobacco and non-tobacco alike—was immense, not too different from that of Wall Street and the National Rifle Association today.

But by the 1990s, the pressure had built on Big Tobacco to acknowledge that they were targeting children to buy, or at least to use, their toxic product. The companies pretty much—finally—told us: We do not target children. We never have. And we will never do it again. They promised to kill off Joe Camel. They pledged no more billboards near schoolyards. They ended the practice of handing out free samples of their brand-name cigarettes.

Big Tobacco was assuredly in a box: they had to stop marketing to young teenagers; well, as it turned out, they did not exactly stop, but they were more surreptitious in their youth marketing and, truth be told, not nearly as effective in creating new young smokers as they had been. So the question remained: How do they find those 1,300 new smokers every single day?

Then I remembered: only three years earlier, in 1991, I had seen Big Tobacco at work . . . in Warsaw. I had a job at the Mershon Center at Ohio State University, training secondary public school teachers and writing curriculum for the Polish Ministry of Education, as they replaced Marxist-Leninist courses with Western civics and democracy classes.

As I looked out my hotel room window in the capital of this former Soviet-satellite state—the Berlin Wall had come down some eighteen months earlier—I saw the first blooms of capitalism, and it wasn't the Prague Spring. Big Tobacco had arrived there first, planting billboard after billboard all over the Warsaw landscape. The billboards looked like the billboards that I used to see in the United States, but with Polish words. Oh, how the Poles had loved to smoke Soviet cigarettes. And, oh, how even more excited they were now to puff on much higher-quality American cigarettes.

Three years later, in 1994, my second year in Congress, at a subcommittee hearing with tobacco executives, it was my turn to ask questions. Looking down the row of tobacco executives, I thanked them for their pledge to back off their most egregious targeting of children—no special promotions of cartoon characters like Joe Camel, no more billboards near schools, no more handing out free samples to teenagers. Would they, I asked them one at a time, make that same pledge in the developing world?

No. No. No. No. No.

Big Tobacco recognized—we all did—the almost unlimited business opportunities for tobacco companies in less developed countries: from the former Soviet Union to India, from eastern Europe to China, from Nigeria to Latin America. Big Tobacco knew that in the developing world, governments had to worry more about malaria than tobacco, that infectious diseases like tuberculosis killed people much more rapidly— and much more directly—than cigarettes. That cholera outbreaks killed people much more quickly than the slow agony of tobacco-induced emphysema. And that while the United States public health community could spend billions to reduce smoking—we did, and rates fell—the developing world would spend its considerably fewer resources on clean water and better sanitation and mosquito nets and condoms and public health education.

There simply were too many intractable public health problems—in China and India and Vietnam and Malaysia and Indonesia and Mexico, densely populated nations with tens of millions of people—and there was little left over to combat Big Tobacco.

Of course, Big Tobacco was not about to give up on the still immensely profitable American market. The tobacco companies knew that they couldn't be quite so obvious in targeting young people. They knew public health officials were emboldened in their anti-smoking campaigns. From the surgeon general's 1964 report that smoking was dangerous through the Waxman hearings, the science on smoking was increasingly clear: smoking was a leading cause of multiple types of cancer, heart disease, and so many other illnesses. The opponents of Big Tobacco, with Bill Clinton in the White House, had succeeded in banning smoking on airplanes. Many states and municipalities were banning smoking in public places. Whistle-blowers at the tobacco companies were going public about reports that were covered up, science that was twisted, experiments and research that were stopped.

But the tobacco companies had allies, lots of them. The elections of 1994 brought a new Republican majority: the new chairman of Waxman's full committee was a Virginian, the new Speaker a Georgian, the new majority leader and majority whip both Texans, the Appropriations chair from Louisiana, the Ways and Means chairman from Texas—friends of Big Tobacco all. And of course the public relations firms, the law firms, the consulting firms, the lobbying firms—all were enlisted because the immense profits of American tobacco companies were at risk. Any action in this Republican Congress ground to a halt—with tobacco-state congressmen and senators leading the charge, or, more precisely, leading the blocking.

But anti-smoking forces, knowing that there was no chance of any help from Congress, took a very different path. Attorneys general from all over the country were working together to sue the tobacco companies on their states' behalf, claiming that tobacco-related illnesses were costing their state governments hundreds of billions of dollars in Medicaid expenditures. And these state officials were immensely successful, winning hundreds of billions of dollars for what turned out to be highly effective anti-smoking campaigns and assistance to the states for health care brought on by tobacco consumption.

It was only when there was a Democratic majority in the House of Representatives, a close to sixty-vote majority in the Senate, and a Democratic president—a decade and a half after the Waxman hearings—that Congress could take action.

For decades, tobacco was considered neither a food nor a drug, and the Food and Drug Administration had said for years that it had no real jurisdiction to regulate tobacco. We passed the Tobacco Control Act that gave the Food and Drug Administration the ability to keep the most toxic tobacco products off the market, and to stand between children and Madison Avenue peddling tobacco companies' toxic wares.

That's the good news: in the face of intense and unrelenting Big Tobacco pressure, government for five decades—sometimes unevenly when conservative legislators addicted to tobacco campaign contributions intervened—did the right thing to protect public health, and smoking rates and death rates have dropped precipitously. A huge victory for our country's children especially. Our nation's public health success in the war on smoking has been remarkable: fifty years ago, at the time of the surgeon general's report, 42 percent of adult Americans smoked (more than half of adult men). Less than 20 percent smoke today. Every year, pretty consistently, the percentage of the population who smokes has declined by about 0.5 percent. And those who do smoke? Fifty years ago, the average smoker smoked almost a pack and a half a day; today he—still more often he than she—smokes less than a pack a day.

But public health's battle with Big Tobacco never ends. Now there are whole new technologies, vaping and, most troubling, juuling, and they come in attractive and delicious flavors. The lobbying effort for e-cigarettes is led by Altria, formerly Philip Morris and now one of the largest tobacco companies in the world. The United States Chamber of Commerce, against the wishes of many of its board members but always driven by its Republican strategists,* continues to help Big Tobacco fight international anti-smoking laws and regulations.

The tobacco fights—physicians and children's advocates up against

---

*It is interesting how many local chambers of commerce take me aside at events and say they disagree with the U.S. Chamber's increased—ahistorical, they sometimes add—partisanship.

powerful executives with multi-billion-dollar marketing budgets—are perhaps emblematic of a fracturing of the consensus on public health generally. Maybe it started with the fringe groups of the 1950s: a few nativist, right-wing groups played on the public's fear of injecting a child with the live polio virus. The John Birch Society, founded by Robert Welch, Harry Lynde Bradley, and Fred Koch (the father of today's ultraconservative activist-billionaire Koch brothers), claimed that the "polio serum has already killed and maimed children," that a "vaccine drive is the entering wedge for socialized medicine by the United States Public Health Service (heavily infiltrated by Russian-born doctors)." Dressing up his arguments a little better while testifying in opposition to President Kennedy's bill to expand vaccinations to polio and diphtheria in May 1962, the John Birch Society activist Clinton R. Miller said that this bill "creates an urgency where none exists . . . and extends the concept of police power."

In those days, the John Birch Society was demonized by the mainstream of both parties; Birchers, after all, had opposed the creation of the United Nations and the World Health Organization and labeled Republican President Dwight Eisenhower a "conscious, dedicated agent of the Communist Conspiracy." Its activism on the fringes of society and politics made little difference. Then.

But today those same forces, even from the same family, have moved from the fringes of American politics to become the financial backbone of one of America's great political parties. Charles and David Koch announced in January 2015 that they and their closest allies planned to spend more than $850 million for Republican candidates in the 2016 presidential, Senate, and House races. Their announcement was made in the first month of the new Republican Senate, enforcing a party discipline that no political party can exert any longer. The suggestion that tens of millions of dollars would be spent against a Democratic opponent in a general election, or in a primary against a Republican incumbent who strayed from the Koch brothers' Tea Party brand of governing, got everyone's attention. And the Koch brothers' influence was easy to see throughout the next two years as Mitch McConnell and Republican senators governed the Senate—on energy policy, on government spending, on tax policy, on environmental regulation. And on public health.

The politics of public health was becoming treacherous; far too many legislators saw public health emergencies as an opportunity for political gain, not as a problem to solve, not as a duty to serve. While even the wealthiest and most insulated members of Congress knew people who suffered from dementia or multiple sclerosis or Parkinson's, few senators knew anyone infected with malaria or Ebola or Zika virus. These illnesses were a problem for people over there, in Africa, or in South America, or surely in Asia. And those who were afflicted, who were dying, were not like us: they didn't look like us; they did not think like we do; they didn't even pray to the same God.

INCREASINGLY, PUBLIC HEALTH threats became opportunities for those who wanted to close borders, to expel immigrants, to defund Planned Parenthood, to shrink the size of government. When the White House and the CDC asked Congress to fund their efforts to combat public health threats, Tea Party congressmen and senators balked. We should not spend government money to fix the lead crisis in Flint, Michigan, or to combat the spread of the Zika virus, or fight Ebola in Africa and the United States. Instead, they wanted to shift funds from other public health investments, or add riders about abortion or tobacco or gun research at the CDC, or weaken the Clean Water Act.

The canary pin I wear, and that I wrote about in Chapter 1, is all about public health, where the role of government is to help everyone—in the United States and abroad—live longer, healthier lives. "The purpose of public health," Dr. Foege wrote, "is to promote social justice." And it must, by necessity, be about an activist government.

But there is good news: a group of senators—Brian Schatz of Hawaii, the Republican physician William Cassidy of Louisiana, Richard Durbin of Illinois, Jeanne Shaheen of New Hampshire, Connecticut Congresswoman Rosa DeLauro, and I—have come together to propose an Emergency Public Health Fund to ensure a prompt, government-wide response to impending health threats. Patterned after the Federal Emergency Management Agency, which supports first responders to respond to natural disasters, it would enable the CDC to plan for and prevent public health crises, without having to go to Congress each time a threat arose. A number of us in Congress have tried to get the White House to support this legislation, and I've also asked the president to think of the opioid epidemic as the major public health crisis that it is; we've asked him to husband all the resources of the federal government, to use the executive's emergency powers, to save thousands of lives—the way we did with tobacco, or smallpox, or polio. Instead, President Trump has issued an unconstitutional emergency executive order for a problem south of the border that he mostly created.

Twentieth-century history teaches us that major investments in public health improve the lives of hundreds of millions of Americans, and save millions of lives around the globe. The question is: Will the twenty-first-century Congress and the White House learn that lesson?

7.

Robert F. Kennedy

A WARRIOR FOR THOSE WITHOUT A VOICE

SERVED IN THE UNITED STATES SENATE 1965–1968

Let us dedicate ourselves to what the Greeks wrote so many years ago: to tame the savageness of man and make gentle the life of the world. Let us dedicate ourselves to that, and say a prayer for our country and for our people.

—Senator Robert F. Kennedy of New York, April 4, 1968, Indianapolis, two hours after the assassination of Martin Luther King

H ISTORY HAS DEFINED ROBERT FRANCIS KENNEDY by his eighty-two-day presidential campaign—not by his service in the United States Senate, not by his staff work for Senator Joe McCarthy, not by his brilliance in running his brother John F. Kennedy's successful presidential race.

In early 1964, in the months after President Kennedy's assassination, it was not at all clear who Robert F. Kennedy was and what his role would be in our nation's political system. Grief overwhelmed him; he had lost his brother, his best friend, his mentor. For weeks and weeks at the Justice Department, he sat for long periods of time in his darkened office with the shades drawn. "I must say," the future RFK press secretary Frank Mankiewicz told Seymour Hersh three decades later, "I have never been as appalled at the sight of a human being since seeing a concentration camp as a nineteen-year-old infantryman. He was so wasted, like he disappeared into his shirt." But he was still the attorney general serving in President Johnson's cabinet, a president for whom he had little respect.

During the first half of 1964, Robert Kennedy was unsure of what to do. He was considering a challenge to the incumbent Republican Kenneth Keating, New York's one-term junior senator. Some also thought LBJ might select him as his running mate in the upcoming presidential race, but he thought it unlikely that LBJ would do so, and was not even sure that he really wanted the position. Yet Jack had chosen Johnson as his running mate in an equally cynical move, recognizing the electoral advantages that LBJ could bring to the ticket. By June, with polling results—polling was much less frequent in those days—showing Johnson with a commanding lead, the president told his brother, Sam, "Look here. I don't need that little runt to win. I can take anybody I damn well please." A bit later, Johnson informed Kennedy that he would not be chosen as his running mate.

It was not until August, a few days before the Democratic National Convention in Atlantic City, New Jersey, that Kennedy decided to be a candidate for senator from New York. With his mother, Rose, at his side, Kennedy announced for the United States Senate at New York's Gracie Mansion. And then the problems began. Liberals didn't trust him: his record of working for the despised Republican Senator Joseph McCarthy, his hostile questioning of labor leaders in racketeering cases as a Senate staffer, and his shaky civil liberties record made New York Democratic activists suspicious. Many dismissed him as a grudge-bearer, wiretapper, relentless prosecutor, never-get-mad-get-even political hack. They grumbled about his ferocious—and many said underhanded—tactics in the 1960 presidential primaries, especially the character assassination of most liberals' favorite candidate, Hubert Humphrey. The belief among some

New York Democrats that he had approved and encouraged Central Intelligence Agency efforts to kill Fidel Castro followed him until the end of his life.

Others pointed out that Eleanor Roosevelt, who had died in late 1962, never really trusted him. She was not a fan of his father, Joseph, nor of his brother Jack; Jack had missed the vote to censure Joseph McCarthy, and Bobby had worked for the anti-Communist demagogue. The more mild critics—many of them officeholders, some of them envious—said simply that Kennedy had not paid his dues.

And New York Republicans and the media were ready for Kennedy's August 25 announcement. Keating said, "As his senator, I would be glad to furnish him a guidebook, road map, and other useful literature about the Empire State which any sojourner would find helpful."

The New York Times editorialized, "Mr. Kennedy apparently needs New York. But does New York need Bobby Kennedy?" One cartoon showed Kennedy carrying a carpetbag and proclaiming, "Ask not what I can do for the State of New York; rather ask what the State of New York can do for me." Newspapers and Kennedy critics thought Bobby opportunistic and ruthless. It was a curious depiction for a human being who, only a short time later, was seen by many of the least privileged people in our country—native Americans corralled into barren reservations, African Americans sentenced to the nation's worst ghettos, Latinos doing backbreaking work for poverty wages for large agribusiness—as the most empathetic political figure of the mid-twentieth century.

Kennedy knew he had some advantages too. He was pretty certain that in 1964 New York voters would decisively reject Barry Goldwater, the Republican nominee for president, and likely anyone else on the ballot with an "R" after their name.

But Keating, much of New York's liberal community believed, was not such a bad senator. He outspokenly supported civil rights legislation. He refused to endorse Goldwater because the Arizona senator was far too conservative. And leftist icons like I. F. Stone, James Baldwin, and Nat Hentoff were supporting Keating. "Democrats for Keating" formed with prominent intellectuals and progressives like Paul Newman,

234 ||| DESK 88

Arthur Schlesinger, Sr., Barbara Tuchman, Joseph Heller, Gore Vidal, David Susskind, and Archibald MacLeish—all critical of Kennedy. And by most accounts, Kennedy was an uninspiring and unimaginative candidate, promising to continue his brother's policies (even though another man was now in the White House) and wanting to build on his brother's legacy.

He was uncomfortable in front of large crowds, often stuttering and monotonic. But, as Lester and Irene David pointed out in *Bobby Kennedy: The Making of a Folk Hero*, he drew larger crowds in upstate New York than had ever assembled in that region to see a politician. At first, Bobby believed the crowds were there for his brother. But once he understood that people were turning out for *him*, he relaxed a bit, and spoke more assuredly and more eloquently. Perhaps the most important quality for good public speaking is the recognition by the orator that people want to hear you; the self-confidence then follows.

As the ten-week campaign unfolded, Kennedy's name recognition and celebrity status, his ample campaign funding, and the surge of support for the Democratic ticket as a whole pointed to a likely victory for the first-time candidate.

Kennedy and his aides also knew how to frame issues. Creating "the box score," Kennedy's campaign selected a dozen votes where liberal New York Republican Senator Jacob Javits and liberal Minnesota Democrat Hubert Humphrey voted one way, and Keating and conservative Republican and presidential candidate Barry Goldwater voted the other way.

On Election Day, even though Bobby and his wife, Ethel, could not vote in their adopted state, voters elected Kennedy to the United States Senate by more than seven hundred thousand votes, one of the largest margins against an incumbent in Senate history. That year and in that state, Keating never had a chance; the Republican nominee for president lost to LBJ by more than 2.5 million votes.

On January 4, 1965, Robert F. Kennedy joined his younger and only remaining brother, Edward M. Kennedy, in the United States Senate. He was seated in the recently added fifth row of desks—the Democrats had increased their already lopsided majority, and the freshmen chose last—alongside Minnesota's Walter Mondale, Maryland's Joe Tydings, and Oklahoma's Fred Harris. Harris and Kennedy came to the Senate in their thirties, Kennedy having been elected at thirty-nine and Harris at thirty-three. From Corrales, New Mexico, in the spring of 2019, Harris told me, "Robert and I were each other's best friends in the Senate, and seatmates all the time we were in the Senate. I saw Robert Kennedy become Robert Kennedy."

But he came to the Senate just fourteen months after his brother's death, and at that time, Robert Francis Kennedy was still—consciously or not—adopting President Kennedy's mannerisms: imitating his speaking style, even wearing his brother's clothes, and following the late president's agenda. His grief weighed heavy, never seeming to leave his slightly stooped shoulders. He arrived in the United States Senate eager to continue the work of his slain brother, but it was not at all clear who he was and what he would do. He believed that his decisive victory was an overwhelming mandate for President Kennedy's domestic and foreign policy.

But something happened to Senator Robert F. Kennedy during his Senate service that made him gentle but driven, focused but sometimes reckless, an idealistic but pragmatic politician who would prove to be one of the most inspiring and charismatic presidential candidates in United States history. What he was able to do in those eighty-two days—beginning with his March 16 announcement in the Senate Caucus Room and ending with his June assassination in the Los Angeles hotel ballroom—was to transform himself into a vessel of hope for millions of Americans, into almost a demigod for the least privileged.

How did he get that way? How did he become the leader who would prompt Sylvia Wright, writing for *Life* magazine at the time, to ask herself repeatedly over the years, "What did he have that he could do this to people?" Or the famed television broadcaster David Brinkley to say that Kennedy was "the only white politician left who could talk to both races"? Or the civil rights activist John Lewis, elected to the United States House of Representatives almost twenty years later, to ask when casting a vote in the House, "What would Bobby do?"

In his Capitol office in the winter of 2010, Congressman Lewis told me, "Bobby Kennedy was the only white politician in America in 1968 who could walk the streets and be met with cheers instead of violence."

Sitting in a Boston restaurant in the early spring of 2009, the former

Democratic national chairman Steve Grossman saw it another way. He observed about elected officials in general, "Politicians are not really liberated until they lose." Whether a state legislator or a United States senator, he or she is then more relaxed, often speaks better, seems more human, and is braver.

But Robert Kennedy was liberated in a different way. His brother's death, and his successful candidacy for the United States Senate, freed him. He was the smallest of the four boys, seeing himself as "the runt of his family's litter," in the words of his advisor and later CBS newsman Jeff Greenfield. At an early age, more so perhaps than the other Kennedy boys, he thought of those outside his social class. His aide Peter Edelman,* who was one of Kennedy's most trusted aides, attributed his empathy to his childhood, when his father—as ambassador to Great Britain—took much more interest in Bobby's older brothers, Joe and Jack.

Surely neither his father's nor his mother's favorite son, he showed occasional early signs of seeing the world through the eyes of others. Bobby chose as the best man at his wedding a working-class friend from school, not exactly a Kennedy thing to do.

But in his early years, and during his brother's 1960 presidential campaign, Robert Kennedy had rarely talked about poverty, apparently thought little about the issues around civil rights, and had done almost nothing to advance the cause of social and economic justice.

Even though President Kennedy had shown only scant interest in addressing poverty in America, Robert invited—perhaps "summoned" might be the better word; he was, after all, the president's brother—the entire cabinet to his Justice Department office to meet with the administration's self-styled "guerrillas," a group of anti-poverty activists sprinkled through several federal agencies. All but Secretary of State Dean Rusk

---

*Edelman, who worked in the Kennedy Justice Department as a young attorney and then in his Senate campaign, tells how he was hired by the new senator after the 1964 election. Leaning against a car in the driveway between the White House and the Old Executive Office Building, Kennedy's first question to the approaching Edelman was, "Are you going to come work for me?"

Edelman: "How much will you pay me?"

RFK: "You can work that out with Ed—"

Edelman: "I have this problem. I am three and a half years out of law school, and I haven't practiced law."

RFK: "I had that problem. I worked it out."

attended. Kennedy closed and locked the doors, and discussed for four hours how they could work together to combat poverty, drawing liberally on the writings of Michael Harrington's *The Other America*.* Here, in part, were the beginnings of the war on poverty.

But through his first forty years, he was mostly someone else's man. His father's influence led him to Joe McCarthy and into prosecutorial-type hearings where he earned the reputation as ruthless and opportunist. The 1960 campaign, brother Jack's victory, and Bobby's appointment as attorney general of course put him in the president's shadow, where critics said he engaged too willingly in wiretapping and compromised too often on civil liberties. And JFK's assassination forced RFK to be his late brother's tribune and carry on his slain brother's legacy. Even in his Senate race a year later and in his early months on the job, he followed the path of his brother.

After the excitement of the presidential race in 1960, the job of attorney general, and the shock of his brother's assassination, Bobby seemed bored in the United States Senate. One day in 1965, as Teddy told me more than four decades later, Ted and Bobby—the younger brother a bit senior on the committee to his older brother—waited several hours for their turn to question a witness. Showing the Kennedy impatience that Ted later tamed, Bobby passed a note to Ted:

> RFK: Is this the way I become a good senator—sitting here and waiting my turn?
> EMK: Yes.
> RFK: How many hours do I have to sit here to be a good senator?
> EMK: As long as it takes, Robby.

THE JOB OF a United States senator—today even more than in 1965—lends itself to insulation and isolation. More often than not, a senator's time is

---

*In my opinion, the best books about poverty, other than Harrington's, written in modern times are Jacob Riis's *How the Other Half Lives*; James Agee's *Let Us Now Praise Famous Men*; Barbara Ehrenreich's *Nickel and Dimed*; Kathryn Edin and H. Luke Shaefer's *$2.00 a Day*; and Matthew Desmond's *Evicted*.

consumed with meetings with other senators, staff, highly educated and generally affluent experts, lobbyists, foreign leaders, and wealthy contributors. In some sense, a senator's social life is no different from most in that it revolves around people like themselves; but in a senator's life, of course, that means socializing chiefly with highly educated, upscale friends, a thin slice of upper-crust society.

But a good elected official does something else. Early in his papacy, Pope Francis exhorted his parish priests to be "shepherds living with the smell of the sheep . . . as shepherds among your flock" with all the biblical connotations. And as we've seen, Lincoln—with his staff telling him that he needed to stay in the White House to win the war and preserve the union and free the slaves—reminded his aides that he needed "my public opinion baths."

And Robert Kennedy *wanted* something different. He knew senators were typically disconnected from the public. Jim Stevenson, who got to know Kennedy intimately, wrote that RFK's toughness was directed inward, representing "a contempt for self-indulgence, for weakness." But even more than many progressives before him, he wanted to expose himself to all that was happening in our country. The more anguish and heartache he witnessed, the more he committed himself to action. The more poverty he experienced, the more he challenged authority. The more pain he saw, the more impatient he was. And the more progressive he became.

Kennedy was now, in some sense, unshackled. He felt liberated to pursue his own calling in the fight for social and economic justice. Frank Mankiewicz, his press secretary in his presidential race, termed it RFK's "free-at-last syndrome." Kennedy was now free to pursue his own legacy, as Arthur Schlesinger, Jr., noted, to be "the tribune of the underclass." He thought more about poverty, Edelman said, and acted upon it more than any other high-ranking public official of his day. He was "always interested in the excluded and the disempowered." Kennedy was "just different, even as a kid," Edelman told me in early 2019.

To be sure, Bobby liked to think his advocacy for the least privileged was a continuation of his brother's legacy, but there is little evidence for that. JFK did indeed run for president as a liberal concerned about the nation's underclass, promising to increase the minimum wage, to pass national health insurance for the elderly, to embark on a decade-long effort to eradicate urban slums, to enact civil rights legislation. Theodore White in *The Making of the President, 1960* explained it this way: "Kennedy's shock at the suffering he was seeing in West Virginia was so fresh that it communicated itself with the emotion of original discovery."

But the new president, as pointed out by the Michael Harrington biographer Maurice Isserman, neglected to mention his domestic agenda in his famous 1961 Inaugural Address to the nation. And according to the Kennedy biographer Richard Reeves, in the spring of 1961, President Kennedy said to former Vice President Richard Nixon, "It really is true that foreign affairs is the only important issue for a president to handle, isn't it? I mean who gives a shit if the minimum wage is $1.15 or $1.25?"

But Bobby *could* point to one poignant example of Jack's interest in the poor, insignificant as history might judge it. John F. Kennedy was an inveterate doodler. During President Kennedy's last cabinet meeting in the fall of 1963, he wrote the word POVERTY on the pad in front of him and scribbled circles around it. After the assassination, the grieving, mourning brother framed the doodle; Bobby pointed to it to reassure others, and perhaps mostly himself, that he was carrying on Jack's work. And that, yes, Jack would have approved.

To New Yorkers, Robert Kennedy's metamorphosis may have begun with a trip through Bedford-Stuyvesant. It was February 4, 1966. A senator for just thirteen months, he took a long, slow walk through the Bedford-Stuyvesant section of Brooklyn, home to 450,000 desperately poor people, one of the largest ghettos in America. "He saw it all," the Kennedy aide Arthur Schlesinger, Jr., wrote: "burned-out buildings, brownstones in abject decay, stripped cars rusting along the streets, vacant lots overflowing with trash and garbage, a pervading stench of filth and defeat."

Ten months later—with Mayor John Lindsay and New York's senior senator, Republican Jacob Javits, in tow—in front of one thousand people in a school auditorium, Kennedy returned to Bedford-Stuyvesant to unveil a development plan. Over the next few years, Bedford-Stuyvesant became, in the words of the sociologist Michael Harrington, "a modest success—which in the context of so many failures, is to say a remarkable success"—new housing and other investment, more entrepreneurial activity and job creation, much improved social services. Eight years later, Javits said that Bedford-Stuyvesant was the place "where the community development corporation idea was born." By then there were thirty-four federally funded and seventy-three privately funded community development corporations.

Kennedy's work on the Labor Subcommittee on Poverty and the Subcommittee on Migratory Labor took him to the Native American reservations of the Great Plains and to the fields of California. On the reservations, he found few textbooks and fewer Indian teachers. "The first American," he told Oklahoma Democratic Senator Fred Harris, himself part Native American, "is still the last American in terms of employment, health, and education."

A month after his February 1966 trip to Bedford-Stuyvesant, Kennedy went to Delano, California, at the request of the United Auto Workers president, Walter Reuther. The subcommittee hearing was to support the Latino labor activists Cesar Chavez and Dolores Huerta in their efforts to unionize farmworkers and to challenge local law enforcement officials who were abusing the community's immigrant families. Right before the lunch break, Kennedy—with his rapier, always-with-a-message wit—instructed local law enforcement officials who were testifying: "Can I suggest in the interim period of time that the sheriff and the district attorney read the Constitution of the United States?"

Kennedy's interest in freedom movements around the world brought him an invitation from the National Union of South African Students to address its annual Day of Affirmation. It took five months before the white apartheid government granted him a visa.

Ethel and Bobby Kennedy arrived in Johannesburg in June 1966. Dr. Hendrik Verwoerd, the Afrikaaner prime minister who still had a firm grip on his divided country, refused to see him and ordered his ministers to stay away. Nelson Mandela had been in prison three years and was to spend twenty-four more there, mostly at the Robben Island fortress.

Kennedy's speech at the University of Capetown was probably his greatest ever, speaking to young people about hope in a country where so few people had hope. Showing the empathy for which he became increasingly known in the United States, Kennedy began his speech:

> I came here this evening because of my deep interest and affection for a land settled by the Dutch in the mid-seventeenth century, then taken over by the British, and at last independent; a land in which the native inhabitants were at first subdued, but relations with whom remain a problem to this day; a land which defined itself on a hostile frontier; a land which has tamed rich natural resources through the energetic application of modern technology; a land which once imported slaves, and now must struggle to wipe out the last traces of that former bondage. I refer, of course, to the United States of America.

And the most famous passage, quoted at his funeral two years and a few days later by his brother Senator Edward M. Kennedy:

> Thus you, and your young compatriots everywhere have had thrust upon you a greater burden of responsibility than any generation that has ever lived . . . Few will have the greatness to bend history itself; but each of us can work to change a small portion of the events, and in the total of all these acts will be written the history of this generation . . . It is from numberless diverse acts of courage such as these that the belief that human history is shaped. Each time a man stands up for an ideal, or acts to improve the lot of others, or strikes out against injustice, he sends forth a tiny ripple of hope, and crossing each other from a million different centers of energy and daring those ripples build a current which can sweep down the mightiest walls of oppression and resistance.

The next day, to a more conservative student audience at Stellenbosch University, he previewed what would become the in-your-face style of his

1968 presidential campaign. In response to a question about race, Kennedy asked, "What the hell would you do if you found out that God was black?"

But it may have been Mississippi that most moved Robert Francis Kennedy.

Marian Wright was no fan of the Kennedy family when the New York senator arrived in Mississippi in 1967 to attend a field hearing examining the work of the Office of Economic Opportunities. The OEO, the command center of Lyndon Johnson's War on Poverty, was established in 1964. It established Head Start and Community Action Agencies, Legal Services and the Job Corps, VISTA and Community Health Centers.

Mississippi's segregationist leaders—notably Senators James Eastland and John Stennis, and Governors Ross Barnett and Paul Johnson— had tried to turn away most of the federal monies directed at the state's enervating poverty, their behavior being not too different from the rejection of federal stimulus money in 2009 by the conservative governors Mark Sanford of South Carolina and Bobby Jindal of Louisiana, and the refusal across almost the entire Old Confederacy to expand Medicaid a few years later.

Wright, a twenty-eight-year-old Yale Law School graduate who'd grown up in South Carolina, found a way to end-run the hidebound and racist state government and bring Head Start services to Mississippi, the poorest state in the nation. Within a matter of a few years, Head Start was the single largest employer in Mississippi—a commentary both on Wright's great organizing skills and on Mississippi's excruciating poverty.

To Wright, Kennedy was a son of privilege whose ambition seemed to trump almost everything else. As attorney general, he had tapped Dr. Martin Luther King's phone. And he'd acquiesced—"senatorial courtesy," she still derisively calls it—in the selection of federal judges in Dixie. Interestingly, because of Eastland's power over the young president, President Eisenhower's southern Republican judges in the 1950s were notably more progressive on civil rights than were President Kennedy's Democratic judges.

Her views about Kennedy began to change when he entered the filthy shack of a poor Mississippi family. He pointedly kept the television cameras out of the family's home. "He tried so hard," she told me forty years later, "to get that child—with his distended belly—to respond." Outside, he asked older children what they had eaten for breakfast that day. Nothing. "Kennedy's anger and pain for that child" were so apparent. On that same day, as she was riding to Cleveland, Mississippi, in the Kennedy motorcade, a police car hit and killed a child's dog, and she saw Kennedy console the child. She saw in him "a spontaneous empathy" that she had rarely seen in a human being, let alone a United States senator born to such great privilege.

The Kennedy aide Peter Edelman, who had met his future wife, Marian Wright, earlier that week, told me that, after Kennedy left that child and his family, he said, "I have been to third world countries, and never seen poverty like this."

At dinner with Connie and me and Peter in the spring of 2009, Marian Wright Edelman told me that Bobby "was open to life, open to suffering." He had a sadness about him—she only knew him after his brother was murdered—and always a curiosity that made him question people, their lives, and their conditions.

And Bobby Kennedy—the wealthy senator from New York, the scion of America's most eminent political family, the privileged young man provided every opportunity by his father—saw something else . . . *felt* something else. The Kennedy biographer Jack Newfield, who personally knew his subject well, wrote, "Kennedy had the almost literary ability to put himself inside other people, to see the world with the eyes of its casualties." Kennedy spoke of "Indians living on their bare and meager reservations with so little hope for the future that for young men and women in their teens, the greatest cause of death is suicide." He described "people of the black ghetto, listening to ever-greater promises of equality and justice, as they sit in the same decaying schools and huddle in the same filthy rooms, warding off the cold and warding off the rats," of "children in the Delta area of Mississippi with distended stomachs, whose faces are covered with sores from starvation." He imagined his own children suffering like these children. "Today in America," he wrote in 1967, "we are two worlds . . . If we try to look through the eyes of the young slum-dweller—the Negro, and the Puerto Rican, and the Mexican-American—the world is a dark and hopeless place."

"Mississippi changed him forever," Atlanta Democratic Congressman John Lewis said. Sitting in his Capitol Hill office in the winter of 2010, Lewis told me, "His empathy came once he was in the Senate. He reminded me of the bantam roosters I raised on the farm in Alabama, the way he fought for what was right."

The head of the farmworkers union, Cesar Chavez, who was distrustful of almost all politicians, said that Robert Kennedy "could see things through the eyes of the poor." Vine Deloria, Jr., a Native American activist who wrote *Custer Died for Your Sins*, said that the rather shy Robert F. Kennedy was a man "who could move from world to world and never be a stranger anywhere." And Schlesinger, who observed Kennedy as friend and advisor for years, wrote, "He appeared most surely himself among those whom life had left out."

Even though LBJ's War on Poverty was beginning to address the suffering—in ghettos, in migrant camps, on Indian reservations—that Kennedy saw, the New York senator believed it fell far short. And even though Kennedy knew that Johnson had moved faster and further than JFK or any other president in addressing both the causes and the realities of poverty, Kennedy was increasingly bitter toward Johnson's reluctance to do more. And the New York senator was increasingly worried about Vietnam and Johnson's escalation of the war at the expense of domestic spending.

In the two short years after President Kennedy's assassination, Johnson had used his considerable legislative skills to convince Congress to enact Medicare, Medicaid, voting rights, equal opportunities and higher education legislation, the Civil Rights Act, and other progressive measures. Kennedy found Johnson's trumpeting of his legislative successes aggravating. He thought Johnson was bragging about his prowess while demeaning the skills of President Kennedy. He believed that Johnson won those victories—whereas President Kennedy could not—primarily because he had such huge liberal majorities after the 1964 elections, not because of his own special gifts. Historians, after all, have noted that after the 1964 elections, Johnson benefited from the first progressive

Democratic majorities in both houses that a Democratic president had enjoyed since Roosevelt had in 1937–1938. Look what happened, Kennedy thought, to Johnson's legislative program after the Republicans picked up several dozen House seats in 1966. Nonetheless, Johnson had immense skills as a legislative leader. And with a number of very strong allies in the House and especially in the Senate, Johnson was willing to use the power of the White House to get his way.

Underlying RFK's criticism of the president was the fact that he just did not like Johnson. Don Riegle, a former Democratic senator and a former Republican congressman from Flint, Michigan, told me of a poignant moment in the months leading up to Kennedy's challenge of Johnson. Watching from the House floor during the 1968 State of the Union, Riegle—who sat on the Republican side of the House chamber—was able to see Kennedy directly during Johnson's address. In the spring of 2009, Riegle told me, "Bobby was smoldering with disdain, with resentment toward Johnson. I could see it all over his face."

The reasons that Robert F. Kennedy finally entered the 1968 race were complicated. He had resisted entreaties from anti-war Democrats and many of his brother's allies. He thought that a race against Johnson would look childish and vindictive—childish in that people would say that RFK believed that the White House belonged to the Kennedy family, vindictive in that he wanted to even some scores with Lyndon Johnson.

The Kennedy spokesman Frank Mankiewicz said, "It was never contemplated that Bobby would become the president pro tempore of the Senate." But Kennedy himself and many of his advisors wanted to wait until 1972, when he would, they thought, have a clearer shot to the nomination and to the White House. But as his opposition to the Vietnam War intensified, and with his growing anger at LBJ's refusal (in Kennedy's mind) to expand the Great Society, it became increasingly difficult for Kennedy to stay on the sidelines.

In early 1968, the vacillating New York senator was greeted by a sign at Brooklyn College: HAWK, DOVE OR CHICKEN? The respected columnist Walter Lippmann said to Kennedy, "If you believe that Johnson's re-election would be a catastrophe for the country, the question you must live with is whether you did everything you could to avert this catastrophe." And not far from his mind were the words from Dante that John F. Kennedy liked to quote: "The hottest places in hell are reserved for those who, in a time of great moral crisis, maintain their neutrality."

Minnesota Democratic Senator Eugene McCarthy, for whom Kennedy and most of his Senate colleagues had little respect, had launched his anti-war challenge to Johnson in late 1967, when no one else would. The Kennedy biographer Arthur Schlesinger, Jr., wrote, "McCarthy, like other brilliant, lonely men, looked down on practically everyone in his own profession." His appeal, especially to young people, was his willingness to stand up to his colleagues. And McCarthy made it easy for others in his profession to dislike him. "Being in politics is like being a football coach," he once said. "You have to be smart enough to understand the game and dumb enough to think it's important." McCarthy had special appeal to white suburbanites and college students.

Jeffrey DeBoer, who loved Bobby and saw him in 1968 in Rapid City, South Dakota, when he was just ten, told me four decades later, "Gene McCarthy, they used to say, had the 'A' students. Bobby had the 'B' students. That was okay with me. I was struggling to be a 'B' student with Bobby."

Two days before the New Hampshire primary, on a private plane bound for Delano, California, Kennedy told Peter Edelman that yes, he would be a candidate for president of the United States. "Four people on a plane," Edelman told me. "The plane takes off and he told us he was running for president. We were just thrilled." Why did he decide to run? "He just couldn't wait until 1972 because of what was happening to the country."

On March 16, 1968, only four days after McCarthy had stunned the political world by almost upsetting the incumbent president of the United States in the New Hampshire primary, RFK announced his candidacy. Just like his martyred brother, he launched his effort in the Senate Caucus Room, which would be renamed the Kennedy Caucus Room after brother Edward's death in 2010. Kennedy detractors, not knowing that he had made known his decision to a few aides before the New Hampshire primary, chalked up Kennedy's announcement to his well-known "ruthlessness and opportunism." RFK had let McCarthy do the dirty work, waiting until the Minnesota senator had softened up LBJ and had proven the president's vulnerability.

NONETHELESS, FOR RFK, the hill was surely steep. As the Kennedy family friend and astronaut John Glenn recounts in *A Memoir*, one of Kennedy's favorite quotes that "defined Bobby's approach to life" was a line popularized by Emerson, "Always do what you are afraid to do." The last time an incumbent president of the United States was denied the nomination of his own party was 1884, when the Republican James G. Blaine was selected over President Chester Arthur; Blaine was then defeated in the general election by Democrat Grover Cleveland. On the March morning of his announcement, Kennedy had little staff, almost no organization, not one delegate, and few elected officials; only Senators Stephen Young of Ohio and Joseph Tydings of Maryland were to come on board over the next few days. Many of the most skilled Democratic campaign strategists in the country had signed on weeks earlier with the McCarthy campaign, and others were afraid to challenge a sitting president.

Johnson and Kennedy's relationship wasn't very good from the days of the 1960 Democratic National Convention in Los Angeles, when Bobby discussed the vice presidency with Johnson on behalf of his brother. They came from very different backgrounds. They saw very different worlds. They neither understood nor trusted each other.

Lyndon Johnson grew up poor in the hill country of Texas, worked his way through Southwest Texas State Teachers College, and taught school in a Mexican American community. He won a seat in Congress, enlisted in the armed services after World War II started, returned to Congress, and then lost once before winning a seat in the United States Senate. The youngest majority leader in American history, Johnson was never an easy man to like. New York Congressman Emanuel Celler, chairman of the House Judiciary Committee, said, "I heard Johnson say one time that he wanted men around him who were loyal enough to kiss his ass in Macy's window and say it smelled like a rose."

Kennedy's path was surely easier, but one strewn with pain and tragedy. Bobby was born to great wealth and had every advantage that privilege can bring. He traveled widely, went to the finest prep schools, joined the Naval Reserve, and graduated from Harvard. Two older siblings were killed tragically in the 1940s, his brother in World War II, his sister in a plane crash in Europe. He worked as counsel to Republican Senator Joseph McCarthy, and managed some of his brother Jack's campaigns. After the painful death of his brother, Kennedy's path to the Senate was relatively easy.

And Kennedy was thought to be moody, enigmatic at times, and abrupt with people. In June 1964, President Johnson, First Lady Lady Bird Johnson, and Attorney General Kennedy were riding together to the newly renamed John F. Kennedy Airport honoring the slain president. After returning to Washington, Mrs. Johnson wrote in her diary that she liked Bobby, but "I haven't the vaguest idea what's going on in his mind."

And Johnson was jealous, insanely jealous of all things Kennedy—the success, the wealth, the glamour, the popularity, the charisma. He resented Jack Kennedy, who he thought was pretty much a failure as a senator. And he loathed Bobby Kennedy, whom he saw as an ingrate and a hypocrite.

And now it was about to get worse.

Sitting in a Mexican restaurant in Austin in the spring of 2009, the former Johnson White House counsel Larry Temple described to me the March 1968 meeting between President Johnson and Senator Kennedy. It was only three days after Johnson had surprised the nation by announcing, "I shall not seek, and I will not accept, the nomination of my party for another term as your president."

When Kennedy arrived at the White House, Temple escorted the New York senator into the cabinet room and offered him a seat directly across the table from the president. Neither feigned warmth toward the other, Temple observed. Temple left the two rivals alone.

Johnson surreptitiously pushed a button underneath the table, turning on a tape recorder. After the abbreviated meeting—it lasted, Temple told me, only fifteen or twenty minutes—the president ordered Temple to get the conversation transcribed. To Temple's great consternation, White House transcribers were only able to hear static on the recording. Kennedy, every bit the poker player that Johnson was, had apparently worn a concealed device that scrambled the president's tape recording. There is an old saying among card players, "If you sit down to a game of poker, and you don't see a sucker, it means you're it." For once, LBJ might have been it.

LBJ told the historian Doris Kearns Goodwin after he left the White House: "And then the final straw: the thing I feared from the first day of my presidency was actually coming true. Robert Kennedy openly announced his intention to reclaim the throne in memory of his brother. And the American people, swayed by the magic of the name, were dancing in the streets."

RFK's campaign, perhaps more than any in the twentieth century, played to the hopes of people. He knew how to play to fear; he had done it with Joe McCarthy, and with his brother warning of the nonexistent missile gap with the Soviet Union during the 1960 presidential race. He had seen Lyndon Johnson in 1964, warning of Goldwater's warmongering and recklessness about nuclear war. This campaign, though, would be about hope—and idealism—and building coalitions. The Kennedys' attractiveness—that of Jack, Bobby, Ted—was their optimism, their ability to appeal to our best instincts, to strive for something better.

The Kennedy charisma is hard to explain. I first saw it as a college student when I visited my brother Bob in Washington when Bob was a naval officer serving under Admiral Hyman Rickover. It was 1971. I was eighteen years old and, I assume, rather easily impressed. We went to a public reception in the Capitol that a number of senators attended. And there was Massachusetts Senator Edward M. Kennedy, the only survivor of the four Kennedy brothers, standing in the middle of the room. Although I did not even meet him on that day, I simply could not take my eyes off of him.

He was handsome, but surely not the most handsome man in the room. He was well dressed, but so was almost everyone else at the reception. His picture was frequently in the paper and his face was often on television, but so were those of a half dozen other senators. What he had was a joie de vivre, a joy of life, that—despite the family's tragedies and almost unspeakable pain—seemed to always shine through.

Thirty-five years later, I saw that vim and vigor again—when talking with Kennedy on the Senate floor; watching him chair his Health, Education, Labor, and Pensions Committee, which he put me on as a first-year senator; laughing in his Senate hideaway when we were waiting for late-night votes; even on the telephone after he was diagnosed with brain cancer.

In his hideaway only a few feet from the Senate gallery, he most enjoyed telling stories about his forty-seven years in the Senate, about Bobby and Jack, and about his childhood. "These," he told Connie and me mirthfully one night as he pointed to the walls, "are *my* family pictures." The people were all identifiable—they were Kennedys, after all—but I had never seen *those* photographs. Another time, Ted invited my twenty-three-year-old daughter Elizabeth and me along with Washington Senator Maria Cantwell to his hideaway after Elizabeth had come to watch us debate the Children's Health Insurance Program from the gallery. She was overwhelmed by his kindness. "He asked me questions . . . and I'm just a college student," she enthused later that night as we walked to my apartment.

Robert Kennedy thought the way a candidate ran for office suggested a lot about how the candidate would serve in office. How could he run a race for president, Kennedy told himself, without challenging voters, without telling people what they needed to hear, without calling on citizens to sacrifice? Anything short of that would ill serve his country and his profession. And "healing a morally wounded nation after an immoral campaign would be impossible," RFK told the biographer Thurston Clarke.

He saw every speech as a chance to educate people. On a plane from Cleveland to Washington on the day after Martin Luther King's assassination, he told Sylvia Wright of *Life*: "For every two or three days that you waste time making speeches at rallies full of noise and balloons, . . . you get a chance to teach people something, and to tell them something they don't know because they don't have the chance to get around like I do, to take them some place vicariously that they haven't been, to show them a ghetto or an Indian reservation."

He told his advisor Frank Mankiewicz that, if he were president, he would convince the networks to produce a documentary depicting the hopelessness of ghetto life. "Show a black teenager, told by some radio jingle to stay in school, looking at his older brother who stayed in school and who's out of a job. Show the Mafia pushing narcotics, put a *Candid Camera** team in a ghetto school and watch what a rotten system of education really is. Film a mother staying up all night to keep threats away from her baby . . . I'd ask people to watch it and experience what it means to live in the most affluent society in history—without hope . . . Let them show the sound, the feel, the hopelessness, and what it's like to think you'll never get out."

As he began his campaign, Kennedy apologized to the voters for two things for which he (and his brother, the martyred president) was responsible: the selection of Lyndon Johnson as vice president at the 1960 Democratic National Convention in Los Angeles; and the beginning of the Vietnam War. On January 20, 1961, there were 685 American advisors in South Vietnam, a limit set by the Geneva Accords. President Kennedy sent advisors to assist the South Vietnamese government and military, and, of course, many believed they played a role in the assassination of South Vietnamese President Ngo Dinh Diem. By the time of the Kennedy assassination, there were more than 16,500 United States military advisors serving in Vietnam.

In the early days, Bobby was a hawk on Vietnam. In Hong Kong in 1962, he said, "The solution [in Vietnam] lies in our winning it. This is what the president intends to do." And then Senator Kennedy had supported the war in 1965—perhaps it was now President Johnson's war, but Senator Kennedy had voted for a supplemental appropriations bill, an implicit vote of confidence in Johnson's handling of the war. Only three senators, courageous and prescient all, voted no: Democrats Wayne Morse of Oregon, Ernest Gruening of Alaska, and Gaylord Nelson of Wisconsin. Morse and Gruening were the only two to vote against the Gulf of Tonkin resolution, and both were defeated for reelection in 1968, Gruening in a primary; Nelson lost twelve years later, in the Republican landslide of 1980.

---

*Then a popular show using a hidden camera catching people doing silly things.

In his first speech after his announcement for president, on March 18, 1968, Bobby told students at the University of Kansas, "Let me begin this discussion with a note both personal and public. I was involved in many of the early decisions on Vietnam, decisions which helped set us on our present path." As he began to speak to the crowd, the Washburn University student and future Congressman Jim Slattery stood nearby. He told me decades later that Kennedy was shaking, unsure of himself, Slattery thought, until he made his apology.

In 1968, at Vanderbilt University in Nashville, Kennedy was taunted by a student who reminded the crowd that RFK promised in 1962 that the war would continue "until we win." The New York senator responded: "I made a mistake in 1962. I would feel better if President Johnson would admit he made a mistake too." The Kennedy advisor and historian Schlesinger wrote that, as late as January 1971, Robert Kennedy was "the only major official in either Democratic administration [JFK's or LBJ's] who admitted publicly to being wrong about Vietnam."

And then he proceeded to tell people what he thought they should hear, not necessarily what they wanted to hear. At the University of Kansas, he talked about the "other Americans," black children in the Mississippi Delta, the barrenness of Indian reservations, the conditions of ghetto life. And what we are as a nation.

> The gross national product—if we should judge America by that—
> counts air pollution and cigarette advertising, and ambulances to
> clear our highways of carnage. It counts special locks for our doors
> and the jails for those who break them. It counts the destruction
> of our redwoods and the loss of our natural wonder in chaotic
> sprawl. It counts napalm and the cost of a nuclear warhead . . . and
> the television programs that glorify violence in order to sell toys
> to our children. Yet the gross national product does not allow for
> the health of our children, the quality of their education, or the
> joy of their play. It does not include the beauty of our poetry or
> the strength of our marriages; the intelligence of our public debate
> or the integrity of our public officials. It measures neither our wit
> nor our courage . . . It measures everything, in short, except that

which makes life worthwhile. And it can tell us everything about America except why we are proud that we are Americans.

In a very real sense, this was his platform, a summary of what he stood for, the issues he would tackle, a blueprint for his presidency.

Woven through his speeches in Indiana and Kansas, in the Deep South and California, in Nebraska and South Dakota were exhortations to end the war, to stop the violence in our cities, to address the disease of enervating poverty—regardless of the audience. He questioned student draft deferments—while speaking to students. He talked about poverty—while speaking to well-fed service clubs in Middle America. Sometimes he was booed for his positions; other times applauded for his political courage. What bothered Kennedy was that the affluent never saw nor wanted to see the crushing poverty in America's cities, in its remote rural areas, and on its Indian reservations. What bothered him most was that working-class kids, many of them young African Americans from the inner cities, fought in Vietnam while more affluent, overwhelmingly white youth were in college. Speaking to students in Omaha, Kennedy demanded, "How many black faces do you see here? The fact is if you look at any regiment or division of paratroopers in Vietnam, forty-five percent of them are black. How can you accept this?"

And his message was hopeful and idealistic. In March, about a week after he announced, he told a crowd, "Together we can make ourselves a nation that spends more on books than on bombs, more on hospitals than the terrible tools of war, more on decent housing than military aircraft."

Most of all, Kennedy thought a campaign like this was morally right and strategically correct. David Murray of the *Chicago Sun-Times* wrote: "He went yammering around Indiana about the poor whites of Appalachia and the starving Indians who committed suicide on the reservations and the jobless Negroes in the distant great cities, and half the Hoosiers didn't have any idea what he was talking about; but he plodded ahead stubbornly, making them listen, maybe even making some of them care, by the sheer power of his own caring. Indiana people are not generous nor sympathetic; they are hard . . . but he must have touched something in them, pushed a button somewhere."

But Bobby Kennedy, in his twelve-week presidential run, had something else.

The three Kennedy brothers attended Harvard and, like so many progressives that this book has described, served in the United States armed forces: the oldest brother, Joseph, was killed in combat in Europe in 1944 during World War II. Jack was badly injured as the commander of PT 109 in the Pacific during World War II; Bobby served in the United States Naval Reserve; and Ted joined the United States Army right after high school before starting college. They were all successful political figures—Jack, who became president of the United States; Bobby, who represented our nation's most populous and important state at the time and was probably the twentieth century's most exciting candidate; and Ted, probably the greatest senator in American history, were all relatively late bloomers, achieving real success mostly after their fortieth birthdays. In their twenties and thirties, none of the three seemed especially likable or serious-minded or empathetic, even though all reached the United States Senate while in their thirties.

Jack, at best only an average senator, came into his own as a presidential candidate when he was forty-two. Bobby did not become his own man until he came out of his brother's shadow to tackle the issues of poverty when he was in his late thirties. For Ted, it was his abysmal run for the White House in 1980 that caused him to turn his full attention to the United States Senate. He was forty-eight at the time and had served in the upper chamber for almost eighteen years.

The presidential candidate Robert F. Kennedy was an idealist, to be sure. But few would have called him that before his Senate years. During my first campaign for the Senate in 2006, I was to appear on *Meet the Press* with my Republican opponent, Senator Mike DeWine. After arriving at the NBC studio in Northwest Washington, Connie and I went immediately to the greenroom to make last preparations for the debate. The moderator, Tim Russert, came to talk for a moment—about the debate, about the Senate race in Ohio, and about my best friend and his John Carroll University classmate, John Kleshinski—and then left to go to another greenroom to visit with my opponent. A few minutes later, after I had walked into the studio itself and sat down on the famous

Meet the Press set, Russert was already in his chair. He said to me, "You know this is the same studio where Kennedy and Nixon debated. Bobby came in early, they tell me, and snuck back to turn up the thermostat." In their previous debate, Nixon had sweated profusely on national television while Kennedy had looked composed, and the television (but not the radio) audience mostly believed that JFK won the debate. Bobby was just trying to repeat the trick.

But Bobby the candidate was a different man. At no time did his idealism and pain and empathy shine more brightly than in Indianapolis on a spring evening in 1968. After LBJ announced his withdrawal from the race on March 31, Kennedy had turned his attention to the Indiana primary and to his two opponents, Eugene McCarthy and Hubert Humphrey. The future Congressman John Lewis—who was beaten up more times than perhaps any other civil rights activist, and believed that Kennedy was "the only political leader addressing the real issues"—had helped set up an event in one of Indianapolis's poorest neighborhoods.

Right before boarding his charter plane from Muncie to the state capital, Kennedy was informed that Martin Luther King, Jr., had been shot in Memphis. After the plane landed, he got the news that the civil rights leader was dead. According to the Kennedy biographer Arthur Schlesinger, Jr., Kennedy seemed to shrink back as though struck physically. He put his hands to his face and beseeched *Newsweek*'s John Lindsay, "Oh God. When is this violence going to stop?"

The Indianapolis police chief told him at the airport that he should cancel the rally. Indianapolis Mayor and future Senator Richard Lugar thought it dangerous for Kennedy and for the city for him to be there. Lugar told me many years later that he counseled the Kennedy staff to call it off. John Lewis, who accompanied Kennedy to Indianapolis, said he "knew we had to come." Kennedy sent his wife, Ethel, to the hotel, and then got in his car for the twenty-five-minute drive to the rally.

It was thirty-seven degrees and windy. The festive crowd of about a thousand, waiting for more than an hour, had not heard the terrible news. Kennedy climbed on a flatbed truck next to an outdoor basketball court, raised his hands, and asked for quiet. Lewis told me years later,

"He was measured. He spoke like someone teaching a class, sounded almost like a priest":

> I have some very sad news for all of you and that is that Martin Luther King was shot and killed tonight. Martin Luther King dedicated his life to love and to justice for his fellow human beings and he died because of that effort . . . For those of you who are black and are tempted to be filled with hatred and distrust at the injustice of such an act, against all white people, I can only say that I feel in my own heart the same kind of feeling. I had a member of my family killed, but he was killed by a white man . . . What we need in the United States is not division; what we need in the United States is not hatred; what we need in the United States is not violence or lawlessness; but love and wisdom, and compassion toward one another, and a feeling of justice toward those who still suffer within our country, whether they be white or they be black. So I shall ask you tonight to return home, to say a prayer for the family of Martin Luther King, that's true, but more importantly to say a prayer for our own country, which all of us love—a prayer for understanding and that compassion of which I spoke.

Violence and rioting engulfed more than one hundred American cities in the ensuing days. Thirty-nine people, most African Americans, were killed, and twenty-five hundred were injured. Some seventy-five thousand National Guard and federal troops were dispatched to our nation's urban areas. Only two major American cities, news reports recounted, escaped widespread violence that weekend. In Boston, after a night of sporadic looting, the singer James Brown—along with newly elected Mayor Kevin White—appealed to city residents to stay away from his concert at the Boston Garden and watch it on a specially arranged public television broadcast from their homes. According to Anthony Lukas in *Common Ground*, only two thousand people showed up at the Garden and watched Brown live, and listened to his words of reason in an arena that held fourteen thousand people. Peter Wolf of the J. Geils Band traveled through Boston's South End that night: "Every window seemed to be watching James Brown." And in Indianapolis, Kennedy's soothing words about Dr. King and his brother—also "killed by a white man"—helped to still a distraught and angry black community and calm the city.

Later that night at his Indianapolis hotel, Kennedy uttered wistfully to his aide Jeff Greenfield, "You know that Harvey Lee Oswald, whatever his name is, set something loose in this country."

Greenfield remembered that the first stories reported out of Dallas on November 22, 1963, had Oswald's first and middle name reversed. "That was the way he remembered it, because he obviously never took another look at it again."

The next day, Kennedy canceled all but one engagement, a speech at the City Club of Cleveland. In those days, the City Club was made up mostly of conservative white businessmen who loved their country and their community, but most of all wanted to protect and defend the status quo. The City Club of Cleveland "is a product of the Progressive Era, founded in 1912." The "Citadel of Free Speech" has attracted the most prominent international figures—artists and scientists, economists and philosophers, and almost every U.S. president since Franklin Delano Roosevelt. But speakers must abide by one inviolate rule, no matter their title or station in life. No exceptions. No matter how important, no matter the circumstances, every speaker must answer questions from the Cleveland audience after the speech.

In Cleveland that day, less than twenty-four hours after the assassination of Martin Luther King, Kennedy delivered his "On the Mindless Menace of Violence" speech before 2,100 people. Speaking for only ten minutes, he reminded the audience of the terrible destruction that was afflicting the America of the late 1960s: the "violence of institutions," the "violence that afflicts the poor," the "slow destruction of a child by hunger," the "breaking of a man's spirit."

> This is a time of shame and sorrow. It is not a day for politics. I
> have saved this one opportunity to speak briefly to you about this
> mindless menace of violence in American which again stains our
> land and every one of our lives.

It is not the concern of any one race. The victims of the violence are black and white, rich and poor, young and old, famous and unknown. They are, most important of all, human beings whom other human beings loved and needed. No one—no matter where he lives or what he does—can be certain who will suffer from some senseless act of bloodshed. And yet it goes on and on.

Why? What has violence ever accomplished? What has it ever created? No martyr's cause has ever been stilled by his assassin's bullet.

No wrongs have ever been righted by riots and civil disorders. A sniper is only a coward, not a hero; and an uncontrolled, uncontrollable mob is only the voice of madness, not the voice of the people . . .

And, true to form, as he almost always did before and after the King assassination, he acquiesced and then he challenged: to white audiences, he denounced violence and then called for an end to injustice; to a black audience, he denounced injustice and then called for an end to violence.

For there is another kind of violence, slower but just as deadly, destructive as the shot or the bomb in the night. This is the violence of institutions; indifference and inaction and slow decay. This is the violence that afflicts the poor, that poisons relations between men because their skin has different colors. This is a slow destruction of a child by hunger, and schools without books and homes without heat in the winter.

This is the breaking of a man's spirit by denying him the chance to stand as a father and as a man among other men. And this too afflicts us all . . . When you teach a man to hate and fear his brother, when you teach that he is a lesser man because of his color or his beliefs or the policies he pursues, when you teach that those who differ from you threaten your freedom or your job or your family, then you also learn to confront others not as fellow citizens but as enemies—to be met not with cooperation but with conquest, to be subjugated and mastered.

After his tearful speech on that April day, an emotional Robert Francis Kennedy walked off the stage without answering questions. For the only time in the City Club's 107-year history, no City Club official tried to enforce the rule that every speaker answer questions.

Kennedy and his aide Greenfield flew back to Washington that afternoon; Kennedy went home to northern Virginia and Greenfield returned to the Capitol. "When I returned to the Hill," Greenfield recalled when I reached him at his Santa Barbara home in the spring of 2019, "I saw sandbags surrounding the Capitol and soldiers with machine guns. It was what you might expect in a third-world country after a coup, not at the United States Capitol." It was the first time federal troops had been ordered to the Capitol since the summer of 1932, when President Hoover ordered Douglas MacArthur to disperse the Bonus Army.

The last sixty days of Robert Kennedy's life took him on a frenetic chase for votes—to Nebraska and Indiana, to Oregon and South Dakota, and to California. He lost only once—in Oregon—the first time that a Kennedy ever lost an election. He brought together a coalition of white ethnics and African Americans, of Latinos and young voters, of peaceniks and union activists. The crowds were huge; the momentum was growing; the nomination looked to be his.

We know how it ended—right before midnight on June 4, 1968, in Los Angeles, after he won the California Democratic primary. Robert Francis Kennedy was assassinated.

But we did not know then what his life—and his death—would mean later. We had to wait forty years for another man in his forties, representing a large state in the United States Senate, to pull together a coalition of young people and African Americans, of Latinos and labor activists and progressives, to inspire us and give us hope.

In addition to his signature on Desk 88, Robert F. Kennedy affixed his name to one other Senate desk, number 24. Desk 24 was the only desk that Senator Barack Obama signed. Each of them served less than four years in the United States Senate.

THOUGHTS FROM DESK 88

F OR TWENTY-FIVE YEARS I had worked for universal health
care for our country. Now, with a new young president, we had
a chance.

It was a rare Saturday night session. More than ninety United States
senators were in their seats—itself an unusual occurrence—as the clerk
called the roll. I thought of all those who had sat at Desk 88 awaiting
this moment: Hugo Black, who wanted to help President Franklin Roosevelt improve health care as part of the Social Security Act; Glen Taylor
and Theodore Green, who worked with President Truman to set up a

national health care system; Albert Gore, Sr., and Abraham Ribicoff, who helped President Johnson enact Medicare for America's oldest citizens; Robert Kennedy and George McGovern, who worked to improve health care for America's youngest citizens. The first hurdles had been cleared almost four months earlier. In the spring, Senator Christopher Dodd—who was filling in for the ailing Edward Kennedy as chairman of the Health, Education, Labor and Pensions Committee—had asked Rhode Island Senator Sheldon Whitehouse and me to draft the language for the so-called public option that would supplement the broader bill's combination of state-run exchanges, subsidies, mandates, and regulations on private policies. The public option, conceived as an alternative to private insurance permitting anyone to enroll in a government-run plan akin to Medicaid, caught the public imagination almost immediately. To its progressive supporters, it would bring insurance costs down, provide competition where there was none, and keep the insurance companies honest. To conservative opponents, the public option was lumbering big government at its worst—resulting in a government takeover of our health care system; the public option was unfair competition for private insurance companies, they said. Standpatters never did explain, however, how a bloated bureaucratic government program—all government programs are, they insist—could outcompete the streamlined, uber-efficient private insurance industry and put them out of business.

We thought the public option was part of a proud American tradition. FDR had crusaded for public power, as a check on an alternative to private utilities that were gouging the public. "The liberty of democracy," the president said, "is not safe if the people tolerate the growth of private power to a point where it becomes stronger than their democratic state itself." FDR and the Democratic Congress set up the Tennessee Valley Authority, serving much of the same South where almost every senator today, mostly Republicans, are opposed to the public option in health care and seemingly most other government programs. And then came the Rural Electrification Administration, bringing electricity at affordable rates to small-town America, where investor-owned utilities showed little interest. As Adam Cohen of *The New York Times* wrote, "The whole New Deal was in a sense just a series of public options": the Farm Credit

Administration, the Federal Deposit Insurance Corporation. And of course, Social Security was "all public and no option."

At the White House in early June, more than a dozen Democratic senators weighed in on the public option. At the conclusion of the one-hour meeting, the president again emphasized the importance of moving forward in June and July, especially in the face of the large health insurance companies' intractable opposition to the health care law generally and the public option specifically. President Obama reiterated his support for the public option when he echoed "the point Sherrod made that the insurance companies are one step ahead of the sheriff."

On June 17, 2009, acting Chairman Dodd gaveled us to order. We were meeting in the Senate's most historic hearing room, the Senate Caucus Room in the Russell Senate Office Building. It was the scene of the *Titanic* hearings almost one hundred years ago, the Joseph McCarthy tribunal, the General Douglas MacArthur and Watergate proceedings, the Supreme Court nominee Clarence Thomas's confirmation hearings, and the site of John Kennedy's 1960 and Robert Kennedy's 1968 announcements for president.

What followed the rap of Chairman Dodd's gavel was government at its best: debate illuminating and passionate; ideas offered and rejected; amendments submitted and approved. Good ideas—coming from all parts of the country and from people in all walks of life—were brought to the committee and discussed.

In late 2007 my mother had told me about the Community Health Access Project (CHAP) in Mansfield, my hometown. A decade earlier, two physicians, Sarah and Mark Redding, a husband-and-wife team who had worked in the Public Health Service in Alaska, were alarmed by the terribly high incidence of low-birth-weight babies in the poorest sections of Mansfield and the surrounding rural areas. The rate of low-birth-weight babies was over 20 percent, more than three times the national average. A low-birth-weight baby costs our health care system tens of thousands of dollars in her first year; the baby often has significant health problems throughout childhood and frequently has some developmental disabilities for life; and of course that does not even count the human cost to the baby and to the family.

Community health workers—a newly licensed profession in many states but, in some sense, one of the oldest professions in the world, as it involves taking care of people—were hired to visit the homes of low-income pregnant women, encourage them to see a physician, and give counseling about nutrition, immunizations, and prenatal care. In Mansfield and in rural Richland and Knox Counties, in only a few short years, the percentage of low-birth-weight babies dropped almost to the national average.

My amendment—which was adopted in the HELP Committee and the House Energy and Commerce Committee and later became law—provided funds to public health departments, community health centers, free clinics, hospitals, and other nonprofits to set up CHAP-like programs. The savings in dollars to our health care system could be in the hundreds of millions of dollars. The humanitarian savings of course will be immeasurable.

In all, every one of the committee's twenty-three members introduced amendments, some four hundred in all; about half became part of the bill. More than 180 Republican-sponsored amendments passed, giving the legislation a distinct bipartisan flavor. The markup went for eleven days—longer than any committee markup in anyone's memory—often until late in the evening. We included the public option in our version of the bill, as did all three House committees that marked up the Affordable Care Act. But on the big questions—the role of government in our health care system, the treatment of workers, the establishment of consumer protections prohibiting insurers from excluding customers with a preexisting condition—the deep ideological difference between the parties carried the day. And on that, nothing much has changed.

We need to look no further than the 1965 passage of Medicare—the same charges of socialized medicine, the same overwhelming Republican resistance in the House of Representatives, the same insurance industry opposition, the same conservative attempts to derail the legislation. The John Birch Society of 1965 had bequeathed its extremism to the Tea Party of 2009—but with more funding . . . this time provided by billionaires. And the far right operatives and their billionaire sponsors had learned something over that half century: the John Birch Society failed to have great influence because it appeared as it was, a top-down wealthy interest group that connected only with the fringe elements of our society. The Tea Party was just as top down, just as wealthy, just as fringe in its politics as the John Birch Society. But it was built to look like a grassroots organization. Hence its influence.

Of course it became more than that. As the rumors spread about government takeover and illegal immigrants, partisan lines hardened. Not that there is anything funny about Republican dirty tricks used to try to defeat the health care bill, but Glenn Beck outdid himself on this one. The always angry and often confused Beck, on his radio show, railed against the coverage of PET scans; like birds flying off a telephone wire, Beck's obedient flock repeated and amplified his confusion. Our office was inundated by claims that our bill provided insurance for Rufus and Biscuit. To be clear, Mr. Beck and your followers: PET—positron emission tomography—is a medical imaging modality. To be fair, maybe Beck himself was joking, gaming his listeners. But the callers to my office were serious—and angry that their tax dollars were going to be spent on, shall we say, cats and dogs.

What began as strong ideological differences evolved into partisan winner-take-all political warfare. South Carolina Senator Jim DeMint sounded the Republican battle cry, "If we're able to stop Obama on this, it will be his Waterloo, it will break him." Both sides dug in.

Conservative appeals to fear accelerated in 2009 as President Obama tried to rally the nation in support of his health care initiative, "the most important thing you will ever do, and I will ever do, in our lives," he told a group of us at the White House in August 2009. Conservatives were trotting out the same old bromides, some that they had used effectively since Roosevelt and Truman—"socialized medicine," "government takeover of our health care," "bureaucrats standing between me and my doctor."

Much of the organized campaign against health insurance reform was aimed at the new president, and much of it was about race. One of the conservative favorites came from Glenn Beck—here he is again: "Barack Obama has a deep-seated hatred for white people."

The misinformation campaign was not confined to the president personally. The far right decided to employ one of politicians' favorite

American pastimes—scaring older people. But there was one problem: very little of the six-hundred-page bill directly affected Medicare and the elderly. Still, the former New York lieutenant governor and conservative commentator Betsy McCaughey came up with an idea: accuse the Democrats of creating death panels. Say that congressional liberals supported euthanasia. "Congress would make it mandatory, absolutely require, that every five years, people in Medicare have a required counseling session that will tell them how to end their life sooner," she told the talk show host and former Republican Senator Fred Thompson, who nodded knowingly, then pronounced it "the dirty little secret" of the Democratic bill.

And, like the echo chamber that it was, the words reverberated far and wide. The columnist Ellen Goodman wrote that the Fox News analyst Peter Johnson called it a "kind of our 2009 *Brave New World*." The abortion-clinic protestor Randall Terry said Democrats were trying to "kill Granny." And, always wanting to get out in front of her followers in order to lead them, the former Republican 2008 vice presidential candidate Sarah Palin posted on her Facebook page: "The America I know and love is not one in which my parents or my baby with Down Syndrome will have to stand in front of Obama's 'death panel' so his bureaucrats can decide, based on a subjective judgment of their level of productivity in society whether they are worthy of health care. Such a system is downright evil."

The GOP opposition tactics mostly worked, and the Democratic response mostly did not. Whether it is opposition to the "death panels" or "the death tax" or the claims that President Obama was a Muslim and born outside the United States, the truth did not much matter. Fox News, right-wing talk radio, *The Wall Street Journal* editorial page—all are always making the same arguments as Republican leadership in Washington. The Democrats have none of that; Fox, talk radio, and *The Wall Street Journal* will say that the liberal mainstream media sides with Democrats and progressives, but they know better.

And there was more. House Republican Leader John Boehner and Republican Policy Committee Chairman Thaddeus McCotter, an ultraconservative from Michigan, solemnly warned that the Democratic bill "may start us down a treacherous path toward government-encouraged euthanasia." Boehner, a Republican from Ohio, was well known in his early House days in the late 1980s and early 1990s as a win-at-any-cost partisan. At a meeting soon after Obama's inauguration, he instructed the top Republicans on House committees, "You're not legislators anymore. You are *guerrilla* warriors." Obama's health care bill "could create a slippery slope for a more permissive environment for euthanasia, mercy-killing, and physician-assisted suicide, because it does not clearly exclude counseling about the supposed benefits of killing oneself."

The only problem with these comments? Our legislation did none of these things. It provided Medicare coverage for senior citizens who want to visit their doctor to talk about a living will and to ask about end-of-life decisions, if they so choose. The language we used came from legislation sponsored by the Louisiana Republican physician Charles Boustany in the House of Representatives and the Georgia Republican Johnny Isakson in the Senate. AARP supported the bill. So did National Hospice and Palliative Care Organization, which helped to draft the legislative language.

I remember my first year in the House of Representatives in 1993. President Clinton and congressional Democrats were attempting to enact health care reform legislation. We heard the same angry response from conservatives about big government taking over our health care system. And the mail cascaded into my office. Several letters came from people complaining that a government takeover of the health care system would ruin what we already have. A lady from Wadsworth, Ohio, wrote: "I don't want big government taking over my health care. Keep the government away. I've been on Medicare for fourteen years and it works."

To many Americans, the market is all-knowing and infallible. Conservatives, Thomas Frank wrote in *One Market Under God*, "believe that markets are a far more democratic form of organization than democratically elected governments." In a system of "market populism," there are no experts, just "divinely inspired markets." Democratic government could not represent our democratic interests, only the market could. "The market, if we would only let it into our hearts and our workplaces, would look after us; would see that we were paid what we deserved; would give us kind-hearted bosses who listened, who recycled, who cared; would bring a democratic revolution to industry that we could only begin to imagine."

The incessant attacks on all things government—at least all things non–Defense Department government—do indeed have an impact. If airlines ran ads attacking one another's safety record, people would quit flying. If the fast-food industry warned of potential *E. coli* outbreaks in their competitors' restaurants, no one would eat at *any* of them.

Yet we know that Medicare is more efficient than private insurance, with administrative costs well under 5 percent. And we know that Medicare and Medicaid never deny care because of a preexisting condition. Yet conservative attacks against anything government made people distrustful of our efforts to reform the health care system.

On July 15 the HELP Committee, on a partisan vote, approved S 3200 13–10 with a public option. I pinched myself that I was there— in the Senate Caucus Room, on Senator Kennedy's committee, casting a vote on the most important bill of my professional life, legislation that I had helped to write.

Unfortunately, the other Senate legislative committee that wrote the health care bill was the Finance Committee, a committee more captive to health insurance interests than any in the Senate, with a chairman, Max Baucus of Montana, whom many Democrats simply did not trust to represent Democratic values. And the Finance Committee—in May, in June, in July, now in August—was not producing any legislation.

On August 4, his forty-eighth birthday, President Obama invited all the Democratic senators to the White House. Many of us were increasingly restless, anxious, bordering on angry. We knew the Finance Committee's slow walk violated every rule of politics we knew; it gave opponents, especially the nation's most powerful corporate interest groups, more time to exaggerate, distort, and outright lie. It exposed senators and representatives in Republican areas to an onslaught of lies and distortions. It illustrated why Lyndon Johnson was right when pushing Medicare through Congress in 1965: "Now look, I've just been re-elected by the overwhelming majority. And I just want to tell you that every day while I'm in office, I'm going to lose votes. I'm going to alienate somebody . . . We've got to get this legislation fast." Johnson wanted the bill out of committee, then to the floor as quickly as possible, then out of conference committee and to his desk so that the opposition could not organize. "For God's sakes, don't let dead cats stand on your porch . . .

"They stunk and they stunk and they stunk. When you get one of your bills out of that committee, you call that son of a bitch up before they can get their letters written."

AND NONE OF us could figure out the endgame, how this lethargic process would help us pass a good health care bill. As we entered August, and four of Congress's five committees—three in the House of Representatives, one in the Senate—had marked up their legislation, it was clear that the Finance Committee was a long way from completing its work. Several weeks earlier, Chairman Baucus from Montana, skipping over two more senior and more progressive members of his committee, had tapped Democrats Kent Conrad of North Dakota and Jeff Bingaman of New Mexico to join Republicans Charles Grassley of Iowa, Olympia Snowe of Maine, and Michael Enzi of Wyoming to negotiate a health care bill. Enzi and Grassley are very conservative, and most Senate Democrats—and overwhelming numbers of House Democrats—believed that the two Republicans had no intention of voting for health care reform that mainstream Democrats and the public could support. Why, the Democratic activists were asking, should these two extremely conservative, small-state senators get to write the health care bill? To most of us, it was clear that these six senators—representing states with a total of thirteen House members and about two-thirds the population of Ohio—were not coming to any agreement anytime soon. Many thought that the negotiations were set up to fail.

Most Senate Democrats figured out quickly that the Republicans were simply stalling. Mike Enzi, criticized by some Republican activists for even talking to the Democrats, acknowledged that the Gang of Six was all about delay. Then, in August, at a town hall in Iowa, Chuck Grassley said we "should not have a government program that determines if we're going to pull out the plug on Grandma." Baucus, to the outrage and consternation of many, invited Grassley back to the negotiating table like the prodigal son. Bad behavior in the United States Senate is rarely punished.

In August, during the congressional recess, the media focused not on the legislation passed by four House and Senate committees—that was already old news. Instead, reporters covered the negotiations among the Gang of Six. The mainstream media, assiduously and breathlessly, documented every utterance of bipartisanship by the Gang of Six. But most Democrats believed that the only way to get bipartisanship was to make further concessions to the insurance industry, then—next to the oil companies and the Koch brothers—the Republicans' most important and generous benefactor. Of course Republicans knew that delay was their best friend: to stop health care, to undercut the president, and to hurt the Democrats politically.

In August and September passions from all sides intensified. Opponents of health reform, led by former Texas Republican Congressman Dick Armey and FreedomWorks—funded mostly by the insurance interests, the Koch brothers, and their far-right billionaire allies—organized "tea parties," to protest "the government takeover of health care." Some members of Congress and some health care supporters in the audience were threatened physically. One angry opponent of health care reform yelled at a woman in a wheelchair, "Go back to Russia." Most of us in the House and Senate had security assigned to us before and during our town hall meetings. Several death threats were aimed my way.

Some Tea Party protestors drew swastikas on posters of the president, complete with a Hitler-like mustache, claiming the Democrats wanted to end freedom as we know it and set up a dictatorship in our beloved country. Republican House Minority Leader John Boehner predicted "less freedom for the American people . . . We're going to have a real fight for how much freedom we're going to have left in America." They shouted that the "czars" in the White House—a common term for top presidential advisors of both parties for more than a decade—were leading us to Russian Communism, although my recollection is that the 1917 Russian Revolution was mostly about the overthrow of the czarist · government.

Rank-and-file Tea Partiers, disproportionately white and elderly, favored the existing retirement programs, as long as the benefits went to people like them. But to Tea Party leaders and funders, disconnected as they were from the working class and middle-class activists, an ideal twenty-first-century America would have no Medicare, no Social Security. I have heard those leaders and funders say this dozens of times. It would mean no interstate highways or publicly funded airports; perhaps they might want to substitute a fully privatized transportation system, which no country in the world has ever been able to accomplish. It would mean a society without consumer protections against unsafe products, no Food and Drug Administration and pure food laws, no prohibitions on child labor and unsafe working conditions, and surely no progressive tax system where the wealthy pay more because they can afford it. The Koch brothers, and their lobbyist allies like Dick Armey, saw a libertarian America with no public safety net for the old, the infirm, the disabled, and the very young.

It makes me think that Tea Party leaders, and the activists whom they often fooled, do not much like America the way we are.

THE FOUNDER OF the modern Democratic Party, Franklin Roosevelt, saw freedom in a very different light. Freedom was not defined by the absence of government, but by the Four Freedoms. In his January 1941 State of the Union address to Congress, the nation's thirty-second chief executive outlined the four freedoms that "everyone in the world" should enjoy: freedom of speech and expression, freedom of religion, freedom from want, and freedom from fear. A government that works to create a society with those freedoms could not abandon its people. That is why Roosevelt helped to establish Social Security and collective bargaining, public works and public health programs, the minimum wage and the Tennessee Valley Authority.

As Republicans delayed day after slow-moving day, Democratic Majority Leader Harry Reid had had enough. He made a decision to keep the Senate in session pretty much every day until Christmas. Only a few times since 1861 had the Senate convened on a Sunday, but Reid wanted the country—and his Republican colleagues—to know that he meant business, that he would do whatever it took to pass real health care reform. During the first couple of weeks of December, Reid, Democratic leadership, and several of the rest of us were trying to round up the sixty votes needed to break a filibuster.

More and more Democrats, especially in the House, where dozens of members in evenly divided districts faced tough elections, were growing uneasy with health care reform. In early November, Bill Clinton, who learned painful lessons about health care battles fifteen years earlier, came to our caucus lunch to reassure us of the importance of passing health care reform. "The American people are optimistic," he told us. "The ratings of Congress and the president will go up the day Obama signs the bill." And all of you will get the political benefits when "health care is off the table" and you can move on to jobs and the economy.

In late November President Obama visited our caucus. "I promise you that—ten years, twenty years, thirty years from now—you will be proud of what you did; that will be your legacy . . . If we fail, you are all going to be featured in an ad with me—like it or not—and you'll be standing alongside a weakened president." He concluded with a tepid pitch for cloture, the resolution requiring sixty votes that would head off any filibuster and move the bill along; many of us were frustrated by the perceived reluctance of the White House to engage more forcefully, maybe even more threateningly, with recalcitrant senators. Progressive Radio's Bill Press opined, "Barack Obama should act more like Lyndon Johnson and less like Mahatma Gandhi."

It was becoming clearer that four Democrats were not going to vote for cloture if the bill contained a public option, or anything resembling a government plan. If we wanted a bill, and even though progressives had compromised far too much already, and even though the caucus was overwhelmingly supportive of the public option, we simply could not get the votes of Joe Lieberman, Blanche Lincoln, Mary Landrieu, and Ben Nelson. Initially, Nelson seemed the most problematic, several times telling the media that he could not support any public plan of any kind. Interestingly, as former President Bill Clinton told me in Toledo a few weeks later, Nebraska is the "only state in the United States where literally everyone pays their electric bills" to a public entity. Nebraska was the home of Senator George Norris, father of the Tennessee Valley Authority.

The majority leader asked ten of us—five progressives (Russ Feingold, Tom Harkin, Jay Rockefeller, Chuck Schumer, and me) and five moderates/conservatives (Joe Lieberman, Landrieu, Lincoln, Nelson of Nebraska, and Mark Pryor)—to work out a compromise on the public option. When Lieberman declined to come to the negotiations, Reid appointed Delaware's Tom Carper.

What could possibly be enough for us to give up one of the central elements of our bill? At the beginning of the meetings, we were not at all sure. But as Friday's hours of negotiations spilled into Saturday's and Sunday's, we thought we could work out an agreement. What united us as Democrats was that we all—to varying degrees—believe in government as a force for good.

A decade earlier, I had been part of a legislative effort with President Clinton, Senator Patrick Moynihan, Senator Kennedy, and Congressman Pete Stark to offer a Medicare buy-in plan. At the age of fifty-five, Americans without insurance could join Medicare by paying a higher-than-normal but affordable premium. We were unable to get congressional Republicans to even explore the idea. Now, Leader Reid asked me to introduce into the negotiations a Medicare buy-in for people who were fifty-five to sixty-four. I told our negotiating group that progressives would be willing to give up a public option that could cover everyone in exchange for a national not-for-profit alternative for those fifty-five and over. We knew that Lieberman, who sent staff to the meeting, had told Reid that he liked the idea of a Medicare buy-in. And he had campaigned in support of a strong Medicare buy-in nine years earlier, when he was the Democrats' vice presidential nominee with Al Gore. By Tuesday, with Nelson mildly supportive and Landrieu and Lincoln on board, we had a deal.

At least we thought we did. Five days later, Lieberman—with no Congressional Budget Office estimate of whether our option would cost taxpayers money and with his facts wrong—went on *Face the Nation* and announced, "You've got to take out the Medicare buy-in." He asserted that "it will add taxpayer costs." No, it wouldn't. "It will add to the deficit." Not true. "It will add to our debt in the future." Wrong again. We had written the compromise so that it would be revenue neutral. And it was a separate, segregated fund, different from the Medicare trust fund.

Lieberman said his opposition was "a matter of conscience," although he had supported a Medicare buy-in only three months before, and told the leader that he could probably support it. It was hard for many of us to accept that opposing a revenue-neutral program to allow fifty-nine-year-olds with a preexisting condition or a sixty-two-year-old who lost her job and her insurance could be a matter of conscience. *The New York Times* editorialized that the Connecticut senator "has taken more than $1 million from the [insurance] industry over his Senate career. In his 2006 re-election campaign, he ranked second in the Senate in contributions from the industry. He doesn't seem to have forgotten that." He did represent Hartford, after all.

I have known Joe Lieberman for a long time. While a senior in college, I took a seminar on state and local politics with the then state senator, who was in those days a young progressive representing a mostly university district. Years later, after voting for the Iraq War and supporting a Republican for president against the first African American Democratic nominee, Lieberman continued his journey down the road to conservative, special-interest politics when he returned to the Senate as a private citizen to sit with and introduce Betsy DeVos and Neil Gorsuch at their confirmation hearings for secretary of education and for the United States Supreme Court. His support for the two far-right Trump nominees brought not one Democratic vote to President Trump's side. He is now a registered lobbyist for the Chinese telecommunications giant ZTE Corporation.

President Obama had asked the Senate to vote on the health care bill before Christmas. We thought we were going to make that deadline, until Lieberman announced his opposition to the Medicare buy-in. The slow walk of the Gang of Six had, in the words of the columnist E. J. Dionne, given Joe Lieberman "near dictatorial powers." And progressives knew that the bill in its present form—with an excise tax on high-quality health plans, with no public option, with no Medicare buy-in—was exactly what Baucus had wanted all along.

A few days before Christmas, at the Executive Office Building—
a few feet from the White House—the president spoke to the Senate
Democrats again: "Everybody's poll numbers are down; Republicans' are
lower than ours. History will vindicate us; the politics will catch up . . .
Seize the moment."

The Senate met twenty-five days in a row. Only once before, during
the terrifying opening months of the First World War in 1917, had the
Senate met that many days in a row. When we passed the bill on December 24, it was the first Christmas Eve voting session since the month after
the Kennedy assassination.

IT SHOULD NOT have been this difficult.

On the Sunday morning in December that Joe Lieberman killed the
Medicare buy-in by changing his mind, I was called into the majority
leader's office, expecting to meet alone with Harry Reid. I walked into
a room with Finance Chairman Baucus, the president's deputy chief of
staff, the majority leader, and HELP Chairman Dodd. In frustration—
largely because of Republican obstruction, underhandedness by a few
Democrats, and the vicious and personal attacks from health care opponents at home—Dodd turned to me and whispered, "We never could
have passed a fucking civil rights bill in this environment."

Then, unbelievably enough, it got worse.

For months and months, the Democrats had held together a frag-
ile and delicate coalition of sixty votes. *The Washington Post*'s E. J. Dionne
wrote that the Senate "acted as though it had unlimited time to pass health
care legislation and ignored how foolish its listless ways appear to normal
human beings. Like a bottle of milk kept out of the refrigerator too long,
the health bill went sour for voters who felt they never heard an adequate
explanation of what was in it."

The slow walk of the Gang of Six and the Finance Committee had
been especially risky because so many things can happen to a group of
sixty men and women whose average age is sixty-three: one senator could
change his mind or try to make an untoward deal; or an incapacitating

illness or accident could befall one of us; or the death of a senator in a state with a Republican governor who would appoint a Republican hostile to health care reform. Any one of those could derail the bill.

Or we could lose a special election in—gasp!—Massachusetts. In mid-January, voters went to the polls to elect a senator to replace Edward Kennedy, who had died the previous summer with his dream of comprehensive health care reform still unfulfilled. With a straight—and handsome—face, the Republican nominee, Scott Brown, labeled himself a populist. Populism, to many in the media, is more about style than substance. Scott Brown fit the role; after all, he wore a barn coat and drove around his state in a beat-up pickup truck. To Washington pundits, it did not matter that he sided with insurance companies in the health care debate and Wall Street on the bank tax issue and with the Chamber of Commerce on all things corporate; after all, they assured us, he looked like a populist is supposed to look.

A real populist believes that government should work to stabilize employment and avoid the huge income inequality that undermines democracy; she believes that the economy exists to serve the people, not the other way around. The people, real populists preach, need government on their side, to stand up against powerful forces—energy conglomerates, pharmaceutical firms, insurance companies. Populism was Franklin Roosevelt railing against "economic royalty" and welcoming their enmity, and Harry Truman standing up to "the gluttons of privilege." And "populist" should never be used to describe a politician who slashes programs for the poor while slashing taxes for the rich. Never.

The Democrats' loss on that night in Massachusetts was the loss of a sixtieth seat—and it decided the final shape of the health care bill. MSNBC's Howard Fineman explained what it meant this way: "Barack Obama gave his [2008] winnings to Max Baucus."

Progressives, of course, wanted more from this bill. As we were working to pass the Affordable Care Act, I visited a community center in Youngstown for a town hall. As we talked about Medicaid and high drug prices, a woman stood and spoke: "I am sixty-three years old. I have two jobs. And don't make a lot of money. Neither of those jobs gives me insurance. I just want to stay alive for a year and a half so I can get on Medicare." Nothing about retirement. Nothing about spending more time with grandchildren. Or taking a short vacation. Just getting to sixty-five so she could finally get decent health insurance, to lift that anxiety that weighs down so many people without insurance.

PRESIDENT OBAMA SIGNED the ACA on March 23, 2010. Since then Democrats have had to beat back unrelenting attacks from the Republican-insurance-companies-Koch-brothers-Chamber-of-Commerce machine. The House of Representatives passed what it called Repeal and Replace (although Republicans never told us what "Replace" actually meant) Obamacare more than fifty times: from the first vote on the first day of the first session of the Congress in January 2011, until the Senate defeated Repeal and Replace during a middle-of-the-night vote in 2017. The roll call began that July night at about 1:00 a.m. I will never forget the sight of one Republican senator after another, each with good health insurance compliments of American taxpayers, standing at his desk and voting to take insurance from tens of millions of Americans. I will never forget. Ever.

Now, nearly a decade after the passage of Obamacare—and in spite of unrelenting opposition from Republican governors, legislators, congressmen, and conservative media and billionaires—eight hundred thousand Ohioans have health insurance; an additional 120,000 young people have been included on their parents' health care plan; and 240,000 older Ohioans have saved more than $750 million on their prescription drugs, an average of $800 per Medicare beneficiary per year. Scores of Ohio seniors have benefited from free physicals and preventive screenings with no copays or deductibles; and all Ohioans have new consumer protections to stop health insurance companies from denying care and terminating health insurance policies.

We know what else we need to do: make Medicare available so that people ages fifty to sixty-four can choose it if they want. Provide a public option, a Medicaid look-alike so that people can choose between public and private plans; the competition from the public plan will surely bring private insurance prices down. Strengthen consumer protections so that insurance companies cannot deny coverage to people with a preexisting condition.

And stop big drug companies' price gouging. Order the federal government to negotiate drug prices with pharmaceutical firms in the same way that the Veterans Administration does now on behalf of seven million veterans. Allow American wholesalers to buy legal drugs from other countries where prices are considerably cheaper. Stop the tax subsidies for drug company advertising.

But all of that would have to wait for another day. History tells us that even the greatest victories do not come all at once, that small victories can lead to larger ones. Over the years, landmark legislation, especially social welfare reforms like Medicare and Social Security, often falls immediately short of expectation. But as the years go by, subsequent congresses and presidents improve them. When it was first adopted, Social Security in the 1930s had glaring gaps in coverage, especially for large numbers of African Americans, and it has seen improvements every decade or so since.

"No reform," Edward Kennedy wrote in *True Compass*, his autobiography that was published a few weeks after his death in 2009, "is ever truly complete. We must constantly keep moving forward, seeking ways to create that more perfect union." He could have written that about any progressive victory in the last one hundred years.

8.

George McGovern

FEEDING THE HUNGRY

SERVED IN THE UNITED STATES SENATE 1963–1981

*Virtually every step forward in our history has been a liberal
initiative taken over conservative opposition: civil rights, Social
Security, Medicare, rural electrification, the establishment of a
minimum wage, collective bargaining, the Pure Food and Drug
Act, and federal aid to education, including the land-grant colleges.*

—Senator George McGovern of South Dakota

THE CONSERVATIVE BARRY GOLDWATER and the progressive George McGovern had two things in common, one of them perhaps meaningful only to my brothers and me. My father, quite improbably, voted for both of them for president. And each, in losing a landslide presidential election, brought tens of thousands of young people into the political process.

McGovern and I were sitting in the Capitol during my first year in the United States Senate. Not unlike other losing presidential candidates—and especially those who lost by almost record margins, as the South

Dakota senator had in 1972—recovery for George McGovern from humiliating political defeat came slowly. Years later, McGovern said, "I
thought the world had died." And the darkness from his loss lifted oh so
slowly. In the wake of Walter Mondale's 1984 landslide loss to Ronald
Reagan, the former vice president asked McGovern, "How long until I
get over this?" McGovern wistfully replied, "I'll let you know when I get
there."

As we talked that night, McGovern told me a story about another
losing candidate, Barry Goldwater. In 1971, as the senator from South
Dakota was considering an anti-war challenge to President Nixon's reelection, he sat down with Senator Goldwater—perhaps at his Desk 88—in
the Senate chamber. McGovern smiled as he recalled the good-humored
senator from Arizona.

After a lengthy conversation, McGovern inquired, "I've always wondered about something, Barry. Why did you come out in opposition to
Social Security in Florida right before the November election?"

He still remembers Goldwater's answer. "I was exhausted. I knew
I wasn't going to win. My staff—most of them less than half my age—
always aggressive, always with the certainty of youth, was always wanting
me to do more. One night in St. Petersburg, Florida, they insisted that I
do one last event. I resisted. They persisted. Finally I relented. So in the
speech that night, I came out against Social Security to get even with my
staff."

George McGovern knew what it was like to lose—for the Senate
in 1960 and again, as an incumbent senator, in 1980, and of course in his
presidential race in 1972. But he won more often, almost always against the
odds—for the House of Representatives in 1956 and 1958, for the United
States Senate in 1962, 1968, and 1974, and in a long string of Democratic
primaries where he outlasted sixteen other Democrats for president in
1972.

Losses aside, it was great consolation to him that so many young
Americans were brought into the political system because of the excitement around his presidential campaign. McGovern recounted to me at
the Capitol many years later, "Tip O'Neill told me, 'I can count a hundred
congressman who are here because of your 1972 campaign.'" I told him

that my first big campaign—after knocking on doors in Massapequa, New York, as a college freshman in support of Democratic Congressman Allard Lowenstein's losing reelection bid in 1970, and helping Henry Parker, New Haven's first African American mayoral candidate, in 1971 in his unsuccessful effort—was the 1972 McGovern crusade; I worked in New Hampshire, Massachusetts, Ohio, New Jersey, and New York in the primaries; and in Ohio, Iowa, and Connecticut in the general election. By Election Day 1972, I had convinced my "less sophisticated political" friends—and myself—that McGovern was actually going to win. He carried Massachusetts and the District of Columbia.

George McGovern—son of a fundamentalist Republican Methodist minister—was described over the course of his career as "old-fashioned and biblical," "pedantic," and "moralistic." He enlisted in World War II, serving his nation heroically as a bomber pilot in Europe, and was a principal subject of Stephen Ambrose's *The Wild Blue*. McGovern had ended up in the Army Air Corps almost by accident.

In the mostly empty Senate dining room on a warm spring day in 2009, McGovern told former Republican Senator John Warner, former Vice President Al Gore, and me the story. "Ten of us at Dakota Wesleyan had taken flying lessons to learn to fly little prop planes. After Pearl Harbor, we got in a car and drove to an enlistment office in Omaha. We saw, once we got there, two recruiting stations—one for Naval Air Corps, one Army Air Corps. The Army Air Corps recruiters were giving out coupons for a free lunch at a downtown cafeteria. We all signed up for the Army Air Corps. We were nineteen, twenty years old . . . and hungry. I never sold out so cheap." McGovern, who named his bomber *Dakota Queen* after his new bride, Eleanor, flew thirty-five missions in Europe, earning the Distinguished Flying Cross and Air Medal with three Oak Leaf Clusters.

World War II taught him much about his country. Almost six decades later he wrote:

> During my years as a combat pilot I read the huge, two-volume tome by Charles and Mary Beard entitled *The Rise of American Civilization*. Lying on an army cot in southern Italy, with only a

candle to light the page, I more than once was still reading when
the call came at 4 a.m. for me to fly another bombing mission
over Nazi Germany. Reading helped take my mind away from
the other pilots and crews who had died. It was also a way to
discover, in some sixteen hundred pages, what America was all
about.

After the war, he graduated from Dakota Wesleyan and earned a
PhD in history and government from Northwestern University. Like
millions of others returning from World War II, he used the GI Bill to
pay for his education. In those postwar years, people knew that government could be a positive force in their lives, and for their country. The GI
Bill provided the opportunity to go to college for millions of Americans
who had served their country. Other veterans chose to buy a farm or start
a business with government-guaranteed, low-interest loans—all together
bringing great prosperity to the nation for decades.

But for black soldiers returning home from World War II, the situation was very different. While we may like to think that Roosevelt had
wanted to create the first major social legislation that did not discriminate
on the basis of race, and the GI Bill was race-neutral on its face, it did not
play out that way. Mississippi Democrat John Elliott Rankin, perhaps
the most virulent racist in Mississippi's segregationist House delegation,
demanded that the bill allow local control and states' rights, which gave
counselors at local VA centers the ability to deny loans, to stonewall job
placements, to push qualified black veterans into trade schools instead
of two-year and four-year colleges. Almost 30 percent of white veterans
went to college on the GI Bill; only 12 percent of African American veterans did. And of course job discrimination and housing discrimination
made it worse, making it so much harder for African American citizens
to build generational wealth.

When I visited Mayor Stephen J. Wukela's law office in Florence,
South Carolina, in the winter of 2019, an African American minister
told me, "Jim Crow may be dead, but it isn't buried yet." Another pastor
retorted, "It's not even dead yet." That is part of the legacy of the housing,
education, and job discrimination that the GI Bill failed to correct.

While in Chicago, McGovern was very active—along with other young, idealistic students and professors—in the 1948 campaign of the progressive presidential candidate Henry Wallace. But by Election Day, disturbed by Wallace's alleged ties to Communists, McGovern did not even bother to vote. Throughout his career, he rarely spoke of his interest in and support of Wallace.

After earning his doctorate, he and his wife, Eleanor, settled with their young family in Mitchell, South Dakota, where George became a professor at his alma mater. Although he had been raised a Republican, "it was my study of history that convinced me that the Democratic Party was more on the side of the average American."

It was never easy for George McGovern or any Democrat to win elections in South Dakota. South Dakota has always been one of the most Republican states in America; in 1940 and 1944, it voted against FDR and the New Deal by the highest percentage of any of the forty-eight states. At the time of McGovern's presidential run, South Dakota had fewer unions than any other state in the nation. It was a state where, in the words of William Greider of *The Washington Post* in 1972, "virulent anti-Communism, not peace, normally won elections."

After the 1952 Eisenhower landslide, the South Dakota Democratic Party, for all intents and purposes, had ceased to exist. The November election had produced just two Democrats in the seventy-five-member South Dakota House of Representatives and not a single one in the thirty-five-seat South Dakota Senate. Since South Dakota had become a state in 1889, Republicans had won fully 90 percent of all state elections.

In 1953, the young professor—just thirty years old—quit his job and took to the road. Imagine the mountain he had to climb: building a Democratic Party in a state with Republicans holding a 73–2 majority in the House and a 35–0 margin in the Senate. Traveling town-to-town, even door-to-door, signing up Democrats and putting their names and important information in a card file, McGovern almost single-handedly built the South Dakota Democratic Party. He filled precinct committee slots, persuaded community leaders to serve as Democratic county chairmen, and recruited candidates for local offices and for the state legislature. He pleaded with and convinced a number of Republicans to help him build the Democratic Party, because the state would be stronger, he asserted, with a viable two-party system. He raised money to operate the party and to pay his own salary, persuading dozens and dozens of South Dakotans to contribute ten dollars a month.

By 1956 he was ready. He had 42,000 names on cards—volunteers, contributors, supporters—an extraordinary number before the days of the internet in a state with fewer than 670,000 people. And he now had an organization in place to launch his long-shot candidacy against the four-term Republican incumbent Congressman Harold Lovre. South Dakota in those days had two House members. Traveling the district—listening and talking—taught him much about South Dakota and its people. And he changed something about himself. He told *Life* magazine years later, "I thought my liberal ideas would be less frightening in such a conservative state if I talked directly in a measured, restrained way. I think that has permanently slowed down my style of speech."

He won that race by ten thousand votes, and was reelected handily against a former South Dakota governor two years later, in 1958. Even though South Dakota had elected only two Democratic senators in its history, his wife, Eleanor, urged him to run for the Senate in 1960: "Anything was better than campaigning for re-election every two years, living with one foot in South Dakota and the other in Washington with a preoccupied husband and five growing children who had no idea where they belonged."

McGovern decided to challenge two-term Republican Senator Karl Mundt, who had not faced significant Democratic opposition in either of his two races for the Senate. To McGovern, this race was an ideological crusade, a battle between good and evil, a look to the future or a return to the dark days of McCarthyism. And McGovern was ready to suit up. He generally saw politics, as his biographer Robert Sam Anson said, "in moral, almost apocalyptic terms; later Vietnam would be that way for him." Besides, as McGovern said later about Mundt, "I hated his guts."

Mundt too saw it as a battle between good and evil; he saw the rise and fall of Joseph McCarthy up close, and he believed that McCarthy was right in facing down Communism and doing whatever it took to win.

•

If a candidate sees himself as the only thing standing in the way of evil, he will do anything to block it. And Mundt did.

As an ally of McCarthy—who had died less than three years earlier—and as a student of McCarthyism, Mundt knew what would work in South Dakota. He labeled Hubert H. Humphrey "McGovern's political godfather." He attacked the war hero McGovern's "soft handling of Communists" and railed against his "kinship with the old familiar types of CIO-PAC candidates." He enlisted the assistance of the always eager FBI Director J. Edgar Hoover, who intoned: "In my own humble opinion, these fearless men, knowing of the scorn and abuse that would be heaped on them by the Communists, pseudoliberals, and others of like ilk, have constantly risen above personal consideration to strike out whenever possible against the treacherous enemy. The Communists, both here and abroad, have long felt the heel of Senator Karl Mundt."

And, right out of the McCarthy playbook, Mundt fabricated the very public endorsement of McGovern by Dave Beck, the corrupt president of the Teamsters. With no shame and much irony, Beck was paying a debt to Mundt for diverting Senate labor investigators from Beck and the Teamsters to "the socialist" Walter Reuther and the United Auto Workers. For good measure, Beck was able to exact revenge on McGovern for the congressman's harsh attacks on Teamster corruption on the House floor. And icing on the cake: Mundt ran ads saying "Hoover endorses Mundt; Beck endorses McGovern."

But McGovern was hardly innocent in the campaign either. Watching Mundt up close—as a professor and two-term congressman—his contempt and enmity for Mundt led him down a path that he later regretted. And of course that disdain and contempt only grew during the course of an increasingly bitter and rancorous campaign.

The two debates between the skillful sixty-year-old president of the National Forensic League and the thirty-eight-year-old winner of the five-state best debater award in college illustrated the sharp differences between the two men. But the outcome was most influenced in the last couple of weeks by attacks on Senator John Kennedy's inexperience and his Roman Catholicism that linked McGovern to the national Democrats.

In the end, Nixon won South Dakota with 58 percent of the vote, and

Mundt edged out McGovern by some fifteen thousand votes. Although most analysts believed McGovern lost because of the presence of the not very popular (in South Dakota) John F. Kennedy on the ballot, McGovern acknowledged later that he was too negative in that race, and could have run a better campaign. Kennedy himself said that he thought he cost McGovern the race. A dozen years later, McGovern acknowledged his own responsibility for the defeat: "I hated [Mundt] so much I lost my sense of balance. I was too negative. I made some careless charges. When the media in the state turned against me, I got kind of rattled. I got on the defensive. I started explaining and answering things I should have ignored."

Soon after the 1960 election, as McGovern's term in the House of Representatives was ending, President Kennedy appointed him the director of the Food for Peace Program. The White House looked to McGovern to enhance American stature in the developing world, understanding that food was a very effective weapon against Communism; helping the poor in the poorest nations might turn those nations toward the United States. "In the Cold War, our grain elevators are more powerful than the mightiest nuclear-tipped missile," McGovern emphasized.

After his trip to South Asia in the early days of his tenure at Food for Peace, McGovern and his staff stopped in Rome for meetings. While there, they had an audience with John XXIII, "the greatest pope in my lifetime," McGovern told me forty-eight years later. At the end of their thirty-minute discussion at the Vatican, the pontiff clasped McGovern's hand and told him, "When you meet your Maker and he asks you, 'Did you feed the hungry?' you can say yes."

Food for Peace sparked McGovern's lifelong interest in world hunger issues. His burning interest, though, was elective politics, where he thought he could make the greatest impact. He returned to South Dakota in 1962—he had never really left—to run for the other South Dakota Senate seat, held by two-term Senator Francis H. Case. Case unexpectedly died in June 1962, and the governor appointed Lieutenant Governor Joseph H. Bottum to the United States Senate in July.

McGovern edged out Bottum by a scant 597 votes. His subsequent two elections, in 1968 and 1974, were easier, in large part because, as polls consistently showed, the voters trusted him. His high school debate coach, according to his biographer Anson, said, "George's colorfulness was his colorlessness." The voters saw a man-of-the people sort of populism, a which-side-are-you-on brand of humanitarianism, a you-and-I-against-the-big-guys kind of progressive politics. It was a philosophy that worked in all times and in all regions of the country: for Hugo Black in the 1920s and 1930s in the South; for George McGovern in the 1960s and 1970s in the Great Plains states; and, dare I say, for me in the industrial Midwest in 2006 and 2012 and 2018. It is also a governing philosophy that works for the middle class and the less privileged. That governing philosophy never means partisanship for partisanship's sake; nor does it mean never working with people with whom you disagree. It does mean, simply, respecting the dignity of work and fighting for those people who need help. Period.

During his first two years in the United States Senate, from his perch on the Senate Agriculture Committee, the new senator from South Dakota teamed up with Republican Representative Bob Dole and Democratic Senator Hubert Humphrey to enact legislation establishing the food stamp program. As they pondered the gargantuan task of the federal distribution of food to the nation's hungry citizens in rural and urban areas alike, something more sensible occurred to them. Why should the government, they asked themselves, try to distribute food to every corner of the nation when a very efficient system—producers, wholesalers, and grocery stores—is already in place? Logically, the food stamp program was set up to allow low-income families to buy reduced-price food at their local stores.

As early as September 1963—before any other member of the Senate, before the assassination of South Vietnam's Ngo Dinh Diem, and while Attorney General Robert Kennedy was speaking out in support of the Vietnam War—McGovern warned of a quagmire in Vietnam and proposed an amendment to cut $2 billion in military procurement. "[It] is a policy of moral debacle and political defeat . . . The contest with international Communism cannot be won in the military arena . . . The failure of our Vietnam policy should be a signal for every one of us in this chamber to reexamine the roots of that policy."

Already, in that speech—which Idaho Senator Frank Church said may have been "the most important address of this session"—McGovern laid out the role that the United States should play in the world. In only his ninth month in the United States Senate, the World War II hero explained that diplomacy and engagement—not always military action—would best serve American interests. "I submit that America will exert a far greater impact for peace and freedom in Asia and elsewhere if we rely less on armaments and more on the economic, political, and moral sources of our strength."

From his work at Food for Peace under President Kennedy to his Senate opposition to the Vietnam War, from his efforts on behalf of America's hungry to his cooperation with former Republican Senator Bob Dole on the international school feeding program—that philosophy informed George McGovern's life.

Although his opposition to the war in Vietnam was a bit uneven in the beginning—he voted for the Gulf of Tonkin resolution in 1964—his courage was evident throughout the 1960s as he spoke out publicly and privately, even as he represented such a conservative state.

By 1967 the future congressman Allard Lowenstein approached McGovern, as he also approached Robert Kennedy and later Eugene McCarthy, to challenge President Lyndon Johnson in the Democratic primary as an anti-war candidate. McGovern declined, choosing instead to seek reelection. After Robert Kennedy's assassination in early June 1968, McGovern—at the request of several in the Kennedy operation—mounted a late challenge to Vice President Humphrey. He announced his candidacy for president a mere eighteen days before the Democratic National Convention in Chicago, knowing full well that he would finish behind both Hubert Humphrey and Eugene McCarthy, but wishing to honor his martyred friend. "At least I have precluded the possibility of peaking too early," he remarked in his South Dakota twang.

His opposition to the war had intensified in the election year of 1968, as the country began to catch up with him. "How we can carry out an objective" of security and peace in Vietnam, the decorated World War II bomber pilot asked colleagues on the Senate floor less than three weeks after Robert Kennedy's assassination, "by dropping more bombs on that one little country than we dropped in all of World War II in the Pacific and on continental Europe escapes me completely. People talk about the blood bath that would follow in the event we decided to reduce our commitment in Vietnam and began to move out. I think that the blood bath is on with a vengeance today."

In October 1969—he had been reelected by a solid margin eleven months earlier even as Richard Nixon won a South Dakota landslide—he spoke at three war moratorium rallies on the same day; the next month he addressed the National Mobilization Committee to End the War, perhaps the largest anti–Vietnam War demonstration of the decade. In 1970 he teamed up with Republican Senator Mark Hatfield of Oregon to offer the Hatfield-McGovern Amendment to cut off military funds for the war.

Addressing his colleagues on September 1, 1970, before the vote, he said:

> Every senator in this chamber is partly responsible for sending
> fifty thousand young Americans to an early grave. This chamber
> reeks of blood. Every senator here is partly responsible for that
> human wreckage at Walter Reed and Bethesda Naval and all
> across our land—young men without legs, or arms, or genitals,
> or faces, or hopes . . . It does not take any courage at all for a
> congressman, or a senator, or a president to wrap himself in the
> flag and say we are staying in Vietnam, because it is not our blood
> that is being shed. But we are responsible for these young men
> and their lives and their hopes . . . So before we vote, let us ponder
> the admonition of Edmund Burke, the great parliamentarian of
> an earlier day: "A conscientious man would be cautious how he
> dealt in blood."

By the next year, during Richard Nixon's third year as president, McGovern pinned the war on the president, who had promised in the 1968 election that he had "a secret plan to end the war in Vietnam." "Fifteen thousand young Americans have been killed since Richard Nixon took office," McGovern told students in Wisconsin, "and their blood is on his hands."

McGovern's legislative efforts, while surely genuine, were probably undercut by his increasingly public plans in 1971 to seek the presidency the next year. A number of senators in both parties were reluctant to give him credit that would help his candidacy. And to some, McGovern's effectiveness as a senator on foreign policy was already in question: Majority Leader Mike Mansfield called him "a loner," according to the Congress Project, and the respected Michigan Democratic Senator Phil Hart, after whom the newest Senate office building is named, said McGovern was "not much of a traditional power within the Senate."

Almost no one, though, questioned his effectiveness on hunger issues. On May 10, 1968, in South Dakota, Robert Kennedy said of McGovern, in large part because of the South Dakotan's work to combat poverty, "Of all my colleagues in the United States Senate, the person who has the most feeling and does things in the most genuine way, without affecting his life, is George McGovern."

When George McGovern came to the Senate in 1963, he had seen poverty and hunger all over the world—in other countries. But it was a moment with his family, he told me decades later, that opened his eyes to the enervating poverty and debilitating hunger that afflicted millions of Americans. One night, he and his family were at home watching a documentary about hunger in the United States. A boy told the interviewer that he was ashamed to be hungry. McGovern said to his daughter, "It's not that boy who should be ashamed. I should be ashamed. I'm on the Agriculture Committee and I didn't even know about this."

In March 1969, McGovern, by then chairman of the Select Committee on Nutrition and Human Need, took the committee on a two-day fact-finding trip to Immokalee, a migrant farming community in southwestern Florida. Several senators in both parties made the trip: Bob Dole of Kansas, Walter Mondale of Minnesota, Marlow Cook of Kentucky, Allen Ellender of Louisiana, Jacob Javits of New York. To McGovern, it was always about hunger, never about partisanship. Vern Goetcheus, a minority party staff member, said, "[McGovern] has strived to maintain a bipartisan image for the committee . . . The success of the committee is due in part to that."

Gerald Cassidy, then a South Florida Migrant Legal Services lawyer and later counsel to the Select Committee in Washington, told me the story many years later. "Most of the workers, perhaps sixty percent, were African American; the rest were migrant workers from the McAllen, Texas, area. Many were afraid to talk to us because the crew leaders and the farmers would have thrown them off the farms," and they had nowhere else to go. The children were not enrolled in school. "McGovern was especially moved by the children and was very kind to them. He put his hand on the children's heads when he talked with them. We saw children who were full of worms and whose bellies were distended. Many hadn't eaten in who knows how long. George is a very quiet man, you know, but in his own quiet way he was very angry. The next day, when he chaired the hearing, he was tough on the farmers' representatives who made this happen and on the county officials who let this happen."

Back in Washington, McGovern said, "Most of the cattle and hogs in America are better fed and sheltered than the families we have visited." As more members of the Senate enlisted in the cause, McGovern was able to make significant strides in increasing the food stamp benefit, expanding the school lunch program, and enhancing other nutrition programs.

McGovern, with the help of several others on the committee, pushed a bill through Congress in 1970 that greatly expanded food stamp eligibility and the size of the program, providing free food stamps for families with very low incomes. And he learned a political lesson that served him the rest of his life. "As long as you talk about welfare, nobody will listen to you. But if you talk about hunger, then you can do something." His efforts led to the creation of the summer feeding program. He later led the charge to expand the school lunch program and, in the mid-1970s, created, along with Bob Dole and Hubert Humphrey, the Women, Infants, Children (WIC) nutrition program for pregnant women and young families. The first pilot opened in Kentucky in 1974; at the end of the year, it was operating in forty-five states. The next year, WIC became a full-fledged national program, along with the Summer Food Service Program.

Today, WIC serves seven million families who—without a doubt—have healthier children than they would without it.

Speaking to his colleagues on the Senate floor, McGovern summed up the importance of his work to alleviate hunger:

"Millions of children in the world, many of them right here in the United States, are doomed to half lives when they enter grade school because malnutrition in their first five years has impaired them for life either physically or mentally."

But most of all, McGovern was confident and hopeful. Again in the Senate chamber:

"The people who manage these lunch programs are serious and dedicated . . . They know and understand the importance of good nutrition for children and they know and understand how to go about providing this good nutrition . . . Our school lunch and milk programs are this nation's finest insurance of a strong, healthy, mentally alert generation of young Americans."

It was the Vietnam War, though, that catapulted George McGovern to national prominence: first, as a last-minute stand-in for his friend Robert F. Kennedy after the assassination in June 1968, when he made his eighteen-day run for the Democratic nomination for president that was never really within his reach. Then, for the next three years, he continued his campaign against the war.

By early 1972 he was more closely identified with opposition to the war than the front runners Hubert Humphrey and Ed Muskie, and of course than Henry "Scoop" Jackson and George Wallace, both of whom supported the war effort. Interestingly, as McGovern pointed out to me almost four decades later, many of those who most strenuously opposed the war had fought in World War II; some, like McGovern, were war heroes. Those who spoke out against the Vietnam War were often called "weak," or "appeasers," or "soft on Communism," and their patriotism was frequently questioned by those who had avoided military service. Those doves like McGovern knew the horrors of war and understood that the decision to undertake it should be made only in the most unavoidable of circumstances. In many cases, it was the hawks who had never served who romanticized war—in their day Stennis and Eastland, for example; then it was Cheney most prominently, and in our day, President Trump, whom my friend war hero Senator Tammy Duckworth called "Cadet Bone Spurs."

McGovern's 1972 presidential race was, in the end, nothing short of disastrous. His idealism and straight talk about the Vietnam War brought tens of thousands of young people into politics, many as first-time, newly enfranchised eighteen-, nineteen-, and twenty-year-old voters. But at least as many union members—especially the more conservative, over-whelmingly white and male members of the building trades unions—turned away. His string of brilliant primary victories as an insurgent candidate in large and small states alike against giants of the Democratic Party—Humphrey, Maine Democratic Senator Ed Muskie, and Wash-ington Senator Henry "Scoop" Jackson—alienated many mainstream Democratic regulars. Later, McGovern quipped, "I opened the doors of the Democratic Party, and twenty million people walked out."

As if the party divisions were not deep enough, three House Demo-crats, including future House Speaker Thomas Foley, illustrated—and reinforced—the unease many insiders felt about McGovern and his abil-ity to win. Right before the Democratic National Convention in Miami Beach—in a remarkably self-serving and self-fulfilling act—they sent out a questionnaire to all Democratic House members that said "George McGovern, if named the Democratic presidential nominee, will have an adverse effect on the continuance of the Democratic majority in the United States House of Representatives in the 1972 congressional elec-tion. Strongly agree, agree, not sure, disagree, strongly disagree." Of the 129 who responded, 79 agreed or strongly agreed.

Then came perhaps the most embarrassing series of events in the campaign. By summer, after he had pretty much secured the nomination, McGovern's chances to win the general election looked dismal. Several prominent Democrats—among them Edward Kennedy and Gaylord Nelson and perhaps his vanquished opponent Ed Muskie—turned down his offer to run for vice president. Running out of time and choices, he turned to a forty-two-year-old Missouri senator, Thomas Eagleton, who had served less than four years in the Senate, and about whom most people knew little. Soon after the convention, the nation learned that Eagleton, only a few years before, had been hospitalized three times for depression and had twice undergone electroshock treatment. McGovern said that he "was one thousand percent" behind Eagleton, only to succumb to pressure and dump him from the ticket almost immediately. McGovern was labeled weak, insincere, and spineless. McGovern's reputation never recovered.

McGovern later regretted how he handled the Eagleton affair. "I would have stood up for him if I had known more about mental illness at the time," he later told me. The stigma attached to mental illness in the early 1970s was far greater than today. And the South Dakota senator was troubled by his own daughter Terry's illness; at the time, she was seeing a psychiatrist who was treating her for depression and alcoholism. She later died, at the age of forty-five in Madison, Wisconsin, never able to overcome her illness.

McGovern's 1972 campaign and its message were hijacked. Playing to Middle America's fears about counterculture and Communism, Nixon dirty tricksters convinced the public that McGovern was the "Triple A candidate," the candidate of amnesty, acid, and abortion—draft dodging, drug taking, loose moral values. McGovern's amateurish campaign—brilliant in the primaries, but bumbling from the Democratic National Convention on—made it easier for the Committee to Re-Elect the President to shape McGovern's feckless image. Because of rancorous floor fights at the chaotic convention, even his masterful "Come Home, America" acceptance speech at the Democratic National Convention was bungled, delivered at 2:48 a.m. Eastern time, hours after most Americans had gone to bed.

It did not matter that McGovern was a war hero, that he was the straitlaced son of a minister, that he worked his way through college and graduate school, that he won elections in the most conservative of states, that he was married to the same woman for decades, that never a whiff of scandal wafted across his career. The Republicans, with a masterful campaign, convinced a majority of voters in forty-nine states that McGovern was reckless and weak, indecisive and unpatriotic, and far out of the American mainstream. Thus was born the "McGovern Democrat."

McGovern was slow to recover from the pain of his humiliating defeat. He returned to the Senate—dejected, unhappy, and diminished. He skipped the Nixon inauguration and was loudly critical—perhaps too loudly, for a defeated presidential candidate—of the reelected president's ethics and policies. He had difficulty settling back into his job. In March he tried to summon up some humor when he told the Gridiron Club, "Ever since I was a young man, I wanted to run for the presidency in the worst possible way—and I did."

Arizona Republican Barry Goldwater, a member of the exclusive club of senators who had lost presidential elections, may have helped the South Dakota senator recover from the humiliating loss. McGovern told a *Washington Post* writer, "Barry said to me, 'You and I got beat badly. Just imagine how awful it must have been for that son-of-a-bitch Nixon, getting so close but losing to Kennedy by a hundred thousand votes.'"

During the next eight years—he was reelected in 1974, a very good year for Democrats as the Republican Watergate scandal unfolded—McGovern may not have been as good a senator as he had been in his first decade. He looked out for his home state agriculture interests, worked for arms control and nuclear weapons reduction, and continued his efforts to eradicate international and domestic hunger. But, he said, "I've noticed one thing about myself as a legislator. Once an idea I've been working on becomes generally acceptable, I'm not nearly as interested in it. I'd rather move on and do some pioneering in another field. I'm afraid I get bored very easily."

McGovern knew he was in trouble as the 1980 election approached. American Embassy employees had been held hostage in Iran since November 1979, angering an increasingly frustrated American public. Ceding the Panama Canal to Panama had been highly controversial. While standing in line at a Sioux Falls supermarket, he told me three decades later, he saw two women standing in front of him paying for their groceries with food stamps, the program that no one in Washington had done more to expand than McGovern. Not having noticed that their senior senator was standing nearby, they were discussing the upcoming Senate race between McGovern and his Republican challenger, James Abdnor. With all the major problems in our economy, one woman said as she handed the clerk the food stamps, "I can't vote for McGovern. He's for too many of those giveaway programs."

Almost everything went wrong for the nation's Democrats that year. Former California Governor Ronald Reagan's landslide win over incumbent Democrat Jimmy Carter helped to bring down big-name Democrats all over the country: Ways and Means Chairman Al Ullman, a twelve-term Democrat from Oregon, and Majority Whip John Brademas, an eleven-term congressman from Indiana, were unceremoniously dumped. Much of an entire generation of Democratic senators was swept out: Washington State's Warren Magnuson after thirty-six years in the Senate; Idaho's Frank Church, who served twenty-four years; and Indiana's Birch Bayh, Wisconsin's Gaylord Nelson, and George McGovern, who each served eighteen years in the Senate.

At the age of fifty-eight, McGovern left elective office, but not public service. He set up an organization, Americans for Common Sense, "a citizens' counterforce to the New Right," lectured at American University, and then bought an inn in Connecticut, which he and Eleanor ran for a couple of years.

But even after he left office, McGovern's reputation as a big-government liberal stayed with him. His name was evoked when Republicans wanted to suggest weakness on national defense, or to decry wasteful government spending, or simply to discredit liberalism. Republicans were calling Michael Dukakis, the 1988 Democratic presidential nominee, "a McGovern Democrat," and Dukakis was responding that he was "not another George McGovern."

Then, eight years after his 1980 Senate defeat, George McGovern had had enough. In June 1988 he wrote an op-ed in *The Washington Post* entitled "This McGovern Democrat Business," a sort of open letter to his four young grandchildren and anyone else who had not been born before his 1972 landslide electoral defeat. Why, he asked, was his name being "used as a kind of swearword"?

It had all started in 1972. Since that campaign, "McGovern Democrat" had suggested weakness on national defense, wrongheaded economics, and a decline in family values. In the 1972 race against President

Richard M. Nixon, McGovern tried to make his campaign about four principles: "ending the war in Vietnam; warning the American people about the significance of Watergate and other forms of political corruption; reforming military spending and national priorities; and calling America home to its constitutional principles and founding ideals." He was convinced then, and for the rest of his life, that he was right—and that the public agreed with him on those principles. Nonetheless, in the early 1990s, the acerbic Newt Gingrich called President Clinton "a counterculture McGovernik," the suffix apparently suggesting something Soviet.

McGovern was rarely partisan for partisan's sake. But he understood that progress—and progressivism—are rarely reached by consensus. His reading of America's greatest historians, notably Charles Beard, told him that conflict—Innovators versus Conservators, in the words of Ralph Waldo Emerson—brought social change. Wealth and status rarely relinquished their privilege. "History is the long and tragic story of the fact that privileged groups seldom give up their privilege voluntarily," Martin Luther King, Jr., once said. Those on top hired legions of helpers—accountants, lawyers, lobbyists, and an occasional newspaper publisher and politician—to stay on top. That is why those in the privileged class—from editors of *The Washington Post* to well-fed Republican congressmen to comfortable businessmen—are so quick to levy the charge of class warfare against anyone who challenges the privileges of wealth.

Nonetheless, George McGovern believed that America's best days were yet to come. "We are on the verge," he wrote in *Harper's* in late 2002, "of the best period in human history." We have made incredible progress in health care and education, in science and energy and transportation, during the twentieth century. And Americans have always believed in "the essential goodness of man," that the conditions of our lives could be improved.

To his last days, McGovern fought for the principles he held dear. Perhaps no former senator worked so fervently to champion the cause of liberalism than did George McGovern. *Webster's Dictionary*, he tells us, defines liberalism as "a political philosophy based on belief in progress, the essential goodness of man, and the autonomy of the individual and standing for the protection of political and civil liberties." Unflinchingly, he wrote,

> Just about every educated person I encounter around the world is a liberal. Almost every working journalist, nurse, and flight attendant leans toward liberalism; nearly every teacher, scientist, clergyman, and child-care worker is a liberal. I can't remember the last time I met an illiberal professor of history, my old profession. How could anybody read history and not be a liberal?
>
> Virtually every step forward in our history has been a liberal initiative taken over conservative opposition: civil rights, Social Security, Medicare, rural electrification, the establishment of a minimum wage, collective bargaining, the Pure Food and Drug Act, and federal aid to education, including the land-grant colleges, . . . guaranteed bank deposits, the Federal Reserve, the Securities and Exchange Commission, the National Park Service, the National School Lunch Program, the Voting Rights Act, and the graduated income tax.

McGovern understood that much of what was best about America had been established by a progressive government—Medicare and safe drinking water laws, Head Start and medical research money provided by taxpayers. And he understood the conservatism that dominated the American political scene in the 1980s, the 1990s, and the first part of the twenty-first century. In his *Harper's* essay, McGovern said,

> Attempts to utilize the powers of government to improve the well-being of ordinary Americans have been shouted down in favor of policies serving only the commercial interests of the nation. In foreign policy the conservatives have tended to be isolationists or unilateralists, distrustful of dialogue with the other nations of the world, quick to resort to military force, and seemingly opposed to international assistance when it does not

involve sending guns and land mines to the odd Asian despot who claims to have converted to Christianity.

McGovern often said, from his earliest days, that he needed to have a passion in his life. In the late 1990s, McGovern put his passion back to work. President Clinton asked the former South Dakota senator to go to Rome as the United States ambassador to the United Nations Agencies for Food and Agriculture. McGovern's name and reputation—known all over the world for his efforts to combat domestic and international hunger—brought new status to the UN program. McGovern, reaching for the ostensibly elusive goal of feeding at least half the world's hungry people, wanted to apply what had worked in the United States to the world at large.

But the food program, which provides emergency food for some 120 million people each year, was falling far short.

Former Democratic Congressman Tony Hall, McGovern's successor in Rome, called it "the best job you could have." In my office in the Hart Office Building in Washington on a warm July day in 2009, he explained how the Western world had, for all intents and purposes, abandoned providing assistance to African agriculture some three decades earlier. By the 1990s, our assistance, more generous than any other country to be sure—we provide half the food aid, including in-kind services and dollars, in the United Nation's emergency assistance program—was all about emergency food, but rarely about agricultural development, leaving Africa in a continually desperate situation. There is no more food produced in Africa today, Hall said, than there was twenty-five years ago.

The former South Dakota senator returned home in 2001 and continued his efforts. When I asked McGovern in 2009 what his passion was now, in his ninth decade of life, he told me succinctly, "McGovern-Dole." In 1999 McGovern wrote an op-ed article in *The Washington Post* that Illinois Democratic Senator Richard Durbin read. A call from Durbin to McGovern, a meeting in the Senate dining room with Dole, who had also left the Senate by then, McGovern, Durbin, Indiana's Richard Lugar, and Agriculture Secretary Dan Glickman, and the George

McGovern–Robert Dole International Food for Education and Child Nutrition Program was born. Pushed in the House by Representative James McGovern (no relation to the former senator), McGovern-Dole aims to provide every boy and girl in the world with a nutritious school lunch. Begun in 2001 as a two-year pilot program, McGovern-Dole provides at least one meal per day for children in dozens of poor countries around the world. In many cases, at the end of each day, the child is given some food to take home to her family. While the struggle for funding annually falls short—especially during the Bush years—the goal is real and someday will be in reach.

Imagine, McGovern told me, if every child in the developing world were provided a free breakfast and lunch; imagine what would happen. McGovern and his old adversary—and ally—Bob Dole understood that the best way to get children, especially girls, to go to school in undeveloped and traditionally conservative nations is to offer them a wholesome, nutritious meal. In dozens of communities around the world, McGovern-Dole has led to local efforts to provide clean water, improved sanitation, HIV/AIDS prevention, and TB testing.

Then I saw it work. In 2013 Connie and I visited Haiti, where we saw McGovern-Dole in action. We visited a school in Port-au-Prince where hundreds of boys and girls were getting their only (for most of them, we assume) hot meal of the day. They all waited patiently until everyone was served.

And it's really no different in the United States. In Ohio some seven hundred thousand children are in the free and reduced breakfast and school lunch program. They eat better during the week, when food is more plentiful and more wholesome. But in the summer, even though all these children are eligible for the summer feeding program, only about seventy thousand of them—about one in ten—participate. And Ohio is no different from the rest of the country. Imagine, McGovern might say, if hundreds of thousands of these children had breakfast and lunch, reading sessions and a music program, during these long summer months.

One morning in 2007, as I was presiding over a quorum call—when no senator is speaking and the chamber is mostly empty—George McGovern entered the back of the chamber by himself. I asked several

301 ||| GEORGE McGOVERN

pages—most of them sixteen and seventeen years old—who were sitting on the steps below the dais if they recognized the man in the back of the hall. None did. I told them it was former South Dakota Senator George McGovern. Still, nothing registered. It was a reminder to me—and to all of us—of what the Roman stoic Emperor Marcus Aurelius wrote almost nineteen centuries ago: "How quickly all things disappear, bodies into the universe, memories of them in time . . . vapory fame . . . Everything lasts only for a day, both that which remembers and that which is remembered . . . Consider that before long you will be nobody and nowhere, nor will any of the things exist which you now see, nor any of those who are now living."

Perhaps so, but millions of children in the poorest countries in the world get at least one good meal a day because of George McGovern.

THOUGHTS FROM DESK 88

N OT LONG AFTER I JOINED THE SENATE, I set my sights on serving on the Finance Committee, which writes tax, trade, health care, pension, and Social Security law. At least by the second decade of the twenty-first century it had become the Senate's most sought-after committee. Some senators are satisfied with other important assignments like Foreign Relations or Appropriations. Others try for Finance and never get chosen. And others fail—once or twice; almost everyone fails at least once to get on the committee—try again, and then get selected to sit on the Finance Committee. I was in the last group. In

2010 and in 2012, Majority Leader Harry Reid, who I thought gave his committee chairs too much say in who was selected for their committees, told Finance Chair Max Baucus that he wanted to appoint me to the Finance Committee. Baucus—who despised my views on trade, didn't much like my record on health care and taxes, and loathed my outspokenness on progressive issues generally—refused each time.

Then came the 2012 elections and the billionaire Koch brothers. Outside groups—Big Tobacco, gun manufacturers, Big Oil, Wall Street—spent $40 million to defeat me, more than had been spent in any United States Senate race in the country's history. By then, Reid believed I had earned a seat on the Finance Committee; he liked it that I was a progressive who did not trim my sails or move to the middle to win an election.

Again, in December 2012, Reid insisted to Baucus that he wanted me on the committee. Baucus again said no. "Max," Reid said, "you either get Sherrod Brown or Bernie Sanders. Which is it going to be?" I was appointed to the Senate Finance Committee in January 2013.

Soon after I joined the Finance Committee, the Capitol Historical Society hosted a dinner for senators on Finance, former Finance staff, and lobbyists who, shall we say, care a lot about the committee—past and especially present. Chairman Baucus spoke, illustrating to the crowd—wittingly or not—how special interests dominate the committee: "When Senator Hatch and I are negotiating, you couldn't tell the difference between Democrats and Republicans."* Senator Lott, the former Republican leader, told us how happy he was now making boatloads of money after his long career in the House and Senate, "after living on a fixed income for thirty-nine years." That would be thirty-nine years averaging well into six figures as a congressional chief of staff, a congressman, and a senator.

And former Senator John Breaux, a moderate to conservative Democrat from Louisiana, told the story of a conversation almost three decades ago that his wife, Lois, had with Carolyn Elizabeth Long, the wife of Breaux's friend and mentor Russell Long, the just-retired chairman of the Finance Committee: "Not much has changed for us," she intoned.

---

*Graham Steele, a brilliant young lawyer who staffed the Senate Banking Committee, told me one day as we left a Washington hotel after a meeting with bankers, "There's the blue team and the red team. But it's usually the green team that wins around here."

"We used to call them constituents. Now we call them clients." That was a long journey from Chairman Long's father's comments; when Huey Long came to the Senate in the mid-1930s, he quipped, "They've got a set of Republican waiters on one side and a set of Democratic waiters on the other side, but no matter which set of waiters brings you the dish, the legislative grub is all prepared in the same Wall Street kitchen." Surely this is why Carter Glass, a conservative Virginia Democrat, referred to Long as "a demagogic screech owl from the swamps of Louisiana."

That Washington speaks with an upper-class accent was never better illustrated than in the 2012 budget agreement. The deal reduced the estate tax for the few very wealthy Americans who are subject to it. Republicans in Congress, with the echo chamber of conservative talk radio, *The Wall Street Journal* editorial board, and Fox News, were successful in naming that tax "the Death Tax"; if you can name the legislation in this town, more often than not, you are the victor.

But under the same 2012 budget agreement, the Earned Income Tax Credit and Child Tax Credit did not fare quite so well. The EITC, which many presidents, including Ronald Reagan, have expanded, is a refundable tax credit, meaning that if you make less than a certain amount of money in a given year, the government will write you a check instead of levying income tax.

It appeals to liberals, as it redistributes wealth to those who work hard and need it, and to some conservatives, as it rewards work. Together with the CTC, the program benefits the twenty-eight million families who earn no more than $55,952 a year. Combined, the EITC and the CTC lift more than nine million people out of poverty. And yet the Budget Agreement posed a mortal threat, calling for the EITC and CTC to expire at the end of 2017. From my new seat on the Finance Committee, I was determined to protect a program that would have made Hugo Black, T. F. Green, or Herbert Lehman proud.

The EITC long enjoyed broad bipartisan support. But by the end of the first decade of the twenty-first century, many Republicans—especially Tea Party enthusiasts—decided they were no longer supportive; to many of them, it smacked of Big Government; why give the working poor special tax breaks? Then, when President Obama and House and Senate

Democrats expanded the credit in 2009 and indexed it to account for in-flation, EITC became—to GOP officials and Republican activists—just another Obama program.

I had personally been an advocate for the EITC for almost twenty years. Having the tax break for low-wage workers was one thing; making them aware of it so they could benefit was another. As a House member, I worked with my staff and local accountants and tax preparers to set up EITC and Child Tax Credit sign-up sites in Elyria, Lorain, Akron, and Brunswick, and encouraged low-income workers—through news re-leases, radio programs, and mailings—to join us. A visit to our EITC sign-up site could mean a $2,500 or $3,000 check in the mail a few weeks later for a single mother with two children and a full-time job. And of course, as with a minimum wage increase, the money is spent in the neighborhood at local businesses, giving an economic boost to the whole community.

Now, as a member of the Senate Finance Committee, I was in a posi-tion to do something about EITC. But the hill was steep. Joined by thirty-five colleagues in early 2013—all Democrats; unfortunately, no Republicans responded to our requests—I introduced the Working Families Tax Relief Act, a bill that would expand the credits and make them permanent, pro-viding crucial benefits and peace of mind to working people.

Republicans—the party, they tell us, of tax cuts—went to work. They couldn't really say that they were against tax breaks for working-class Americans, not when their "pro-growth policies" always featured big tax cuts for the "job creators." A number of Republican senators said that they supported the Earned Income Tax Credit, but they claimed that it was rife with fraud; and we just can't expand it—worthy as it might be—when that many people are cheating. We countered that there was more sleight of hand among the wealthiest taxpayers.

In the fall of 2014, in my second year on the Finance Committee, I proposed a trade: Democrats would agree on making some pro-business provisions in the tax code permanent in exchange for making the ex-panded EITC and CTC permanent too. Our momentum was growing as the election approached, but we did not yet have the support we re-quired, nothing close to the sixty votes needed in the Senate to pass.

Then came the 2014 elections, where we lost nine seats—and control of the chamber. Democrats were stunned, uncertain, and in disarray. Unbeknownst to rank-and-file Democratic senators, even to most of us on the Finance Committee, some in Democratic leadership were negotiating with House Republicans on a major tax bill—to renew dozens of tax provisions and make permanent a number of corporate tax breaks. Lots of things for lots of interest groups, a total of $400 billion in tax breaks. But missing? The EITC and CTC.

On the Friday after Thanksgiving, someone leaked the negotiations to us. I spent most of the weekend on the phone—with Assistant Democratic Leader Richard Durbin, with Obama budget director Shaun Donovan, with Treasury Secretary Jack Lew, with White House Chief of Staff Denis McDonough, with other Senate colleagues. None knew about the secret negotiations. All were alarmed that a vital and effective anti-poverty effort could be jettisoned, even with Democrats still in control of the Senate during the lame duck session. We spoke with President Obama, and by Monday, we had prevailed upon him to issue a veto threat, clearing the deck for a new start in 2015.

As we planned our strategy to make the EITC/CTC permanent, we knew one thing: as much as Republican leaders had grown to *dislike* these refundable tax credits that benefited low-wage workers, they *liked even more* the corporate tax breaks that so many of their contributors wanted. To hold our ranks together, Ron Wyden, the senior Democrat on the Finance committee, and I persuaded Democratic senators to commit to the mantra "no corporate tax breaks unless EITC and CTC are permanent."

To keep the momentum going, we organized colleagues to make floor speeches, to hold news conferences, to speak out in Finance Committee discussions. We invited an Ohioan who would benefit from our efforts to the State of the Union to sit in my designated gallery seat in the House of Representatives. We emphasized the dignity of work. I had regular discussions with House Democratic Leader Nancy Pelosi, who was very effective at holding her Democratic members together and reaching out to Republican leadership in the House. Pelosi, I might add, will go down as the best legislative leader since LBJ . . . or beyond. By the summer of 2015, leaders in the party and on the Finance Committee were telling the Democratic caucus, "we are not agreeing to any corporate tax extensions, any corporate tax breaks without permanent EITC/CTC." Even with Republicans now controlling both houses of Congress, we knew we had won—on behalf of many millions of working families.

To save face, Republicans insisted on tightening up some eligibility rules, which we were glad to do—they called it "program integrity." Near the end of the year, the Republicans accepted a permanent EITC/CTC. Unfortunately, we could not convince them to index the child tax credit, nor expand the credits for workers without children. We will of course continue to try, as we go on fighting for the dignity of work. But in making the Earned Income Tax Credit permanent, I knew we had won a great victory for working Americans. Our work fulfilled Martin Luther King's vision that no work is menial if it is adequately compensated. There is nothing I've done in the Senate I'm more proud of.

FURTHER THOUGHTS FROM DESK 88—ABOUT 2020 AND BEYOND

ELECTION NIGHT 2018 WAS JOYOUS. I had convincingly won reelection to my third Senate term with our nationally acclaimed message emphasizing the dignity of work; our victory was larger than in 2012, taking by seven points a state Hillary Clinton had lost by eight points two years earlier. National Democrats won overwhelming victories, picking up forty House seats, the biggest Democratic gains since Watergate. The Great Lakes industrial states—the heartland—elected Democratic governors in Wisconsin and Minnesota and Pennsylvania and Illinois.

And the future looks promising. Nationally, millennials voted in historically large numbers, and voted overwhelmingly for Democrats, by margins better than two-to-one.

But election night 2018 was sad too. Four of my Senate colleagues—Joe Donnelly, Claire McCaskill, Heidi Heitkamp, Bill Nelson; friends all—lost, in states where the rural vote swamped them. Every other state-wide Democratic candidate in Ohio—all of whom I know and like, all well qualified, all deserving better—lost their races. Democrats in Ohio have won only once in the last seven governor's races. We have, because of redistricting, only about a third of the legislature; and, of Ohio's sixteen congressional districts, Democrats hold only four. In fact, there are more Republican congressmen—congressmen, yes, all white men—from Ohio than there are in the entire fifty-three-seat California delegation.

In my race, we won only sixteen of Ohio's eighty-eight counties. These included all of the state's metropolitan areas, which we took mostly by huge margins—Cleveland, Columbus, Cincinnati, Toledo, Akron, Dayton, Youngstown-Warren. We were victorious in smaller counties with large state universities—Bowling Green, Ohio University, Kent State. And we won all the counties that border Ohio's Great Lake.

That's it. We lost medium-sized industrial city after medium-sized industrial city, small town after small town, rural community after rural community. Pretty much all of them. And we lost many of those counties big, by more than 40 percentage points in a few, and more than two-to-one in more than a dozen of them. The geographical divide between the parties is big, and getting bigger.

So what's next for Democrats? Do we just run up the margins in the big cities and suburbs and turn out large numbers of young people? Do we just count on demographic changes that suggest long-term Democratic dominance? Bill Clinton and Barack Obama each won Ohio and Iowa twice. But in 2016, Hillary Clinton did better in North Carolina and Georgia and Arizona than she did in Ohio. She did better in Texas than in Iowa. Do we in Ohio and in rural and small-city America just wait, sit back, and expect to win the Senate and the electoral college because demographics and times, they are a-changin'?

Of course not. While demographics and population growth in

metropolitan areas spell long-term doom for a reactionary, hidebound Republican Party, Democrats must aggressively go after voters outside of the large cities, and outside, shall we say, of our comfort zone. After my 2018 election night speech where I said that Democrats should look at our Ohio victory as a "blueprint" for 2020 and beyond, Connie and I thought about how we could inform the Democratic narrative and influence the national debate. Too many Democrats believe that we have to choose between campaigning to our progressive base and talking to working-class voters, many of whom might not think of themselves as progressives. Surely, it is a false choice—and a certain ticket to defeat. Instead, we should continue to talk to our base—never compromising on women's rights and civil rights, or gay rights or the environment. We never cave to the gun lobby. But we must listen to workers, and learn about their lives. We must make a special effort to reach out to women and people of color, always recognizing—even in twenty-first-century America—their challenges are even greater because of decades of discrimination.

As we listen to working-class voters, it is important to remember that Emerson's Conservators were not just the rich grasping tight to their privilege, but small-town people resisting the land of the unknown. There is an inherent pour-in-and-harden conservatism in small-town America, a suspicion perhaps of big-city ways, a fear above all that the constant change in the cities might infect their way of life in the countryside.

Rural and small-town voters don't think either party is going to do anything for them, but they vote Republican because they think Democrats will do something *to* them: take their guns, or raise their taxes, or enact an environmental law that will put them out of work. These communities have felt job loss, they watch their children leave, they have seen drug addiction in their own and their neighbors' families. They have been abandoned by Wall Street and large corporations that invest in metro areas and ignore small towns and rural areas. And they see a distant federal government with no plan to help them.

So people's cynicism about their government grows, fed by one party and one quasi-government-run television network: the narrative comes from Republicans and Fox News, and also from right-wing talk radio and *The Wall Street Journal*: government doesn't care; government is corrupt; government can do nothing right; and Democrats are the party of government. Small-town and rural Americans believe little of what Democrats say; they rarely trust government to do the right thing; they question the intentions and morality of elected officials. I will never be one who says that people in rural and small-town America vote against their own interest; who am I to say what is their self-interest? But we as progressives have work to do.

Earning voters' trust is part of that work. During the 2000 campaign, as I've recounted elsewhere, I visited the Ford Plant in Avon Lake and drank coffee in the cafeteria with several workers. The one Bush supporter told me that while he knew his candidate was hostile to labor, he couldn't vote for Gore because he "wants to take my gun." When one of his co-workers replied, "Well, Sherrod has the same position Gore does," he said, "Yeah, but at least Brown is fighting for the stuff I care about."

TODAY, AS BEFORE, Democrats need to show up in these communities. We should talk some history, including the history discussed in this book. We should tell the canary story and discuss how government can be on their side. We can explain how the federal government improved their lives from Hugo Black's Fair Labor Standards Act to unemployment insurance and the right to collective bargaining. We can tell the story of rural electrification, and emphasize how those fights still matter—for example, in the struggle to bring broadband to rural communities, where their children too often don't have access to the internet and their small businesses can't sell their products online. We should promote, as former Iowa Governor and Agriculture Secretary Tom Vilsack advocates, a "natural resources economy" where annual crops provide the raw materials for a sustaining, decentralized economy. In this vision, we would pay farmers to use their land to help address the threat of climate change, and employ plant-based by-products to replace fossil fuels in the production of plastics and other materials.

And of course Democrats should talk about Medicare, Medicaid, and Social Security, and how Republicans opposed their creation decades ago, and how progressives still fight for them, and conservatives try to cut and privatize them. And we should point out—elections are always about contrasts—how Republicans in Washington cut taxes on rich people in 2017 and proposed in the ensuing years to pay for the hole in the federal budget by cutting Medicare and Social Security.

We must talk about a White House that looks like a retreat for Wall Street executives, where big banks get their way, where Wall Street has abandoned small-town investments for more lucrative big-city pastures, where the White House has not lifted a finger to fix our pension system and help the more than one million workers who could lose half of what was promised them. We should listen to these voters' concerns, and engage with them on ways to address the opioid public health crisis and to create economic growth in their communities.

As America prepares for another presidential election, we must show who *we* are and show who *they* are. President Trump and congressional Republicans preached a pro-worker populism, but when they left the pulpit they sat in corporate America's front pew, taking money out of the collection plate. Virtually everything they do has enriched their corporate special-interest friends: cutting taxes for the rich while proposing to cut Medicare and Medicaid to pay for them; a special corporate tax break that provided a 50-percent-off coupon for companies that shut down in Manchester or Des Moines and relocate in Mexico or China; relaxing rules for for-profit colleges while squeezing community colleges, state universities, and liberal arts schools. Siding with internet providers over consumers, Big Oil over the environment, the Gun Lobby over high school students. Even Trump's signature promises to make our approach to trade do more for American workers have masked his support for his grifter friends who profit from tax and trade policies that are worse than those he inherited from his corporate and free-trade-oriented predecessors.

And of course the Supreme Court. Reactionary forces in Washington have nominated a Supreme Court that puts its thumb on the scales of justice, favoring large corporations over workers, Wall Street over consumers, health insurance companies over sick people. In the end—and this has been the story for years—the Republican Party and its billionaire funders care fundamentally about three things: tax cuts for their wealthy donors, weaker consumer and environmental rules for their corporate sponsors, and young, far-right federal judges who will tip the scale against unions and women's rights and voting rights; they are—fundamentally and principally—a party that cares more about property than workers.

As the 2020 elections draw near, progressives can never let Trump and conservatives hide behind their language of divisiveness and obfuscation. Dr. William J. Barber II, a North Carolina civil rights activist, told *The New York Times* the religious far right hijacked the term "evangelicals" to make what they are saying sound theological when it is really not; it is "clearly Christian nationalist, extreme in its views." As my wife, Connie Schultz noted in her review of Michael D'Antonio and Peter Eisner's *The Shadow President: The Truth About Mike Pence*, the authors describe the religious leader of his party as "the most successful Christian supremacist in American history."

It is pretty simple: President Trump and Vice President Pence and their enablers in Congress play to fear. They promote a racist, phony populism. They attack people and institutions that their base detests and fears. Fox, *The Wall Street Journal*, and right-wing talk radio preach a daily gospel of grievance as they marinate in their resentments. They train their listeners and readers to think of themselves as victims.

Instead, progressives offer something else—the dignity of work and the dignity of community. We must go everywhere—to metro areas where Democrats do very well, and to small towns where Democrats get slaughtered, where the politics is the most difficult. We show up with our story—America's story—about the dignity of work, about the dignity of community, about our canary.

THE DIGNITY OF WORK

The German constitution tells its people that "dignity of man is inviolable. To protect it and respect it shall be the duty of all public authority." The French Revolution, the American Revolution, and, in our time, Ukraine's Revolution of Dignity spoke to the dignity of work, rejecting the disregard and humiliation that characterized the status quo.

History teaches us that when work is honored and workers are respected, freedom and self-government thrive.

In late January 2019, Connie and I set out on our Dignity of Work Listening Tour. As we visited the four early presidential states, we listened—the first requirement of understanding the Dignity of Work. Dee Albritton of Fast Forward, a community-based nonprofit in Columbia, South Carolina, told us, "Our clients have been invisible and unheard for far too long." She spoke on behalf of disabled veterans and people struggling with addiction: the poet Darious Sanders, a combat marine, who had attempted suicide seven times, read his poem about the "strain in my voice," telling us that veterans are "more than a painting on the wall." We listened to Gillet Hood, homeless at seventeen, who now held two jobs, and who taught *us* about "worker's integrity," about going the extra mile. We heard from Glendella Jackson, a laundry worker for the Veterans Administration, whose arthritis meant less work time and more economic challenges.

Ms. Albritton advocated for them, to be sure, but could have been speaking for millions of other invisible hard-working Americans whose pay is inadequate and benefits are sparse, and whose workplace schedules are not their own.

She could have been speaking for cooks and retail workers, for custodians and service works, for security guards and farmworkers—usually the lowest paid with the fewest benefits and the most unpredictable work schedules, and often laboring in unsafe conditions. Rarely do they have the benefit of a union.

At an AFL-CIO event in southwest Ohio a few years ago, a half-dozen middle-aged women, proud new members of the Service Employees International Union, were eating dinner at a table near the front of the banquet room. They were the bargaining team that had signed the first contract for the 1,200 union workers who cleaned office buildings in downtown Cincinnati. I joined them for part of the dinner and asked what it meant for them to have a union.

"For the first time in my life," the woman seated next to me said, "for the first time in my fifty-one years, I will have a paid one-week vacation."

Some of the most invisible workers clean federal facilities, prepare

food for federal workers and the visiting public, and keep federal buildings safe for staff and the public. But they work for contractors, not directly for the government. During Trump's partial government shutdown
of 2018–19, 800,000 federal workers were either furloughed or deemed
"essential" and made to work without pay. Classifying workers as "essential" or "nonessential" is in itself an insult to the employee and the dignity
of work. After Trump backed down and reopened the government, the
800,000 federal employees received back pay; the contract workers, many
earning $14 or $15 an hour, got nothing. Majority leader McConnell and
Trump, despite our efforts, refused to help.

From Waterloo, Iowa, to New Hampshire's North Country, from
Las Vegas to Florence, South Carolina, we met workers who fought for a
living wage, who aspired to be in the middle class, who struggled to stay
in the middle class, and who believed—as the Culinary Workers Union
in Las Vegas directed—that "one job should be enough."

These workers told us that we must recognize their contributions to
our communities: the food they grow and prepare, the cars they build,
the sick people they heal, the restrooms they clean, the buildings they
construct, the children they nurture, the military they join. We heard
from Anne Grassie, who has worked in child care in Laconia, New
Hampshire, for decades, that child care should be considered "a public
good": just as government invests in transportation or public parks, it
should invest in kids' earliest years. We know that markets can create
great wealth in our society, provide good-paying jobs for workers, and
produce high-quality goods for consumers. But not always. Millions of
working families cannot afford child care. And hundreds of thousands of
child care workers are not earning a living wage. If we are a country that
values its children and respects the dignity of work, then we must invest
in child care, and think of it as a public good.

At the beginning of dinner or lunch speeches, I often thank the
servers, people who are seldom noticed and rarely thanked. Afterward—
usually to the annoyance of my always-in-a-hurry staff—I try to meet
them, ask them their names, and learn something about their lives. It
makes me a better senator and, Connie says, a better human being.

I notice that those who serve—as waitresses and bank tellers and security guards and drivers and hotel workers—often have a name tag pinned to their uniform, usually bearing only a first name. These workers typically address the public as Mr., or Ms., or . . . Senator. I will always ask the server her last name, and address her that way. If I'm Mr. Brown or Senator Brown, they are Ms. Jackson and Mr. Kleshinski. I taught my daughters—Emily, a legal services immigration attorney, and Elizabeth, a Columbus city councilmember, and Caitlin, who advocates for low-income families—to do the same. Another enduring lesson from my beloved mother.

Pope Francis puts it succinctly: "We don't get dignity from power nor money or culture. We get dignity from work." And so we celebrate the dignity of all work, and respect the dignity of all workers. Martin Luther King, martyred five decades ago while advocating for some of the most exploited employees in America, sanitation workers in Memphis, said: "If a man is called to be a street sweeper, he should sweep streets even as Michelangelo painted, or Beethoven composed music or Shakespeare wrote poetry. He should sweep streets so well that all the hosts of heaven and earth will pause to say, 'Here lived a great street sweeper who did his job well.'"

Dignity of work suggests not just a say in the workplace, but a sharing of the wealth that workers and their labor create. The Alabama-born Hattie Canty, a daughter of sharecroppers, led the longest successful strike in U.S. history, a six-and-a-half-year action beginning in 1991 against the New Frontier Hotel in Las Vegas. She said: "The labor movement, and the civil rights movement, you can't separate the two of them." In the words of Dr. King, who spoke about labor rights as fluently as civil rights, "The most dynamic and cohesive liberal forces in the country are the labor movement and the Negro freedom movement."

DR. KING INSTRUCTED US that "no labor is really menial unless you're not getting adequate wages." In the decade after the Great Recession, corporate profits soared, executive compensation exploded, and worker productivity rose, yet workers' wages were all too often stagnant; hard work simply was not paying off. Wall Street makes billions, the average bank teller earns less than $30,000 a year, temporary workers are hired who can easily be fired, and business too often sees workers as a cost to be minimized.

When we talk about work, we talk about everyone. When we restore value to work, we lift up everyone. If work is honored and respected, workers feel valued; and when they know our society believes in the dignity of work, and their employers believe in *their* dignity of work, workers are empowered as citizens. That strengthens our communities, our nation, and our democracy.

When I delivered my "Working Too Hard for Too Little" address, presenting our Dignity of Work blueprint at Ohio State's John Glenn College of Public Affairs in early 2017, I sought to encapsulate a lifetime of my own work, and a vision of the future. The challenges to work and community are greater than ever as corporations shave off benefits for their employees, as some companies misclassify their workers or insist they be independent contractors or, in some cases, force them to work off the clock. Corporations are engaging in increasingly sophisticated practices to keep unions out of the workplace. And the gig economy, where more and more people are cobbling together multiple jobs to survive, poses a whole new set of difficulties.

At the same time, workers are facing a more hostile government, where Congress and the courts and numerous state legislatures are stripping them—union and nonunion alike—of their rights in the workplace.

But government, progressives insist, has a major role to play in restoring value to work and respecting its dignity. Start with wages: We must raise the federal minimum wage, which has not risen since 2009. Ensure that workers are paid the overtime they earn, by restoring the overtime rule that Labor Secretary Acosta eviscerated. Pass equal pay for equal work laws. And update our labor laws so that workers can join a union and collectively bargain for wages and benefits.

We must also come together with most of the rest of the democratic nations on earth to provide paid family leave and sick days. And credit time off to raise children or care for aging parents toward earning Social Security benefits.

It is also imperative to extend the reach and size of the Earned Income Tax Credit and the Child Tax Credit. And while we are at it, we should allow workers who qualify for the EITC an advance on their credits, at no extra cost to the government, of up to $500 a year, so fixing a car to go to work doesn't land the worker at the payday lender's doorstep.

THE DIGNITY OF COMMUNITY

T he South African Constitution tells its people that "everyone has inherent dignity and the right to have their dignity respected and protected." It speaks to the acknowledgment of the intrinsic worth of human beings. It tells us, historic translations of Matthew 25 aside, that no human being is worth less than another. No matter their title. No matter their station. Ever. Or, as Robert Browning wrote, "All service ranks the same with God . . . there is no last nor first."

The dignity of community is undermined when President Trump invokes an angry phony populism where some get ahead by pushing others down. He and his party divide people to prop up the powerful. They confuse popularity with populism. Real populism is not *these* people versus *those* people, but all people. Real populism is never racist, never anti-Semitic, never gaining for some at the expense of others. It never excludes, but embraces. It never slashes programs for the least privileged while bestowing tax breaks on the rich. Populism is never about giving more money and power to those who have much. For many of us, our commitment to stronger communities is rooted in our faith, and we should never be afraid to talk about that faith. This faith speaks to the dignity of work as well as the value of community. The Hebrew Bible respects what we today would call hourly wage earners: "The Lord your God may bless you in all the work of your hands" (Deuteronomy 24:19). And nearly every faith tradition honors the dignity of community. If you're a progressive and a Christian, you can do no better than the Sermon on the Mount, the "best political speech ever written," House Speaker Tip O'Neill liked to say: "Blessed are the merciful for they shall obtain mercy. Blessed are the peacemakers, for they shall be called children of God."

The Sermon on the Mount with the Beatitudes is bookended by the Old Testament's Micah 6:8, which tells us how to live and how to serve others, an admonition for which progressives strive: "Do justice, love kindness, and walk humbly with God." To the Muslim, "The Companions of the Garden" tells us that the owner of the orchard first shares his bounty with the poor.

The dignity of work is far more than a slogan. It is not simply about winning elections. It's about who we are. And it's about how we must govern, seeing our country and our economy and our government through the eyes of workers.

THE CANARY

The canary represents the fight we make, and must make every generation. None of the progress that the canary symbolizes came easy for working Americans. Progressives—in their union halls and church basements, in their veterans' lodges and in their civil rights organizations—took on the most powerful people in our country, endured great sacrifice, and overcame the opposition of those clinging to their privilege. This book has concentrated on the achievements of those fortunate enough to serve in the United States Senate. But progress has always depended as well on the ordinary people doing ordinary work who've overcome the most entrenched, well-heeled interests in Washington and in state capitols all over our nation. It was their fight for the dignity of work that created a vibrant middle class in this country. They brought us civil rights and safe drinking water, the forty-hour workweek and the weekend, protections for children and the disabled, human rights and women's rights, collective bargaining and overtime, Social Security and Medicare, unemployment insurance and Medicaid.

I wore the canary pin long before I laid eyes on Desk 88. Someday, when I leave the Senate, other senators will sit at this desk where I have chronicled its occupants and the Senate's progressive history, and there will surely be women and people of color among them. They will carry on this mission.

Their success—their ability to carry on the progressive tradition, to bend the arc toward justice—will depend on the activists of the future, in union halls and church basements, and in civil rights and gay rights organizations.

Desk 88 is the story—past and future—of all of them.

Epilogue

CARVING A PLACE IN HISTORY

I T WAS TIME TO SIGN MY NAME ON DESK 88—now twelve years in the United States Senate, ninety minutes before the beginning of my third term. It was my grandson Leo Sherrod Brown-McDonald's sixth birthday—he'd been born on January 3, 2013, the day I was sworn in for my second term.

My family—our daughters, Emily, Elizabeth, and Caitlin, and their husbands, with six of our seven grandchildren in tow—walked onto the Senate floor; it was the first time there for a number of them. Desk 88 and the other ninety-nine desks are arranged in a half circle facing the presiding officer—Democrats to the left, Republicans to the right. The desks in the Senate chamber are mostly trapezoidal, because the original forty-eight desks in the Old Senate chamber were shaped to form a perfect semicircle facing the presiding officer. The middle aisle separates the assigned seats of the two parties. Desk 88—and I—have moved to the back of the hall, on the aisle, closest to the door; this location allows me, with the long cord attached to the microphone, to walk into—and on occasion up and down—the aisle when I speak.

Forty-eight of the desks in the Senate chamber today were crafted by the New York cabinetmaker Thomas Constantine and installed in the Old Senate chamber in 1819. Constantine, who emigrated from England with his family when he was two, was already a master craftsman when the House of Representatives retained him, at age twenty-seven, to make its furnishings. Official Washington was so enamored of Constantine's work that President James Monroe's vice president, Daniel Tompkins, offered Constantine—and his workshop—an unbid contract to craft forty-eight desks and forty-eight chairs. He had only six weeks to fill the order and was promised handsome payment to do it. Constantine had made tables for the House of Representatives, where several congressmen were seated at each, but the Senate order called for a separate desk for each senator—already speaking to the power and status of the United States Senate even in those early days.

Constantine was paid $34 for each desk, and $48 for each chair. Of course, the chairs, while well made and durable, do not last as long as the desks. Only three of his original chairs still exist, none of them any longer in the Senate chamber. Two are in private collections; one is being restored and will be displayed in the Capitol. Retired or defeated senators are allowed to purchase their chairs from the government.

All one hundred desks are constructed of solid mahogany, with the drawers made mostly of poplar and pine. Most of the mahogany came from a now deforested Haiti. In the early 1800s, Haiti was a relatively prosperous nation. The United States of America, itself of course a slave-holding nation in the first half of the nineteenth century, did not recognize Haiti, a country of former slaves who had overthrown their French colonial masters, until we ended slavery in our country during the Civil War. Beginning in the 1830s, senators requested that mahogany writing boxes be added atop the desks; after all, most senators, without offices in the Capitol in those days, did much of their work in the Senate chamber at their desk. And they needed a place to store the books and the papers that they were accumulating. Only one desk today—that of Daniel Webster—has no writing box. According to the Senate curator, Webster refused to alter his desk because if his predecessors could manage with a smaller desk, so could he.

History swirls around every one of the one hundred desks in the Senate chamber, especially the original forty-eight. Five of them are "reserved": the Democratic leader sits in the front row, a tradition that the Arkansan Joseph Robinson began in 1927; across the aisle sits the Republican leader, a custom that began with Oregon Senator Charles McNary in 1937; the Henry Clay Desk is occupied by the senior senator from Kentucky (that desk may be assigned to Kentucky's junior senator if the senior senator serves as a party leader, as is now the case); the Daniel Webster Desk is assigned to the senior senator from New Hampshire (even though Webster served in the Senate from Massachusetts, he was born in New Hampshire and was a representative from New Hampshire). Jeanne Shaheen, the first woman in American history to serve as both a governor and a senator, now occupies the Webster desk.

The other "reserved" desk is the Jefferson Davis Desk, which carries a special history. Mississippi's junior senator, Jefferson Davis, was assigned to it in the 1860s at the outbreak of the Civil War. He was a West Point graduate, soldier, congressman for less than a term, slaveholder, unsuccessful candidate for governor of Mississippi, and President Franklin Pierce's secretary of war. After Mississippi and other southern states seceded from the Union, Davis, now a traitor to his sworn country, left the United States Senate, and was elected president of the Confederate States of America and inaugurated in February 1861. Two months later, U.S. troops were bivouacked in the U.S. Capitol; some were temporarily encamped in the Senate chamber. Isaac Bassett, who had started as a page in 1831 and worked in the Senate for more than six decades, recounted what happened:

As I entered the Senate, I heard a noise, as if someone was splitting wood. I looked over on the Democratic side of the chamber and behold! There was a crowd [of] soldiers with their bayonets, cutting one of the desks to pieces. I hollered at the top of my voice. "Stop! What are you doing?" Several answered, "We are cutting that damn traitor's desk to pieces." I ran in among them and told them it was not his desk, that it belonged to the government. "You were put here to protect, and not to destroy!" They stopped immediately and said I was right, they thought it belonged to Jefferson Davis.

The desk was rebuilt; a small bayonet mark from its battering was preserved. The senior senator from Mississippi, now Republican Roger Wicker, occupies it today.

Before each new Congress, in December and January after the election, staff members move the desks according to election results. In late 2006, after Democrats gained six seats in the November election, a half dozen desks were unbolted and moved from the Republican side to the Democratic side. In that election, Democrats won a razor-thin majority of 51–49.

Two years later, after the 2008 elections, seven more desks were moved to the Democratic side. Then on April 28, 2009, Pennsylvania Republican Arlen Specter switched parties; so another desk on the Republican side was unbolted and moved; and then in July with the seating of the Minnesota Democrat Al Franken—after a protracted series of recounts and court battles—a sixtieth desk was squeezed among the desks on the Democratic side of the aisle.

Oh. And there's the candy desk. In 1965 on the Republican side of the chamber, California Senator George Murphy, perhaps known better for his acting and dancing than for his legislating, decided to fill his drawer with candy. He made the candy available to his colleagues, most of whom walked by his desk in the back of the hall as they entered the chamber. Democrats, not to be outdone, designated their candy drawer in a secretary's desk in the back of the chamber. West Virginia Senator Jay Rockefeller filled the candy drawer on the Democratic side for a number of years before his retirement in 2014. We had better candy back then.

The tradition of carving names on the inside of Senate desks began early in the twentieth century. Some senators over the years migrated throughout the chamber, staking claims on each desk as they moved. Harry Truman—ten years in the Senate, ten desks, ten signatures— comes most prominently to mind. So do Alaska Senator Ted Stevens, who signed seven desks, and Virginia segregationist Harry Byrd, Sr., who marked nine different Senate desks. John McCain of Arizona signed five. Senate records show that West Virginia's Harley Kilgore signed the most desks—fourteen—followed by Alabama's Lister Hill and Iowa's Guy Gillette, who each signed twelve different desks, including Desk 88. Why did they feel the need to switch desks? I have no idea. I plan to remain at Desk 88 throughout my Senate career.

Most senators sign just one, and many wait until near the end of their Senate service. On the last day of session in 1978, after other senators had left the chamber, Minnesota's Muriel Humphrey, who succeeded her late husband in the United States Senate and served for about ten months, stayed behind for a few minutes. According to Alan Fruman, then the Senate's assistant parliamentarian, she quietly sat down at her desk and carved a simple "M + H" in front of "Humphrey" in the desk that her husband, Hubert, had occupied immediately before her.

Others seem almost reluctant. Vermont's Patrick Leahy, elected to the Senate in 1974, has not yet signed his desk, although he says he plans to do it before he leaves. Majority Leader Harry Reid waited until near the end before he signed his. New Mexico's Pete Domenici, who apparently sat in the same desk during his entire thirty-six years in the Senate, retired in December 2008 and declined to sign his desk. Wayne Allard, a quiet ultraconservative Republican from Colorado, looked at this tradition with a more jaundiced view. Retiring in 2008 after twelve years in the Senate—desk unsigned—he told Sarah Abruzzese of *Politico*, "I'm not going to deface public property."

Like his father, Al Gore, Jr., sat at Desk 88, but he never signed it. Wanting to know why, I called to find out. "I thought about signing the desk, but I left in a rush," he told me. Presidential nominee Bill Clinton, in the summer of 1992, selected the two-term Tennessee senator to be his running mate; Gore apparently never looked back. Until now. "You think they would let me sign it?" he asked.

There is always a story. Gary Richardson had made Barack Obama his project. Soon after the Illinois Democrat joined the Senate in 2005, the six-foot-four African American chief chamber attendant had urged the Senate's only African American to sign his desk. Again and again. Finally, in the middle of the presidential primary season, during one of Obama's infrequent trips to the Senate floor, Gary saw his chance. "Senator Obama, either you or Senator McCain or Senator Clinton is going to be the next president of the United States. You need to sign your desk." He then handed the junior senator from Illinois a Sharpie.

Obama took the pen, replied warmly to Richardson with a simple "Okay," and walked onto the floor. Obama was immediately called away by some other senators, and Gary thought he had again lost his chance. But later, Richardson walked over to the desk, opened the drawer, and saw Barack Obama's mostly illegible signature scrawled inside it.

A few months later, after President-elect Obama announced his selection of Hillary Rodham Clinton for secretary of state, Senate Curator Diane Skvarla told me, "I don't want to make history. But I wanted to make sure that Senator Clinton's office knew that she would have the opportunity to sign the desk before she left." On the last day of session in December, the cloakroom staffer Meredith Mellody cleared out Clinton's desk, brought the desk drawer into the cloakroom, and handed the New York senator a Sharpie, and she signed her name in big black letters.

OVER THE LAST dozen years, Desk 88 has become a second home: I have now worked with and alongside almost two hundred different senators, a few who were appointed to fill a vacancy for only a few months, others who served a term or two and were defeated or retired, and others who grew into giants of the Senate with names like Lugar and Kennedy, Byrd and Mikulski, Inouye and Levin.

On some days when I worry about my country—when Trump pulled out of the Paris Agreement on Climate Change, or when the Supreme

Court struck down crucial provisions of the Voting Rights Act, or when the special interests have their way with McConnell on a corporate tax giveaway—I walk into an empty Senate chamber and sit at Desk 88. Pulling out the drawer, I think about the progressive giants who have sat at "my desk." I see the carved reminders of the great victories for our nation: the fight for collective bargaining and the dignity of work waged by Hugo Black, or the battle for civil rights undertaken by Kennedy and Taylor, or how George McGovern, the only one of the eight whom I actually knew, fed millions of children in the poorest countries in the world.

TWO YEARS INTO this dark time for our country, Connie and I thought it was time to celebrate these victories with our children and grandchildren. Of course, our grandchildren—none older than six—were more excited that morning about riding the Senate subway than watching Grandpa carve his name in an old piece of furniture. As my family and I entered the Senate cloakroom next to the Senate chamber, we were greeted by Melinda Smith, curator of the Senate. Wearing light blue surgical gloves, she had removed the drawer from Desk 88, placed it on a table in the cloakroom, and arranged alongside it a pencil, an awl, and a black marker.

The sense of history, the joy of grandchildren, the Margaret Mead dictum that wisdom and knowledge are passed from grandparent to grandchild, the challenge of self-government, the responsibility of passing a better world to the next generation—all filled my head as I peered into the desk drawer.

Surrounded by our grandchildren, I began—first with the pencil for the initial draft, next with the awl to cut the letters, and then with the Sharpie—to carve and print "Sherrod Brown—Ohio." Alongside Black and Green and Taylor and Lehman and Gore and Proxmire and Kennedy and McGovern.

All of the grandchildren ran their fingers over the new engraving. Four-year-old Jackie told her mother, "It felt scruffy."

I picked up the drawer. Then—accompanied by Leo, Jackie, Carolyn, Milo, Ela, and Russell—I walked a few feet onto the Senate floor and slid the drawer back into Desk 88.

BIBLIOGRAPHY

Author interviews and conversations with: Arod Taylor, Steve Grossman, Kathleen Barber, Meredith Mellody, Rick Jacobs, Gary Richardson, Rick Carne, Mark Shields, Diane Skvarla, Peter Edelman, Senate historian Richard Baker, Luci Baines Johnson, Byron Krantz, Larry Temple, Chuck Todd, Paul Volcker, Jeff Greenfield, Larry Temple, Joanne Carter, Ben Barnes, Senate historian Kate Scott, Senate historian Donald Ritchie, Thomas Frieden, Paul Quinn, Mayor Stephen Wukela, D. A. Henderson, William Foege, Marian Wright Edelman, Gerald Cassidy, Jeffrey DeBoer, William Lynn III, Peter Edelman, Thomas Quinn, Senator Jack Reed, Senator Sheldon Whitehouse, Senator Tammy Baldwin, former Congressman Bart Gordon, former secretary of agriculture Dan Glickman, former Iowa governor Tom Vilsack, former congressman and ambassador Tony Hall, Senator Pat Leahy, Senator

Christopher Dodd, Senator Herb Kohl, the late Senator George McGovern, the late Senator Edward Kennedy, Senator Richard Lugar, Senator Richard Durbin, Congressman Ron Kind, Congressman James Sensenbrenner, Congressman John Lewis, Congressman Peter DeFazio, former Senator Bill Nelson, Congressman Bob Inglis, former Senator George McGovern, former Senator Fred Harris, former Senator Donald Riegle, the late Senator John Glenn, former Congressman Paul Todd, former Congressman Lee Hamilton.

Ackerman, Kenneth D. *Dark Horse: The Surprise Election and Political Murder of President James A. Garfield.* New York: Carroll & Graf, 2003.

Akerlof, George, and Robert Shiller. *Phishing for Phools: The Economics of Manipulation and Deception.* Princeton, NJ: Princeton University Press, 2015.

Algeo, Matthew. *Harry Truman's Excellent Adventure: The True Story of a Great American Road Trip.* Chicago: Chicago Review Press, 2009.

Allen, Thomas H. *Dangerous Convictions: What's Really Wrong with the U.S. Congress.* New York: Oxford University Press, 2013.

Alter, Jonathan. *The Defining Moment: FDR's Hundred Days and the Triumph of Hope.* New York: Simon & Schuster, 2006.

Ambrose, Stephen. *The Wild Blue: The Men and Boys Who Flew the B-24s over Germany.* New York: Simon & Schuster, 2001.

American Banker

American National Biography

Anson, Robert Sam. *McGovern: A Biography.* New York: Holt, Rinehart and Winston, 1972.

Antin, Mary. *The Promised Land.* New York: Penguin Classics, 2012. First published 1912.

Baicker, Katherine, Claudia Goldin, and Lawrence F. Katz. "A Distinctive System: Origins and Impact of U.S. Unemployment Compensation." National Bureau of Economic Research Working Paper 5889. January 1997.

Baradaran, Mehrsa. *How the Other Half Banks: Exclusion, Exploitation, and the Threat to Democracy.* Cambridge, MA: Harvard University Press, 2015.

Beard, Charles. *An Economic Interpretation of the Constitution of the United States.* New York: Free Press, 1965. First published 1913.

Bennet, Michael. *The Land of Flickering Lights: Restoring America in an Age of Broken Politics.* New York: Atlantic Monthly Press, 2019.

Bernstein, Mark. *John J. Gilligan: The Politics of Principle.* Kent, OH: The Kent State University Press, 2013.

———. *McCulloch of Ohio: For the Republic.* New Bremen, OH: Crown Equipment Corporation, 2014.

Biddle, Wayne. *Dark Side of the Moon: Werner von Braun, the Third Reich, and the Space Race.* New York: W. W. Norton, 2009.

Black, Conrad. *Franklin Delano Roosevelt: Champion of Freedom.* New York: Public Affairs, 2003.

Black, Hugo, Jr. *My Father, a Remembrance.* New York: Random House, 1975.

Blumenthal, David, and James Morone. *The Heart of Power: Health and Politics in the Oval Office.* Berkeley: University of California Press, 2009.

Bowles, Chester. *Promises to Keep: My Years in Public Life, 1941–1969.* New York: Harper & Row, 1971.

Bowling, Kenneth, and Helen E. Veit., eds. *The Diary of William Maclay and Other Notes on Senate Debates: March 4, 1979–March 3, 1791.* Baltimore: Johns Hopkins University Press, 1988.

Bradbury, Ray. *Fahrenheit 451.* New York: Simon & Schuster, 1993. First published 1953.

Bradford, William. *Bradfords History "Of Plimouth Plantation."* Boston: Wright and Potter, 1898, americanjourneys.org/pdf/AJ-025.pdf.

Brands, H. W. *Andrew Jackson, His Life and Times.* New York: Doubleday, 2005.

Bryson, Bill. *At Home: A Short History of Private Life.* New York: Doubleday, 2010.

Buckley, Christopher. *Losing Mum and Pup: A Memoir.* New York: Twelve, 2009.

Byrd, Robert C. *The Senate, 1789–1989.* Washington, DC: Government Printing Office, 1989.

Caro, Robert A. *Master of the Senate.* New York: Alfred A. Knopf, 2002.

Cash, W. J. *The Mind of the South.* Garden City, NY: Doubleday, 1941.

Cassidy, John. *How Markets Fail: The Logic of Economic Calamities.* New York: Farrar, Straus and Giroux, 2009.

Chace, James. *1912: Wilson, Roosevelt, Taft, and Debs—the Election That Changed the Country.* New York: Simon & Schuster, 2004.

Chang, Ha-Joon. *Bad Samaritans: The Myth of Free Trade and the Secret History of American Capitalism.* New York: Bloomsbury Press, 2008.

Chernow, Ron, *Grant.* New York: Penguin Press, 2017.

Clarke, Thurston. *The Last Campaign: Robert F. Kennedy and 82 Days That Inspired America.* New York: Henry Holt, 2008.

Clinton, Hillary Rodham. *Hard Choices.* New York: Simon & Schuster, 2014.

Crespino, Joseph. *Atticus Finch: The Biography: Harper Lee, Her Father, and the Making of an American Icon.* New York: Basic Books, 2017.

———. *Strom Thurmond's America.* New York: Hill and Wang, 2012.

David, Lester, and Irene David. *Bobby Kennedy: The Making of a Folk Hero.* New York: Dodd, Mead, 1986.

Deloria, Vine, Jr. *Custer Died for Your Sins: An Indian Manifesto.* New York: Collier-Macmillan, 1969.

Diemer, Tom. *Fighting the Unbeatable Foe: Howard Metzenbaum of Ohio, the Washington Years.* Kent, OH: Kent State University Press, 2008.

Dionne, E. J., Jr. *They Only Look Dead: How Progressives Will Dominate the Next Political Era.* New York: Simon & Schuster, 1996.

Donato, Pietro di. *Christ in Concrete: A Novel.* Indianapolis and New York: The Bobbs-Merrill Company, 1939.

Downey, Kristin. *The Woman Behind the New Deal: The Life of France Perkins, FDR's Secretary of Labor and His Moral Conscience.* New York: Nan A. Talese/Doubleday, 2009.

Drury, Allen. *A Senate Journal, 1943–1945*. New York: McGraw-Hill, 1963.

Dunne, Gerald. *Hugo Black and the Judicial Revolution*. New York: Simon & Schuster, 1977.

Edelman, Peter. *Searching for America's Heart: RFK and the Renewal of Hope*. Boston: Houghton Mifflin, 2001.

Elliott, Carl, Sr., and Michael D'Orso. *The Cost of Courage: The Journey of an American Congressman*. Tuscaloosa: University of Alabama Press, 1992.

Fadiman, Clifton, ed. *The Little, Brown Book of Anecdotes*. Boston: Little, Brown, 1985.

Faroohar, Rana. *Makers and Takers: How Wall Street Destroyed Main Street*. New York: Crown Business, 2016.

Fitzgerald, F. Scott. *The Great Gatsby*. New York: C. Scribner's Sons, 1924.

Flake, Jeff, *Conscience of a Conservative*. New York: Random House, 2017.

Foege, William H. *House on Fire: The Fight to Eradicate Smallpox*. Berkeley: University of California Press, 2011.

Frank, Thomas. *One Market Under God: Extreme Capitalism, Market Populism, and the End of Economic Democracy*. New York: Doubleday, 2000.

———. *What's the Matter with Kansas? How Conservatives Won the Heart of America*. New York: Henry Holt, 2004.

Freeman, Joanne B. *The Field of Blood: Violence in Congress and the Road to Civil War*. New York: Farrar, Straus and Giroux, 2018.

Fukuyama, Francis. *Identity: The Demand for Dignity and the Politics of Resentment*. New York: Farrar, Straus and Giroux, 2018.

Galbraith, John Kenneth. *The Great Crash, 1929*. Boston: Houghton Mifflin, 1954.

Gelles, Edith B. *Abigail and John: Portrait of a Marriage*. New York: William Morrow, 2009.

Gessen, Masha. *The Future Is History: How Totalitarianism Reclaimed Russia*. New York: Riverhead Books, 2017.

Gilbert, Martin, ed. *Churchill: The Power of Words: His Remarkable Life Recounted Through His Writings and Speeches*. Boston: Da Capo, 2012.

Gillette, King C. *The People's Corporation*. New York: Boni and Liveright, 1924.

Glenn, John, with Nick Taylor. *A Memoir*. New York: Bantam Books, 1999.

Goodwin, Doris Kearns. *Leadership in Turbulent Times*. New York: Simon & Schuster, 2018.

———. *Team of Rivals: The Political Genius of Abraham Lincoln*. New York: Simon & Schuster, 2005.

———. *The Bully Pulpit: Theodore Roosevelt, William Howard Taft, and the Golden Age of Journalism*. New York: Simon & Shuster, 2013.

Gore, Albert, Sr. *Let the Glory Out: My South and Its Politics*. New York: Viking, 1972.

Gould, Lewis. *The Most Exclusive Club: A History of the Modern United States Senate*. New York: Basic Books, 2005.

Greene, Graham. *The Comedians*. New York: Viking, 1965.

Greenspan, Alan. *The Age of Turbulence: Adventures in a New World*. New York: Penguin, 2007.

Griffith, Robert. *The Politics of Fear: Joseph R. McCarthy and the Senate*. Lexington: University Press of Kentucky, 1970.

Gruening, Ernest. *Many Battles: The Autobiography of Ernest Gruening*. New York: Liveright, 1973.

Gunther, John. *Inside USA*. New York: Harper & Bros., 1947.

Hall, Tony, and Tom Price. *Changing the Face of Hunger*. Nashville, TN: W Publishing Group, 2007.

Hamilton, Alexander, James Madison, and John Jay. *The Federalist Papers*. 1788.

Hamilton, Virginia Van der Veer. *Hugo Black: The Alabama Years*. Baton Rouge: Louisiana State University Press, 1972.

Harrington, Michael. *The Other America: Poverty in the United States*. New York: Macmillan, 1962.

Heilbroner, Robert. *The Worldly Philosophers: The Lives, Times and Ideas of the Great Economic Thinkers*. New York: Simon & Shuster, 1952.

Heller, Anne C. *Ayn Rand and the World She Made*. New York: Nan A. Talese/ Doubleday, 2009.

Hersh, Seymour. *The Dark Side of Camelot*. Boston: Little, Brown, 1996.

Hochschild, Adam. *The Unquiet Ghost: Russians Remember Stalin*. New York: Viking, 2004.

Hoover, Herbert. *The Challenge to Liberty*. New York: C. Scribner's Sons, 1934.

Ingalls, Robert P. *Herbert H. Lehman and New York's Little New Deal*. New York: New York University Press, 1975.

Isserman, Maurice. *The Other American: The Life of Michael Harrington*. New York: Public Affairs, 2000.

Johnson, Haynes, and Harry Katz. *Herblock: The Life and Work of the Great Political Cartoonist*. New York: W. W. Norton, 2009.

Jones, Doug. *Bending Toward Justice: The Birmingham Church Bombing That Changed the Course of Civil Rights*. New York: All Points Books, 2019.

Keith, Caroline H. *For Hell and a Brown Mule: The Biography of Senator Millard E. Tydings*. Lanham, MD: Madison Books, 1991.

Kennedy, Edward M. *True Compass: A Memoir*. New York: Twelve, 2009.

Kennedy, Robert F. *To Seek a Newer World*. Garden City, NY: Doubleday, 1967.

Keynes, John Maynard. *The General Theory of Employment, Interest, and Money*. San Diego: Harcourt, Brace, Jovanovich, 1964. First published 1936.

Khoury, Rana. *As Ohio Goes: Life in the Post-Recession Nation*. Kent, OH: Kent State University Press, 2015.

Kuttner, Robert. *The Squandering of America: How the Failure of Our Politics Undermines Our Prosperity*. New York: Vintage Books, 2008.

Lakoff, George. *Don't Think of an Elephant! Know Your Values and Frame the Debate: The Essential Guide for Progressives*. White River Junction, VT: Chelsea Green, 2004.

Langer, Adam. *My Father's Bonus March*. New York: Spiegel & Grau, 2009.

Lee, David D. "Senator Black's Investigation of the Airmail, 1933–1934." *The Historian*, Spring 1991.

Leuchtenburg, William. "A Klansman Joins the Court." *University of Chicago Law Review*, Autumn 1973.

Levine, Erwin. *Theodore Francis Green: The Rhode Island Years, 1906–1936*. Providence: Brown University Press, 1963.

Liebling, A. J. *The Earl of Louisiana*. New York: Simon & Schuster, 1960.

Liu, Eric, and Nick Hanauer. *The True Patriot*. Seattle: Sasquatch Books, 2007.

Lockard, Duane. *The Politics of State and Local Government*. New York: Macmillan, 1963.

Longley, Kyle. *Senator Albert Gore, Sr.: Tennessee Maverick*. Baton Rouge: Louisiana State University Press, 2004.

Loomis, Erik. *Out of Sight: The Long and Disturbing History of Corporations Outsourcing Catastrophe*. New York: The New Press, 2015.

Lowitt, Richard. *George W. Norris: The Triumph of a Progressive, 1933–1944*. Urbana: University of Illinois Press, 1978.

Lowenstein, Roger. *America's Bank: The Epic Struggle to Create the Federal Reserve*. New York: Penguin Press, 2016.

Lukas, J. Anthony. *Common Ground: A Turbulent Decade in the Lives of Three American Families*. New York: Vintage, 1985.

Luttwak, Edward. *Turbo-Capitalism: Winners and Losers in the Global Economy*. New York: HarperCollins, 1999.

Malamud, Bernard. *The Fixer*. New York: Farrar, Straus and Giroux, 1966.

Marcus Aurelius. *Meditations*. Project Gutenberg ebook, gutenberg.org/ebooks/2680.

Matthews, Chris. *Bobby Kennedy: A Raging Spirit*. New York: Simon and Schuster, 2017.

Matthews, Donald. *U.S. Senators and Their World*. Westport, CT: Greenwood Press, 1960.

Maugham, W. Somerset. *Of Human Bondage*. New York: G. H. Doran, 1915.

Mayer, Jane. *Dark Money: The Hidden History of the Billionaires Behind the Rise of the Radical Right*. New York: Doubleday, 2016.

McKean, David. *Tommy the Cork: Washington's Ultimate Insider from Roosevelt to Reagan*. Hanover, NH: Steerforth, 2004.

McPherson, Larry. *A Political Education: A Washington Memoir*. Austin: University of Texas Press, 1995.

Merrell, Susan Scarf. *Shirley: A Novel*. New York: Blue Rider Press, 2014.

Mondale, Walter. *The Good Fight: A Life in Liberal Politics*. New York: Scribner, 1970.

Morgenthau, Ruth. *Pride Without Prejudice: The Life of John O. Pastore*. Providence: Rhode Island Historical Society, 1989.

Neuberger, Maurine. *Smoke Screen: Tobacco and the Public Welfare*. Englewood Cliffs, NJ: Prentice-Hall, 1963.

Newman, Roger. *Hugo Black: A Biography*. New York Pantheon, 1994.

Odenkirk, James. *Frank Lausche: Ohio's Great Political Maverick*. Wilmington, OH: Orange Frazer Press, 2005.

Oshinsky, David. *A Conspiracy So Immense: The World of Joe McCarthy*. New York: Free Press, 1983.

Parini, Jay. *Promised Land: Thirteen Books that Changed America*. New York: Doubleday, 2008.

Paterson, Thomas, ed. *Cold War Critics: Alternatives to American Foreign Policy in the Truman Years*. Chicago: Quadrangle Books, 1971.

Patterson, James T. *Mr. Republican: A Biography of Robert A. Taft*. Boston: Houghton Mifflin, 1972.

Perlstein, Rick. *Nixonland: The Rise of a President and the Fracturing of America*. New York: Scribner, 2008.

Peterson, F. Ross. *Prophet Without Honor: Glen H. Taylor and the Fight for American Liberalism*. Lexington: University Press of Kentucky, 1974.

Phillips, Steven. *Brown Is the New White: How the Demographic Revolution Has Created a New American Majority*. New York: The New Press, 2016.

Piketty, Thomas. *Capital in the Twenty-First Century*. Cambridge, MA: The Belknap Press, 2014.

Pressler, Larry. *U.S. Senators from the Prairie*. Vermillion, SD: Dakota Press, 1982.

Proxmire, Ellen. *One Foot in Washington: The Perilous Life of a Senator's Wife*. Washington, DC: R. B. Luce, 1964.

Purdum, Todd S. *An Idea Whose Time Has Come: Two Presidents, Two Parties, and the Battle for the Civil Rights Act of 1964*. New York: Henry Holt, 2014.

Rand, Ayn. *Atlas Shrugged*. New York: Random House, 1957.

Riffe, Vernal G., Jr. *Whatever's Fair: The Political Autobiography of Ohio House Speaker Vern Riffe*. Kent, OH: Kent State University Press, 2007.

Rintels, David. *Clarence Darrow: A One-Man Play*. Garden City, NY: Doubleday, 1975.

Ritchie, Donald, "Making Fulbright Chairman: or How the Johnson Treatment Nearly Backfired." *The Society for Historians of American Foreign Relations*, September 1984.

Robenalt, James D. *January 1973: Watergate, Roe v. Wade, Vietnam, and the Month That Changed America Forever*. Chicago: Chicago Review Press, 2015.

Roosevelt, Theodore. *An Autobiography*. New York: Macmillan, 1913.

Rosenfeld, Richard. "What Democracy? The Case for Abolishing the United States Senate." *Harper's*, 2004.

Rosling, Hans. *Factfulness: Ten Reasons We're Wrong About the World—and Why Things Are Better Than You Think*. New York: Flatiron Books, 2018.

Rothstein, Richard. *The Color of Law: A Forgotten History of How Our Government Segregated America*. New York: W. W. Norton, 2017.

Russo, Richard. *Elsewhere: A Memoir*. Alfred A. Knopf, 2012.

———. *Straight Man*. New York: Random House, 1997.

Schlesinger, Arthur M., Jr. *Robert Kennedy and His Times*. Boston: Houghton Mifflin, 1978.

Shannon, David A. "Hugo LaFayette Black as United States Senator." *Alabama Law Review* vol. 36, no. 3, Spring 1985.

Sides, Hampton. *Hellhound on His Trail: The Stalking of Martin Luther King, Jr. and the International Hunt for His Assassin*. New York: Doubleday, 2010.

Sinclair, Upton. *A World to Win*. New York: Viking, 1946.

———. *The Jungle*. New York: Doubleday, Page, 1906.

Sirota, David. *Hostile Takeover: How Big Money and Corruption Conquered Our Government*. New York: Crown, 2006.

———. *The Uprising: An Unauthorized Tour of the Populist Revolt Scaring Wall Street and Washington*. New York: Crown, 2008.

Slayton, Robert A. *Empire Statesman: The Rise and Redemption of Al Smith*. New York: The Free Press, 2007.

Sloan, Richard S. *Revenge of America's Unemployed*. Self-published, BookBaby, 2017.

Smith, Adam. *An Inquiry into the Nature and Causes of the Wealth of Nations*. 1776. Project Gutenberg ebook, gutenberg.org/ebooks/3300.

Snyder, Timothy. *On Tyranny: Twenty Lessons from the Twentieth Century*. New York: Tim Duggan Books, 2017.

Solberg, Carl. *Hubert Humphrey: A Biography*. New York: Norton, 1984.

Stegner, Wallace. *Joe Hill: A Biographical Novel*. Boston: Houghton Mifflin, 1950.

Steinbeck, John. *The Grapes of Wrath*. New York: Viking, 1937.

Stokes, Lou. *The Gentleman from Ohio*. Columbus: Trillium/The Ohio State University Press, 2016.

Stone, Irving. *Clarence Darrow for the Defense, a Biography by Irving Stone*. Garden City, NY: Doubleday, Doran, 1941.

Swift, Earl. *The Big Roads: The Untold Story of the Engineers, Visionaries, and Trailblazers Who Created the American Superhighways*. Boston: Houghton Mifflin, 2011.

Swint, Kerwin C. *Mudslingers: The Top 25 Negative Political Campaigns of All Time*. Westport, CT: Praeger, 2006.

Sykes, Jay G. *Proxmire*. Washington, DC: R. B. Luce, 1972.

Taylor, Glen. *The Way It Was with Me*. Secaucus, NJ: L. Stuart, 1979.

Thomas, Norman. *Great Dissenters*. New York: Norton, 1961.

Tolstoy, Leo. *Resurrection*. New York: Dodd, Mead, 1900. First published 1899.

Tye, Larry. *Satchel: The Life and Times of an American Legend*. New York: Random House, 2009.

Vance, J. D. *Hillbilly Elegy: A Memoir of a Family and Culture in Crisis*. New York: Harper, 2016.

Weil, Andrew. *Why Our Health Matters: A Vision of Medicine That Can Transform Our Future*. New York: Hudson Street Press, 2009.

Wessel, David. *In Fed We Trust: Ben Bernanke's War on the Great Panic*. New York: Crown Business, 2009.

Westen, Drew. *The Political Brain: The Role of Emotion in Deciding the Fate of the Nation*. New York: Public Affairs, 2007.

White, Philip. *Whistle Stop: How 31,000 Miles of Train Travel, 352 Speeches, and a Little Midwest Gumption Saved the Presidency of Harry Truman*. Lebanon, NH: ForeEdge, 2014.

White, Theodore H. *The Making of the President, 1960*. New York: Atheneum, 1961.

Woodward, C. Vann. *Tom Watson: Agrarian Populist*. New York: Macmillan, 1938.

Young, Stephen M. *Tales Out of Congress*. Philadelphia: Lippincott, 1964.

Zinn, Howard. *A People's History of the United States: 1492–Present*. New York: Harper & Row, 1980.

Zito, Salena, and Brad Todd. *The Great Revolt: Inside the Populist Coalition Reshaping American Politics*. New York: Crown Forum, 2018.

Zola, Emile. *Germinal*. New York: Alfred A. Knopf, 1991. First published 1885.

ACKNOWLEDGMENTS

Often before I go to sleep, I recite to myself the words of the thirteenth-century Persian poet Rūmī:

> *In generosity and helping others, be like a river.*
> *In compassion and grace, be like the sun.*
> *In concealing others' faults, be like the night.*
> *In anger and fury, be as if you have died.*
> *In modesty and humility, be like the earth.*

In tolerance, be like the sea.
Appear as you are, or be as you appear.

Thank you to Reverend Doug Tanner and Rabbi Jack Moline and Joan Mooney and my friends at Faith and Politics, who deepened my knowledge of Rūmī and help me explore my faith and place in the world, and to my colleagues Tammy Baldwin and Tom Udall and Sheldon Whitehouse and Mazie Hirono and Chris Coons and Tim Kaine for their kindness and compassion.

To twelve million Ohioans—those millions who vote for me and those who don't—thank you for the opportunity to serve all of you in the United States Senate. What a privilege it is to represent America's premier swing state.

After ten years in President Barack Obama's former Senate office, we now occupy John Glenn's former space, both of them in the Hart Senate Office Building. I love our office's weekly legislative meetings. I thank our diverse, young, talented staff, who remind me—even in dark times for our country—of the vibrancy and strength of the experiment we call America. And our Ohio offices, oh how they care and advocate and fight for people, especially when they know that we are the last best hope for so many. Sarah Benzing and Jeremy Hekhuis and Jenny Donohue and Mary Topolinski and John Ryan and Alea Brown and Joe Gilligan and Ann Longsworth-Orr—thank you for mentoring them. And thank you to our Banking Committee staff, led by the very able and kind Laura Swanson. True public servants, all.

Thank you to John Ryan and Tom O'Donnell and Joanna Kuebler and Pam and Joe Kanfer and Diane Feldman and Kimberly Padilla and Jack Dover and Kim Kauffman and John Hagner and Melissa Wideman and Allan Berliant and Deborah and Ron Ratner and Jennie Rosenthal and Paul DeMarco. Without them, someone else would be sitting at Desk 88. And thank you to everyone who worked so hard under the leadership of Sarah Benzing and Justin Barasky to help me keep that seat in 2012 and 2018.

Mark Powden and Jay Heimbach and Meghan Dubyak and Katie

Mulhall Quintela and Josh Kramer and Denny Wojtanowski: thank you for your insight.

Thank you to Chuck Scotch, who, with his rototiller, kept me grounded—in the garden and on the road. And thanks to Janet Newey for the oasis.

Our 2019 Dignity of Work tour to Iowa and New Hampshire and Nevada and South Carolina gave me a deeper understanding of this great nation. It could not have happened without the genius of Jenny Donohue and Sarah Benzing and Adam Magnus. And I couldn't have survived any of it without Diana Baron holding all things Washington together.

Thank you to the Senate historians Richard Baker, Donald Ritchie, and Kate Scott; they have taught my colleagues and me much in regular five-minute presentations at our weekly Democratic luncheons. Dr. Baker helped inspire *Desk 88*; Dr. Scott has been especially generous with her studied insights.

For more than a decade I worked on this book, and for ten years I wondered if I really had a book. Then along came Gail Ross, who believed that maybe a senator could actually write. And how she pulled it all together!

Thank you to Alexander Star, who taught me far more than I'd ever known about publishing, gave me one good idea after another, and did it all with the speed of a Red Sox pinch runner. With each step toward publication, he created in me the anticipation of a Cleveland Indians playoff victory.

Thanks also go to Julie Tate, whose remarkable skill and immense knowledge made this book sharper and better.

And to Dr. Elizabeth Hinton, who, with Midwestern simplicity, made me think more and understand much—how lucky are the students who get to listen to her every week.

Thank you to production editor Nancy Elgin for her attention to detail; to Richard Oriolo for designing the book; to Rodrigo Corral for designing the jacket; and to Leon Nixon for recording the audiobook. And to Ian Van Wye for never missing anything.

Thank you to my older brother Charlie, who got all this started. On

Election Night 1974, after helping me run my successful race for the Ohio state legislature, he asserted: "I'm not going to do this again; if you lose in two years, I will kick your ass. Or if you win with more than 60 percent, I will also kick your ass because it means you are not standing up on the tough issues." A lesson learned, Brother.

And to my beloved oldest brother, Bob, who kept this book project alive with gentle prodding, big-brother advice, and Phi Beta Kappa–level insight on all things. Clearly in the top 90 percent of any class.

Thank you to Emily and Elizabeth for the joy you have brought to my life. For years, you were the most important reason I got up in the morning. And to Caitlin and Andy—what a stroke of good fortune to be joined with you almost twenty years ago. And Alex and Matt and Patrick and Stina, how rich you have made our lives, and made the world around you more just.

And how could I not conclude with thanks to Connie Schultz, who has encouraged me to be a more skillful writer, but—way more—has made me a better father, a kinder husband, a more engaged grandfather, and (maybe) a more unselfish human being. And oh, how I look forward to *Erietown*, so that all of America will come to know this brilliant new novelist.

INDEX

A NOTE ABOUT THE AUTHOR

Sherrod Brown, Ohio's senior U.S. senator, has dedicated his life in public service to fighting for what he calls "the dignity of work"—the belief that hard work should pay off for everyone. He resides in Cleveland with his wife, Connie Schultz, a Pulitzer Prize–winning columnist and author. They are blessed with a growing family, including three daughters, a son, and seven grandchildren.